T0358581

Prevention
and
Crisi
Management

Lessons for Asia from the 2008 Crisis

Prevention
and
Crisis
Management

Lessons for Asia from the 2008 Crisis

Editors

Steven Rosefielde
The University of North Carolina, USA

Masaaki Kuboniwa
Hitotsubashi University, Japan

Satoshi Mizobata
Kyoto University, Japan

World Scientific

NEW JERSEY • LONDON • SINGAPORE • BEIJING • SHANGHAI • HONG KONG • TAIPEI • CHENNAI

Published by

World Scientific Publishing Co. Pte. Ltd.

5 Toh Tuck Link, Singapore 596224

USA office: 27 Warren Street, Suite 401-402, Hackensack, NJ 07601

UK office: 57 Shelton Street, Covent Garden, London WC2H 9HE

British Library Cataloguing-in-Publication Data
A catalogue record for this book is available from the British Library.

PREVENTION AND CRISIS MANAGEMENT
Lessons for Asia from the 2008 Crisis

Copyright © 2013 by World Scientific Publishing Co. Pte. Ltd.

All rights reserved. This book, or parts thereof, may not be reproduced in any form or by any means, electronic or mechanical, including photocopying, recording or any information storage and retrieval system now known or to be invented, without written permission from the Publisher.

For photocopying of material in this volume, please pay a copying fee through the Copyright Clearance Center, Inc., 222 Rosewood Drive, Danvers, MA 01923, USA. In this case permission to photocopy is not required from the publisher.

ISBN 978-981-4374-13-2

In-house Editor: Zheng Danjun

Typeset by Stallion Press
Email: enquiries@stallionpress.com

Printed in Singapore by World Scientific Printers.

For David Rosefielde

CONTENTS

vii

PREFACE

This compendium is an outgrowth of a series of symposia devoted to the 2008 global financial crisis and its impact on Asia held at Kyoto and Hitotsubashi Universities in 2009 and 2010, funded by the Japan Foundation's Center for Global Partnership. Steven Rosefielde, Masaaki Kuboniwa, and Satoshi Mizobata, the project directors, coordinated a large team of experts across the globe with the participation of Kyoto and Hitosubashi Universities' Institutes of Economic Research, the University of North Carolina, the Stockholm School of Business, the Economies in Transition department of the Bank of Finland, and Trento University.

The symposia and this volume were designed to illuminate the character, complexities, and implications of the crisis and its aftermath as benchmarks for gauging Asia's futures. Although, three years have elapsed since the NBER declared America's "recession" ended in 2009, hard times have lingered raising the specter anew of a double dip recession or worse, as well as the possibility that long term global economic potential has been significantly diminished for a variety of profound reasons.

This volume delves into these new concerns, spotlighting the neglected issue of crisis prevention. It builds on the foundation laid in *Two Asias: The Emerging Postcrisis Divide*, World Scientific Publishing, 2012, reexamining the 2007–2009 financial crisis, subsequent developments, theoretical issues, options, outlooks and the prevention factors. The research reveals that the risk of fresh and severer crises is higher than previously supposed due to the emergence of new factors, and the global community's disinterest in constructing effective crisis prevention early warning systems.

The volume's principal finding is that the causes of the 2008 global financial crisis run deeper than initially behaved and pose governance challenges that cannot be met merely by doing more of the same: deficit spending, expanding the money supply, pretending to tighten financial regulations and burdening systems with mandates and stultifying regulations. The problem is planetary, affecting both Asia and the West, although specifics vary. Early warning systems of the type devised by the International Monetary Fund (see Chapter 6), and country specific variants thereof cannot remedy the danger, but should prod leaders into soberly reviewing their economic governance strategies.

ACKNOWLEDGMENTS

The editors wish to express their gratitude for the invaluable assistance of many institutions and individuals who made our project possible. First and foremost our greatest debt is to the Japan Foundation's Center for Global Partnership, which generously funded two brainstorming conferences and two symposia at Kyoto and Hitotsubashi Universities, critical for grapping with the manifold aspects of the 2008 financial crisis and its aftermath. The Kyoto Institute for Economic Research, the Hitotsubashi Institute for Economic Research, University of North Carolina, the Stockholm Institute of Transition Economics (SITE, Stockholm School of Economics), the Economies in Transition Department of the Bank of Finland (BOFIT), and the University of Trento all provided precious support. We also wish to thank the conference and symposia participants, both attendees and those contributing from afar, as well as Emiko Horibe (KIER), Nancy Kocher (UNC), and Huan Zhou who coordinated meetings, typed manuscripts, and compiled this volume. We acknowledge all these contributions with our deepest appreciation.

LIST OF CONTRIBUTORS

Steven Rosefielde is Professor of Economics at the University of North Carolina, Chapel Hill and a co-director of the Japan Foundation's Center For Global Partnership project on *Two Asias: The Emerging Postcrisis Divide*. He received his Ph.D. in Economics from Harvard University, and is a member of the Russian Academy of Natural Sciences (RAEN). He has taught in Russia, China, Japan, and Thailand. Most recently, he published *Russia in the 21st Century: The Prodigal Superpower*, Cambridge University Press, 2005, *Masters of Illusion*, Cambridge University Press, 2007 (with Quinn Mills), *Russia Since 1980*, Cambridge University Press, 2008 (with Stefan Hedlund), *Rising Nations*, Amazon, 2009 (with Quinn Mills), *Red Holocaust*, Routledge, 2010, *Democracy and its Elected Enemies: American Political Culture and Economic Decline*, Cambridge University Press, 2012, and *Asian Economic Systems*, World Scientific Publishing, 2012.

Assaf Razin is the Friedman Professor of International Economics, Cornell University, Professor Emeritus, Tel Aviv University, and Research Associate in the NBER, CEPR, and Cesifo. Assaf Razin's recent books include: *Labor, Capital, and Finance: International Flows*, Cambridge University Press, (September, 2001; with Efraim Sadka); *The Decline of the Welfare State: Political Economics of Demography and Globalization*, 2005, MIT Press (with Efraim Sadka); *Foreign Direct Investment: Analysis of Aggregate Flows*, Princeton University Press, November 2007 (with Efraim Sadka); *Migration and the Welfare State: Political-Economy*

Policy Formation, MIT Press, (June 2011; with Efraim Sadka, and Benjarong Suwankiri).

Yoji Koyama taught Comparative Economic System and Russian and East European Economies at Niigata University (Japan), where now he is Professor Emeritus. He was a visiting scholar in Belgrade from October 1978 through March 1980 under the Yugoslav government fellowship scheme and a visiting professor at the Faculty of Management, the University of Gdansk for a month in September–October 2005 under the exchange program of the Polish Academy of Sciences and the Japan Society for Promotion of Sciences. He authored several Japanese books including *A Study of Yugoslav Self-managed Socialism: Movement of the Regime of the 1974 Constitution* (in 1996), and *The EU's Eastward Enlargement and South Eastern Europe: Transition to a Market Economy and Small Countries' Strategies for Survival* (in 2004) and two English books including *South Eastern Europe: A Quest for Stabilization of the Region after the Breakup of the Former Yugoslavia* (in 2003). He graduated from the University of Tokyo, Faculty of Liberal Arts in 1967. He holds a B.Sc in Liberal Arts, an M.Sc in International Relations and a Ph.D. in Economics.

Daniel Quinn Mills provides thought leadership in several fields including leadership, strategy, venture capital, finance, economics, and geopolitics. He is an expert on the differences between Asian and Western leadership styles and has just published a chapter on the topic in the American Management Association's *Handbook of Leadership*, which has been chosen as the best business book of 2010. He has been a director of publicly listed firms and is currently a director of several closely held private corporations. During the Viet Nam War, Mills spent several years in Washington, D. C. helping to control inflation. Simultaneously he taught at MIT's Sloan School of Management. Thereafter he taught for many years at the Harvard Business School. He has done consulting and speaking in the following countries: U.S., Canada, U.K., Indonesia, Ireland, France, the Netherlands, Germany, Switzerland, Italy, Russia, Israel, China, Japan, Malaysia, Brazil, Columbia, Mexico, Singapore, South Africa, Kuwait, the United Arab Emirates, Saudi Arabia, Vietnam, and Australia. He has been a member of the National Innovation Council of Malaysia — a ministry-level council chaired by the Prime Minister. Mills earned his M.A. and Ph.D. from Harvard, both in economics. He received his undergraduate degree from Ohio Wesleyan. Throughout his career, Mills has been an influential author. His most recent books are *The Financial Crisis of 2008–2010*, Amazon, 2010, and *Rising Nations* (with Steven S. Rosefielde) Amazon, 2009. Previously he published *Masters of Illusion: Presidential Leadership, Strategic Independence and America's Public Culture* (with Steven S. Rosefielde), Cambridge University Press, 2007.

Torbjörn Becker is the Director of the Stockholm Institute of Transition Economics (SITE) at the Stockholm School of Economics. He is also chairman of the board of the Kyiv Economic Institute in Ukraine and the Center of Economic Analysis in Poland, and a member of the board of the Swedish International Development Cooperation Agency (Sida) and the International faculty committee at the International School of Economics in Tbilisi, Georgia. Prior to his current position he worked at the International Monetary Fund (IMF) in Washington D.C. for nine years. In this capacity, his research and policy work focused on international financial architecture issues and particularly on how emerging markets can protect themselves against adverse shocks and what role IFIs could have in preventing and resolving crises. Recently he has coauthored *Maintaining Financial Stability in an Open Economy: Sweden in the Global Crisis and Beyond*, SNS förlag, Stockholm; *Whither Growth in Central and Eastern Europe? Policy lessons for an integrated Europe*, Bruegel Blueprints, Brussels; "Country insurance: The role of domestic policies", in *Macrofinancial Linkages: Trends, Crises, and Policies*, International Monetary Fund, Washington D.C. His previous research has been published in leading academic journals including the *Journal of Monetary Economics, the Journal of International Economics* and the *International Journal of Finance and Economics*. More generally, his work covers macroeconomics, international economics, financial markets, debt management, fiscal policy and development issues. He holds a Ph.D. in economics from the Stockholm School of Economics and has also studied at U.C. Berkeley and the Manchester Business School.

Huan Zhou is a Ph.D. candidate in the Economics Department, University of North Carolina-Chapel Hill. Her research fields are Macroeconomics and International Economics. Her current research focuses on global imbalances.

Jonathan E. Leightner is Professor of Economics at Augusta State University. He has taught courses on China's economy at the Johns Hopkins University — Nanjing University Center for American and Chinese Studies (in Nanjing, China) and at Chulalongkorn University (in Bangkok, Thailand). His research focuses on Asia, especially China, Japan, and Thailand. He is the creator of Bi-Directional Reiterative Truncated Least Squares, a new regression technique that accounts for the influence of omitted variables without knowing, modeling, or finding proxies for them.

Akio Kawato is lecturer at Waseda University. He was a career diplomat in the Ministry of Foreign Affairs of Japan, 1970 to 2004, with the last posting being Ambassador of Japan in the Republic of Uzbekistan. He was Chief Economist, Development Bank of Japan 2004 to 2006, and after retiring founded an international opinion site www.japan-world-trends.com (in English, Japanese, Chinese, and Russian). Kawato was educated at Tokyo University with international relations as major, the Graduate School at Harvard University with M.A. in Soviet Studies, and was a Fellow at Moscow State University with Russian literature as his major. His publications include: *Will the Soviet Society Change?* (in Japanese) The Simul Press, 1988; *The Rise or Fall of the Soviet Union* (in Japanese) The Simul Press, 1989; *Building a Bridge to Russia* (in Japanese) The Simul Press, 1995, "За даль земли---повесть об Илье" (epic novel against the background of the Soviet's fall) Vagrius, 2001 (Japanese original was published by Soushisha in 2002. English translation was published 2010 in Kindle Amazon as *"Land of Legend, Land of Dream"* under the pseudonym Akira KUMANO)

"The Exit of the Modern Values" (in Japanese) Soushisha, 2004 *"How Japan's Diplomacy Ticks"* Soushisha, 2005 Many articles on China are published on the site: (in English). Available at: http://www.japan-world-trends.com/en/theses/the_world/china/index.php?page=1

Eric Fisher is a Professor of Economics at California Polytechnic State University and a Visiting Professor at Chulalongkorn University. He has published in economics, political science, and physics. He pioneered the work on generational accounting in open economies, and he has applied his ideas in publications about Japan and Korea. Fisher has been a Visiting Professor at the Institute for Social and Economic Research at the University of Osaka and also at Australian National University. He has won several professional honors, including having been elected the Secretary of the International Economics and Finance Society. He has served on the editorial boards of the *Journal of Economic Integration*, the *Journal of Money, Credit, and Banking*, the *Journal of International Economics*, and *Economics Bulletin*. His doctorate in economics is from the University of California at Berkeley, and his undergraduate degree in philosophy is from Princeton University.

Jong-Rong Chen received his doctoral degree from University of North Carolina at Chapel Hill in 1987. Since then, he has been working at Graduate Institute of Industrial Economics, National Central University (NCU), Taiwan. He was promoted to a Full Professor in 1993. He served as Chairman of Department of Economics, NCU in 1992–1993, and Director of Graduate Institute of Industrial Economics, NCU from 1993 to 1997 and from February 2007 to January 2009. He has visited Economic Research Center, Nagoya University, Japan, from May 1996 to October 1996 as a Visiting Research Fellow, Kennedy School of Government, Harvard University, USA, as a Visiting Fellow from July 1998 to July 1999, and Institute of Economics, Academia Sinica from January 2005 to June 2005 as a Visiting Scholar. Currently, he serves as the editorial board member of three Taiwanese Social Science Index Journals, *Journal of Social Science and Philosophy* (2007–2009, 2009–2011), *Taiwan Economic Policy and Forecasting* (2003–2005, 2005–2007, 2009–2011), and *Taipei Economic Inquiry* (2000–present). He has been elected as Board Member of the Taiwan Economic Association, the major economic association in Taiwan, in 1998–1999, 2001–2002, 2004–2005, 2008–2009, and 2010–2011. On average, he has been a PI for at least one project from National Science Council of Taiwan for the past 22 years.

Yun Chen is an Associate Professor at School of International Relations and Public Affairs, Fudan University, Shanghai, China, and is well known as the author of *Transition and Development in China: Towards Shared Growth*, Farnham, Ashgate Publishing, 2009, and as the co-author of *Transition, Regional Development and Globalization: China and Central Europe*, New Jersey and Singapore, World Scientific Publishing, 2010 (with Ken Morita).

Ken Morita is a Professor at the Faculty of Commercial Sciences, Hiroshima Shudo University, Hiroshima, Japan, and is also an Emeritus Professor, Hiroshima University, and is well known as the author of *Economic Reforms and Capital Markets in Central Europe*, Farnham, Ashgate Publishing, 2004 and as the co-author of *Transition, Regional Development and Globalization: China and Central Europe*, New Jersey and Singapore, World Scientific Publishing, 2010 (with Yun Chen).

Masumi Hakogi is Professor Emeritus at Tohoku University and Hiroshima University of Economics. He received his PhD from Osaka University in 1971 and has published widely on international trade and East European development issues. His publications and research papers include: *Economics of the Socialist Countries* (with J.S. Berliner and H.G.J. Kosta), "Environmental Problems, Foreign Capital and Technology in Central Eastern European Countries", "On the Way to Europe: Central and Eastern Europe's Economic Development", "EU's Environmental Policy and Responses by Central Eastern European Countries", etc.

Teerana Bhongmakapat is Professor of Economics and, presently, Former Dean of the Faculty of Economics, Chulalongkorn University in Thailand. He received his Ph.D. in Economics from the University of Wisconsin at Madison in 1988. He was advisor to Deputy Prime Minister and Minister of Commerce. He has served in various important national committees on economic policy formulation. He was the intellectual initiator of the BIMST-EC, a sub-regional economic cooperation between Bangladesh, India, Myanmar, Sri Lanka, and Thailand. He is on the editorial board of *International Journal of Economic Policy in Emerging Economies*, and regional editor of *International Journal of Trade and*

Global Markets. Dr. Teerana Bhongmakapat has published numerous books, articles, and research publications, mostly in the area of macroeconomic policy and trade. *Happiness Development for the Modern Society* and *The Dance of Capital: From Crisis to Crisis* are his most recent books.

Masaaki Kuboniwa is a Professor at Institute of Economic Research, Hitotsubashi University in Tokyo. He received the degree of honorable doctor from Central Economics and Mathematics Institute of the Russian Academy of Sciences in 2003, and was named a Leontief Medal laureate by the Russian Academy of Natural Sciences in 2004. He has published numerous articles in Japanese, English, and Russian economic journals, and is the author of *Quantitative Economics of Socialism,* Oxford University Press, 1989, *Development of Capitalism in Russia* (with Evgeny Gavrilenkov, Maruzen, 1997), and *Economics of Intergenerational Equity in Transition Economies* (with Yoshiaki Nishimura, Maruzen, 2006).

Satoshi Mizobata is a Professor and Vice-director at the University of Kyoto, Kyoto Institute of Economic Research. His research areas are comparative studies in economic systems, corporate governance and business organization, and the Russian and East European economies, focusing on the enterprises and market structure. He is editor of *The Journal of Comparative Economic Studies in Japan* and a member of the Executive Committee. His recent works include: *Melting Boundaries: Institutional Transformation in the Wider Europe*(co-edited with K.Yagi), Kyoto University Press, 2008, "Diverging and Harmonizing Corporate Governance in Russia," in John Pickles ed., *State and Society in Post-socialist Economies*, Palgrave-Macmillan, 2008, and *Varieties of Capitalisms and Transformation*, Bunrikaku, 2008.

INTRODUCTION

A crisis is an acute state of disequilibrium threatening to spin out of control. Crises are not only traumatic but also raise the specter of even worse things to come unless contained and effectively managed. Economic crises take diverse forms, from wage, commodity, hard asset, banking and financial bubbles to growth retardation, recessions, depressions, mass involuntary unemployment, bankruptcies, debt default and deflation. In extreme cases they may cause civil unrest, regime and systems change.

All these disorders should be preventable. The invisible hand is supposed to continuously resolve partial disequilibria (Walrasian price and Marshallian quantity adjustments mechanisms). It often does, but the history of crises demonstrates that market rigidities, speculative gambits and accommodative government policies frequently incapacitate the invisible hand, allowing disequilibria to intensify.

The trick therefore to successful crisis prevention and management policies is not preaching the counsel of perfection that markets should be comprehensively competitive, but identifying why some anti-competitive markets instigate destructive speculation and what can be done to forestall bubbles.

Which subsets of these factors, including the null subset, appear to best explain the Japanese, Asian and 2008 world financial crises and are most likely to recur?

Part I provides a fact profile that serves as a platform for investigating this important matter. Chapter 1 (Rosefielde and Razin) and Chapter 2 (Rosefielde and Razin) deal respectively with the Asian currency and financial crises of the 1990s, and the 2008–2009 global crisis. Chapter 3 (Koyama) expands the crisis framework by considering the plight of West

Balkan transition states. Chapter 4 (Rosefielde and Razin) probes the causes of the daunting sovereign debt problems of Portugal, Ireland, Italy, Greece and Spain (PIIGS), and Chapter 5 (Rosefielde and Mills) parses prospects for an American triggered global debt default. Part II carries the analysis to the next level by delving into the issue of prevention. Becker surveys the evolution of the IMF's prevention guidelines, evaluates their effectiveness and considers prevention prospects more broadly (Chapter 6). He finds a disheartening disinterest in advancing prevention science within the International Monetary Fund, a result confirmed in Part III for counterpart efforts in individual nations and regional associations. The duty to prevent appears to take a back seat to "business as usual" macroeconomic management. Governments, intergovernmental organizations and supranational entities have concocted stress tests, devised automatic stabilizers and emergency intervention protocols, but neglect early warning monitoring, and the institution building needed to connect crisis risk with competing priorities.

Zhou and Rosefielde (Chapter 7) explore the problem by documenting the threat posed by accumulating global imbalances, explaining how they could usher in a 1930s style epoch dominated by protectionism and deglobalization. Leightner (Chapter 8), Kawato (Chapter 9) and Fisher (Chapter 10) examine the nuances. Yun Chen and Morita (Chapter 11), and Jong-Rong Chen, Rosefielde and Hakogi (Chapter 12) then probe whether an Asian economic community or supranational Asian Union can reduce crisis risk. Finally, Bhongmakapat (Chapter 13) pushes the envelope by explaining how Buddhism can be harnessed to enhance global stability. Rosefielde, (Prospects) finally summarizes the current state of crisis prevention and management in Asia and across the globe, and evaluates near-term prospects. With respect to Asia, this volume finds that although China alone at the moment seems ripe for an internally generated Japanese 1990 style crisis, the rest of the region appears vulnerable to the vicissitudes of globalizing economic governance (liberal, rent-seeking and protectionist aspects) and excessive western leveraging. The danger of Asian paralysis, crisis and decline is higher than it should be because there are few if any effective early warning programs in place for predicting crises and intervening in a timely fashion. This failure is not primarily technical. Although, forecasting is imperfect, governments have sufficient analytic tools and investigative authority to discover emerging speculative dangers before they become critical. Moreover, they have the power to nip crises in the bud but, as the compelling evidence demonstrates, often choose not to do so. Becker attributes their dereliction of duty to political expediency, and most contributors to this volume agree with this view.

PART I

CRISES 1990–2010

CHAPTER 1

ASIAN CURRENCY AND FINANCIAL CRISES IN THE 1990S

STEVEN ROSEFIELDE AND ASSAF RAZIN

Asia was beset by three major economic crises during 1990–2010: (1) the Japanese financial crisis of 1989–1990; (2) the 1997 pan-Asian financial crisis; and (3) the global financial crisis in 2008–2010.

The first two were primarily caused by local and regional policies. Both could have been prevented by the Asian authorities and were ultimately resolved by them with some foreign assistance. The global financial crisis was an entirely different matter. Although Chinese dollar hoarding contributed to accumulating planetary disequilibrium, the epicenter of the crisis was Wall Street. The shock that followed devastated Asian exports but, with the exception of Japan, did not have long-lasting contractive Keynesian multiplier effects. This chapter recounts the Japanese and Asian financial crises, evaluates whether they could have been dealt with better at the time and assesses the adequacy of reforms designed to prevent and mitigate recurrences.

1.1. Japan's Financial Crisis: The Lost 1990s and Beyond

Japan was hit by a speculative tornado during 1986–1991, commonly called the *baburu keiki* (bubble economy). It was localized, brief, and devastating, with allegedly paralytic consequences often described as *ushiwanareta junen* (two lost decades). The phenomenon was an asset bubble within an otherwise healthy economy, distinguished by low inflation and robust growth. Speculation was particular rife in land and stocks, but also extended to Japanese antiques and collectibles (such as high-quality native ceramics and lacquer ware).

The Nikkei 225 (*Neikei Heikin Kabuka*) stock market index, which rose from below 7,000 in the early 1980s to 38,916 on December 29, 1989, plummeted to 30,000 seven months later, continuing to fall with fits and starts thereafter before reaching a 27-year low on March 10, 2009, at 7,055. It was approximately 8,600 mid may 2012. At its height, Japan's stock market capitalization accounted for 60% of the planetary total, now it is a pale shadow of its former glory. The real estate story was similar. Condo prices increased 140% between 1987 and 1991, on top of already globally sky high values, then plummeted 40% by 1994.[1] At the bubble's apex, the value of a parcel of land near the Emperor's Tokyo Imperial Palace equaled that of the entire state of California. By 2004, prime "A" property in Tokyo's financial district had slumped to less than 1% of its peak, with the total destruction of paper wealth mounting into the tens of trillions of dollars. The speculative frenzy predictably ended badly but also displayed uniquely Japanese characteristics.

The technical cause of the crisis was financial; an institutional willingness to accommodate domestic hard asset speculation in lieu of low, zero and even negative returns on business investment and consumer savings accounts. Corporations and households piled up immense idle cash balances during the miraculous "Golden Sixties," and subsequent prosperity through 1985 (Johnson, 1982). They were encouraged to believe that the best was yet to come despite diminishing returns to industrial investment, and therefore seized on stock and real estate speculation as the next great investment frontier. They succumbed to what savvy Wall Street insiders called a "bigger pig" mentality, persuading themselves that fortunes were at their fingertips because whatever price little pigs paid today for stocks, real estate, and collectibles, there always would be bigger pigs tomorrow, willing to pay more. Banks capitulating to the frenzy began binge lending, rationalizing that clients always would be able to repay interest and principal from their capital gains, until one fine day when they ruefully discovered that there were no bigger pigs at the end of the rainbow. This

---

[1]Bloomberg, Real Estate Economic Institute, Japan, Home Price Indices, as of March 18, 2009.

epiphany, coupled with a panic-driven free fall in assets values and capitalization, left bankers both in a predicament and a quandary.

The predicament was that government regulation required them to write down the book value of their assets, contract loan activity, and pressure borrowers to meet interest and principal repayment obligations, even if this meant driving clients into bankruptcy. The quandary was that Japanese cultural ethics strongly discouraged maximizing bank profits at borrowers' expense (Rosefielde, 2002, 2013). The Japanese are trained from birth to communally support each other through thick and thin, subordinating personal utility and profit-seeking to the group's well being. Watching out first for number one is never the right thing to do, as it is in competitive, individualist societies. Tough love is not an option; burden sharing is the only viable course,[2] which in this instance meant refusing to "mark capitalizations to market," seeking government assistance and stalling for time hoping that with patience, clients' financial health ultimately would be restored.

The judgment was not wrong. Japanese corporations operating under the same cultural obligation immediately began earmarking revenues from current operations for debt reduction at the expense of new capital formation and refrained from new borrowings to cover the gap. Banks, for their part, not only maintained the fiction that outstanding loans were secure but also provided cash for current corporate operations and consumer loans at virtually no cost above the bare minimum for bank survival. Moreover, they kept their lending concentrated at home, instead of seeking higher returns abroad.

These actions averted the broader calamities that typically accompany financial crises. Japan did not swoon into hyper depression (GDP never fell, growing 1.7% per annum during 1990–1993),[3] or experience mass involuntary unemployment. The country was not swept by a wave of

---

[2]Westerners once knew this, but have forgotten. See Benedict (1946). *cf.* C. Douglas Lummis, C. Douglas, "Ruth Benedict's Obituary for Japanese Culture," 2007. Lummis contends that Benedict failed to comprehensively study culture among all social strata and, like Sigmund Freud, was inspired by literature and art. This is correct, but does not negate most of her insights. Available at: http://www.japanfocus.org/-C__Douglas- Lummis/2474.

[3]A hyper depression is any depression greater than the Great American Depression of 1929. See Angust Maddison, *The World Economy: Historical Statistics*, Geneva: OECD, 2003, Table C3-b, p. 298.

bankruptcies. There was no capital flight, sustained yen depreciation, deterioration in consumer welfare (Sawada *et al.*, 2010), or civil disorder. There was no need for temporary government deficit spending, long-term "structural deficits," "quantitative easing," comprehensive financial regulatory reforms, or high-profile criminal prosecutions. Interest rates already were low, and although the government did deficit spend, arguably it did not matter in a Keynesian universe because Japanese industrial workers in large companies were employed for life (*shushin koyo*). For pedestrians on *hondori* (Main Street) who blinked, it seemed as if nothing had happened at all beyond a moment of speculative insanity.

However, matters look very differently to western macro-theorists and Japanese policymakers, particularly those who erroneously believe that structural deficits and loose monetary policy are the wellsprings of sustainable rapid aggregate economic growth (as distinct from recovery). Their prescription for Japan's "toxic asset" problem was to bite the bullet, endure the pain, and move on swiftly to robust, ever-expanding prosperity. Given ideal assumptions, writing off nonperforming loans and shunning problematic loans is best because it does not sacrifice the greater good of maximizing long-term social welfare for the lesser benefits of short-term social protection. Advocates contend that the Japanese government fundamentally erred in condoning bank solicitude for endangered borrowers, and abetting banks with external assistance because these actions transformed otherwise healthy institutions into "zombie banks" (the living dead),[4] unable to play their crucial role in bankrolling investment, technology development and fast track economic growth.

Their claim has merit[5] but also is seriously incomplete. It is true that Japanese growth has been impeded by "zombie banks," deflation, the

---

[4]Caballero, Hoshi, and Kashyap contend the zombie banks crowd the market and the resulting congestion has real effects on the healthy firms in the country. They find the cumulative distortionary impact of investment and employment to be substantial. See Ricardo J. Caballero *et al.* (2006). *cf.* Akiyoshi and Kobayashi (2008). For a detailed historical review of the Japanese banking crisis see Kanaya and Woo (2000).

[5]Miyajima and Yafeh (2007). The authors find that small, undercapitalized firms were the primary victims of the credit crunch. These firms contribute little to Japanese productivity growth, undercutting the claim that the financial crisis caused Japan's two lost decades.

"liquidity trap" conjectured by Paul Krugman in the 1990s,[6] faulty banking policy (Akiyoshi and Kobayashi, 2008), and the aftermath of stock and real estate market speculation, but this not the whole story because other factors should have been stimulatory. Japan is more competitive vis-à-vis the rest of the world today on a real exchange rate base than it was in 1990. Japanese inflation during the 1990s and 2000s has been nonexistent, while it was in the mid single digits abroad. Moreover, the government has tenaciously pursued a zero interest, loose credit policy, in tandem with high deficit spending that has raised the national debt to 229% of GDP. If Japan's growth retardation were really primarily due to insufficient "zombie bank" credit, government stimulus should have mitigated much of the problem.

There is a better explanation for Japan's two lost decades that has little to do with two concurrent and isolated speculative incidents, one in the stock market, the other in real estate with scant sustained effects on production and employment. The advantages of Japan's postwar recovery and modernizing catch up diminished steadily in the 1980s and were fully depleted by 1990, when its per capita GDP hit 81% of the American level. Thereafter, Japan's culturally imposed, anticompetitive restrictions on its

---

[6]Paul Krugman contends that after Japan's bubble burst savings rose (consumption collapsed) and the natural interest rate (needed for full employment general equilibrium) turned negative, the money interest rate reached the lower bound of zero, rendering monetary policy impotent. The actual real interest rate immediately after the crash and for decades to come often was slightly positive; the combined effect of modestly falling prices (due partly to collapsed demand and retail liberalization in an otherwise *keiretsu* price-fixed environment), and a zero money interest rate. This created a small Keynesian output gap (albeit with negligible unemployment) that was addressed with fiscal deficit spending, but it is still possible to argue that deflation and a "liquidity trap" kept, and still keep Japan's GDP and employment below its full competitive potential. Krugman contends that Japan's "liquidity trap" was the first manifested since the Great Depression, and sends a signal to monetary authorities like Ben Bernanke to be alert to the danger. He recommends that Japan's and America's output gaps should be closed with quantitative easing (central bank purchase of medium- and long-term government securities) and nurtured inflationary expectations through a Phillip's mechanism. The suggestion is sound in principle (albeit controversial) for contemporary America. Japan's institutions prevent its economy from attaining natural output levels. There may be a gap between Japan's achieved and potential institutionally constrained GDP, but it is impossible to reliably measure these gaps. See Krugman (1998), Krugman (2010), *cf.* Stiglitz (2010), *cf.* Aoki and Saxonhouse (2000).

domestic economic activities became increasing pronounced, causing its living standard to diminish to 73% of America's norm.[7] Japan, at the end of the 1980s, was poised to fall back, with or without a financial crisis, and it is in this sense that the two lost decades are being erroneously blamed on the bubble and its "zombie banking" aftermath.[8] Yes, there were eye-popping speculative stock market and real estate price busts, but they were not the national economic debacles they are usually painted to be, either in the short or intermediate term.

This interpretation raises a larger issue that cannot yet be resolved, but nonetheless is worth broaching. Does Japan's fate presage China's future? When the advantages of catch up are depleted, its population grays,[9] and the delusion of permanent miraculous growth subsides, will the end of days be punctuated with a colossal speculative bust, followed by uncountable lost decades? Perhaps not, but still it is easy to see how history may repeat itself.

1.2. The 1997 Asian Financial Crisis and Out of Region Spillovers

The Asian Financial Crisis which erupted in 1997 was a foreign capital flight–induced money and credit implosion.[10] It began as a run on Asian

---

[7]Rosefielde (2010). Available at: www.ggdc.net/Maddison/oriindex.htm; Russia, China 1991–2008 (EU benchmark).

[8]It is unclear whether Krugman ascribes Japan's second lost decade of 2000–2010 to his conjectured "liquidity trap."

[9]Japan's population growth had slowed noticeably by 1990, was still positive when its financial crisis hit. Deaths first began exceeding births in 2007, and the trend will not be swiftly reversed. Demographers are currently forecasting that more than one in three Japanese will be over 65 years in 2055, with the working age cohort falling by over a third to 52 million. Immigration could alleviate the pressure, but the Japanese are resolutely opposed to it because of unvoiced fears of being inundated by the Chinese. The long-term demographic prospect for China, including the possibility for expanded immigration, mimics the Japanese pattern due to Deng Xiaoping's one child per family policy, and xenophobia. See Eberstadt (2007) and Eberstadt (2010).

[10]Stiglitz (1996), Radelet and Sachs (1998), Rajan and Zingales (1998), and Fratzscher (1998). Rajan and Zingales contend that "hot" money in Asia is white hot, because in the absence of the rule of contract law, in a relationship-based culture, short-term foreign investors are especially wary.

banks by foreign short-term depositors and expanded into an assault on government foreign currency reserves, sending shock waves as far as Russia's and Argentina's shores.[11] Banks were decimated by acute insolvency. They did not have the cash on hand to cover mass withdrawals of short-term deposits because these funds had been lent long, sparking asset fire sales, slashed capitalizations, and credit and money contractions, which in turn triggered widespread business failures, depressions, and mass unemployment. Thailand's GDP plummeted 8%, Indonesia's 14%, and South Korea's 6% in 1997–1998.[12] Foreign capital flight (repatriation of short-term deposits), compounded by insufficient government foreign currency reserves, soon compelled steep devaluations that increased import costs, reduced "command national income," (domestic purchasing power including "command" over foreign imports), disordered balance sheets, and otherwise diminished real national consumption.

These events, unlike Japan's financial crisis eight years earlier, were triggered by foreign capital flight rather than domestic stock and real estate meltdowns, and were not quarantined. The crisis started in Thailand, spreading rapidly to Indonesia, South Korea, Hong Kong,[13] Malaysia, and the Philippines, with lesser reverberations in India, Taiwan, Singapore, and Brunei, but fledgling market communist regimes in China, Vietnam, Laos, and Cambodia were spared runs on their banks and foreign currency reserves by stringent state banking and foreign exchange controls. They experienced secondary shocks from diminished regional economic activity, but otherwise escaped unscathed.

The root cause for the runs on Asia's banks and foreign reserves lay in foreign-financed Asian economic development, and East–West interest rate differentials. After World War II, Asia became a magnet for both foreign direct and portfolio investment, driving foreign debt-to-GDP ratios above 100% in the four large ASEAN economies (Thailand, Malaysia,

---

[11]Argentina's money supply contracted sharply because constitutionally its money base was tied peso for peso to its foreign reserves, which wreaked havoc on business activity when hot money fled the country under its fixed foreign exchange regime.

[12] Angus Maddison, *The World Economy: Historical Statistics*, Geneva: OECD, 2003, Table C3-b, p. 298.

[13]Hong Kong's currency board, however, was successfully defended by massive foreign reserve sales, and purchases of private equities.

Indonesia, and the Philippines) during 1993–1996, and causing local asset market prices to soar (real estate and stocks). Rapid, near double-digit GDP growth contributed to the asset boom, inspiring confidence that investments were safe because Asia's miracles were expected to continue for the foreseeable future. The annual GDP growth rates of Thailand, South Korea, and Indonesia during the decade preceding the Asian financial crisis were 9.6%, 8.2%, and 7.2%, respectively.[14] At the same time, Asia's high interest rates attracted the "carry trade"; short-term borrowing of low-yielding currencies like the Japanese yen, and their subsequent short-term investment in high-yielding foreign bank deposits and similar liquid debt instruments. Short-term "hot" money (including large sums from Japanese financial institutions searching for positive returns on near money instruments well after Japan's financial crisis ended) poured into the region, creating what increasingly came to be perceived as a pan-Asian bubble economy, exacerbated by "crony capitalism",[15] severe political corruption and instability (especially Thailand, Malaysia, and Indonesia).

Foreign investors steeled by their faith in Asian miracles at first were not perturbed by the frothiness of the Orient's markets, but the swelling bubble, compounded by surging current account trade deficits, undermined their confidence. Speculators, hot money carry traders, and other investors gradually grasped that the high returns they were reaping could be wiped out by catastrophic devaluations, and began planning for the worst, realizing that those who fled early would preserve their wealth and those who dallied would be left holding an empty bag. The incentive to flee was increased further by developments outside the region. The U.S. Federal Reserve Chairman Alan Greenspan began nudging U.S. interest rates higher to deter inflation, creating an attractive safe haven for hot money hedging, made more appealing by the prospect of an appreciating dollar.

---

[14]Maddison, *Op.Cit.*

[15]Crony capitalism is a vague term often used to describe market economies, especially in the Third World, where business depends heavily on patronage in closed privileged networks of officials, relatives and friends that thrive even though under other circumstances their companies would fail the competitive test. These systems are considered morally hazardous, corrupt, inefficient, and ripe for disaster. See Pempel (1999).

The precise combination of factors that ignited full throttle capital flight is open to dispute. Southeast Asian export growth dramatically slowed in the Spring of 1996, aggravating current account deficits. China started to outcompete its regional rivals for foreign directly invested loanable funds. The domestic asset bubble began to pop with stock and land prices in retreat, forcing large numbers of firms to default on their debts. No doubt for these and many other reasons, including asymmetric information (Mishkin, 1999), opacity, corrupt corporate governance, and "crony capitalism"; foreign investors rushed for the exits in early 1997, symbolically culminating in the Thai government's decision on July 2, 1997, to abandon its fixed exchange rate, allowing the value of its baht to "freely" float. Over the course of the next year, the baht's value fell 40%. The Indonesian, Philippine, Malaysian, and South Korean currencies swiftly followed suit, declining 83%, 37%, 39%, and 34%, respectively.

Devaluation, stock and real estate market crashes, bankruptcies, mass unemployment, wilted interest rates, and heightened risk aversion dissolved the fundamental disequilibria that had beset the region before the fall, only to be immediately replaced by urgent new priorities. Downward spirals had to be arrested, economies stabilized, and steps taken not only to achieve rapid recovery but also to foster structural changes supporting long-term modernization and growth. Thai economic planners and their counterparts elsewhere in the region had a coherent overview of what needed to be done (mundane partisan squabbles aside) but, unlike the Japanese seven years earlier, sought external foreign assistance from the International Monetary Fund, the World Bank, the Asian Development Bank, and individual nations, including China, to finance balance of payments deficits and facilitate structural adjustment.[16] Japan did not run a current account deficit during its crisis, did not need foreign exchange rate support or structural adjustment assistance funding, and

---

[16]Introducing changes to a nation's economy: the promotion of exports; liberalization, through a reduction in government subsidies in order to bring domestic prices more in line with world prices; privatization of public-sector institutions to improve the technical efficiency of production; and the controlling of inflation through currency devaluation, and/or by restricting the rate of increase of the money supply, which means reducing budget deficits and therefore cutting public services.

therefore relied entirely on its own resources, whereas the dependency of noncommunist developing Asia on the developed West was placed in stark relief. The region of course could have gone alone; however, its aspirations for fast track convergence and counter crisis stimulus were clearly tied to its integration into the global financial system, and perhaps acceptance of some bad IMF conditionality.

Much ink has been spilled over whether Washington Consensus style monetary and fiscal stringency, combined with mandated economy opening structural reforms imposed by the International Monetary Fund, helped or harmed Asia.[17] This issue is important, but only so for present purposes insofar as structural reforms increased or diminished the likelihood of future crises. The evidence to date on balance, despite strong claims to the contrary, favors the regional decision to follow the IMF's tough love advice. Asia accepted fiscal austerity and monetary restraint. It liberalized, amassed large foreign currency reserves, maintained floating exchange rates, and prospered. After enduring a protracted and perhaps excessively painful period of adjustment, Asia not only resumed rapid growth within the IMF's framework, but when push came to shove in 2008, weathered the global financial shock wave better than most. It appears that although global financial liberalization does pose clear and present speculative dangers as IMF critics contend, the risks can be managed with prudence and discipline.[18]

Some have suggested that Russia provides a cogent counter Washington Consensus example because having liberalized after its own financial crisis in 1997, and recovered, its economy was crushed by the 2008 financial crisis. The claim however is misleading on a variety of grounds. There simply are too many dissimilarities for the Russian case to be persuasive. Unlike Asia, Russia was mired in hyper depression when it defaulted on

---

[17]The term Washington Consensus was coined by John Williamson in 1989 to describe 10 standard reforms advocated in Washington DC for ameliorating crises and promoting sustainable growth in developing countries. These reforms include fiscal discipline, structural investments (in education, etc.), tax rationalization, market-determined interest rates, competitive exchange rates, trade liberalization, privatization, deregulation, and rule of law. See Williamson (2002), *cf.* Blustein (2001).

[18]Stiglitz (2011) argues that controls can dampen the destabilizing effects of productive and financial regional and global integration. See also Lee and Jang (2010).

its sovereign Euro-denominated debt in 1997. It never received significant sums of direct and/or hot money inflows into the private sector during the Yeltsin years, had a floating peg exchange rate, and received no IMF support after the rouble collapsed. Consequently, it is fatuous to lump Russia in the same basket as Asia.[19] Asia's and Russia's systems and contexts are too disparate for them to be pooled together. The same argument for different reasons applies to Argentina during 1999–2001. The Russia and Argentinian crises were both linked to sovereign debt issues, but their problems and roles within the global economic and financial system place them in separate categories.

Clarity in this regard is essential for gauging the historical significance of the Asian financial crisis. Some like Niall Ferguson contend that Asia's financial crisis was the first tremor of the second globalization age that emerged after the Bretton Woods international monetary and financial order collapsed in the late 1970s, early 1980s; weakly implying that future crises will mimic Asia's experience. (Ferguson, 2008; 2010) This is implausible. Asia's crisis provides an object lesson on the broad danger posed to a wide variety of economies in various stages of economic

---

[19]Vavilov (2010), Rosefielde (2011) "Review of Vavilov's, The Russian Public Debt and Financial Meltdown," and Rosefielde (2005) *cf.* Shleifer and Treisman (2004). The only thing that really links Russia's 1998 financial crisis to Asia's is the demonstration effect. When the Asian bubble burst in July 1997, Europeans started to reassess Russia's creditworthiness, after being assured by Anders Aslund, the IMF, World Bank, and the G-7 that Russia had become a "capitalist market economy" on the road to recovery. The real story is that Yeltsin officials after scamming their own people innumerable times, including the infamous 1996 "Loan for Shares" swindle of the millennium, began a massive issue of GKO (*Gosudarstvennoye Kratsrochoye Obyazatel'stvo*; government short-term obligations) designed to entice foreign hot money by paying 150% interest, at a time when it could not cover its budgetary expenses with tax revenues hopelessly in arrears. Yeltsin insiders knew that the obligations could not be met, but also saw opportunities for self-enrichment and played the situation that way. They secured a 22.6 billion IMF rescue package on July 13, swapping GKOs for long-term Eurobonds to string the process out, before finally repudiating their GKO and Euro-denominated obligations, and abruptly devaluing on August 17, 1998. In the Asian case, foreign capital fled because private sector risks had increased. By contrast, in the Russian case it fled because carry traders realized that the Russian government was intent on ripping them off. The only question was when, not if, the Kremlin would strike. See Goldman (2003), Aslund (1995), and Rosefielde and Hedlund (2009).

development by overly exuberant international financial liberalization, but does not offer a blueprint about how things must unfold.[20]

1.3. Prevention

Japanese and Asian policymakers not only failed to prevent their respective crises but also were complicit in creating the bubbles that overwhelmed them. This failure to prevent cannot be attributed to an absence of early warning signs or a faulty understanding of the rudiments of economic stabilization.

The Japanese had ample warning throughout the 1980s that the nation was at risk for a hyper bubble, concentrated in the financial and construction sectors. The Nikkei 225 index nearly tripled during 1982–1987 and more than quintupled in 1982–1990. Real estate prices and collectibles followed the same trajectory, while consumer prices were tame and GDP expanded at a rapid clip (5% per annum). This segmentation of the real consumer economy from the real estate and financial sector simplified the prevention task. A multitude of price (interest rate), quantity (licensing, permits, etc.), and regulatory measures (suspension of margin privileges) could have tempered the speculative fever without distorting production and arresting economic growth.

Japanese authorities and market participants moreover should have realized quickly that rising asset prices could not be explained by any sensible estimate of foreseeable future rates of return.[21] The great real estate and stock price ascent was propelled by euphoria, not rational expectations.

---

[20]The rebirth of financial globalization, and the possibility of serial crises of increasing intensity, evoke memories of Rudolf Hilferding's Marxist classic *Das Finanzkapital*, 1910, but the fit is inexact because Hilferding stressed the international capitalist concentration of financial power, rather than the competitive variety evident today.

[21]Shigenori Shigatsuka, "The Asset Price Bubble in Japan in the 1980s: Lessons for Financial and Macroeconomic Stability, in Real Estate Indicators and Financial Stability", *BIS Papers* No. 21, International Monetary Fund, 2005, pp. 42–62. Jose Scheinkman and Wei Xiong, "Overconfidence and Speculative Bubbles," *Journal of Political Economy*, Vol. 111, 2003, pp. 1183–1219.

Various factors contributed to this euphoria, including aggressive behavior by financial institutions, financial deregulation, inadequate risk management, the introduction of the Capital Accord (banking system restructuring 1988), protracted monetary easing, taxation and regulations fostering land price inflation, Tokyo's rise as an international money center, the Plaza Accord,[22] enthusiasm for high tech Japan,[23] and prattle about the Japanese miracle.[24]

Japanese leaders, for diverse reasons, found it convenient to portray the nation as a phoenix, reborn from the ashes of WWII in a new and better form. The story line varied, but the essence was that, thanks to Japan's superior communalist culture and planning, the nation had forged an innovative technocratic model that surpassed the western competitive paradigm, capable of crisis-free, fast-track economic growth and perpetual prosperity.[25] Although Paul Krugman later successfully debunked these miraculous claims, the fable had the twin effect of blinding policymakers who had a duty to protect against bubbles and providing grist for the mill of market speculators who gladly urged new entrants, Ponzi scheme style, to throw good money after bad in the dizzying pursuit of capital gains. Moreover, the cozy relationship among politicians, speculators, financiers, banks, and *keiretsu* further impeded timely preventative intervention.[26]

---

[22]The Plaza Accord was an agreement among the U.S., West Germany, France, Britain, and Japan to appreciate the yen and the deutsche market signed at the Plaza Hotel, Manhattan, in September 1985. The expectation of an appreciating yen attracted hot money from abroad into Japanese direct and portfolio investments, fueling rising prices in these assets.

[23]Hugh Patrick and Larry Meissner, *Japan's High Technology Industries: Lessons for Industrial Policy and its Limitations*, Seattle: University of Washington Press, 1986. Sheridan Tatsuno, *The Technopolis Strategy: Japan, High Technology, and the Control of the Twenty-First Century*, New York: Prentice Hall, 1986.

[24]Chalmers Johnson, *MITI and the Japanese Miracle: The Growth of Industrial Policy 1925–1975*, Stanford: Stanford University Press, 1982. Aaron Fosberg, *America and the Japanese Miracle*, Chapel Hill, NC: University of North Carolina Press, 2000. Paul Krugman, "The Myth of Asia Miracle," *Foreign Affairs*, November/December 1994, Vol. 73, No. 6, pp. 62–79.

[25]Masahiko Aoki, *Information, Incentives and Bargaining in the Japanese Economy*, Cambridge: Cambridge University Press, 1988.

[26]A conglomeration of businesses linked together by cross-shareholdings to form a robust corporate structure.

This suggests that Japanese policymakers should consider devising "cultural stress tests" alerting themselves to present dangers they prefer to ignore, and bracing them to act in the common interest when tradition favors accommodating powerful groups. The issue has not arisen again during the subsequent two lost decades (going on three) because euphoria has been replaced by risk aversion and leaders can no longer gull themselves into believing that the East belongs to Amaterasu.[27] But China could benefit from Japan's cautionary tale.[28]

Drawing lessons about prevention from the Asia crisis, extended to include Russia and Argentina, requires a nuanced understanding of specific conditions in each affected country. The Russian case is clearest. Citizens must somehow find a way to discourage their leaders from issuing sovereign debt with the intention of defrauding foreign investors. For East Asia, emboldened by its "Asian values" rhetoric, prevention (*ca.* 1996) boiled down to a failure to anticipate the ferocity of hot money contagion and take appropriate defensive measures, including prudently liberalizing financial markets, improving information and transparency, reducing incentives for excess private risk taking in lending, promoting more flexible exchange rate regimes, insulating the domestic financial systems from short-term capital inflows (through tax disincentives and tight regulation), amassing sufficient foreign currency reserves, and creating international regimes for coordination and mutual surveillance.[29] East Asia subsequently learned most of these lessons the hard way. Its currencies now are more flexible (dirty float) and its foreign currency reserves are ample, although it continues to run significant current account surpluses, suggesting that currencies remain undervalued. Also, it would be a mistake to suppose that policies working in a globalization era will remain appropriate if polarities reverse and the world shifts toward protectionism and de-globalization.

---

[27] Amaterasu is the Japanese Shinto sun goddess, and the original female progenitor of the Japanese Imperial family.

[28] Kazuo Ueda, "Japan's Bubble, The USA's Bubble and China's Bubble," *China and World Economy*, Vol. 19(1), 2011, pp. 47–62. Wei Xiong and Jialin Yu, "The Chinese Warrants Bubble," *American Economic Review*, Vol. 101(6), 2011, pp. 2723–2753.

[29] Manuel Montes, "Lessons from the Economic Crisis in Asia," *Asia Pacific Issues*, No. 35, March 1998, pp. 1–8.

Finally, it seems wise to avoid making strong judgments about Japan's and East Asia's crisis management strategies. It is always possible to claim that if Tokyo had adopted alternative fiscal, monetary, and regulatory policies its performance after 1990 would have been even worse, but it is difficult to see why Japan deserves high crisis management marks. Government and business have experimented with innovative ways to reinvigorate the economy, without conspicuous success and if there is a magic bullet, it has eluded everyone's detection.

It is interesting to speculate whether Japan would have been afflicted with more than two decades of dyspeptic growth had it arrested the bubble at an early stage. On one hand, the extraordinary length of Japan's postcrisis bust raises the possibility that demographic, political, institutional, and anticompetitive structural factors were determinative, and would have slowed growth to a crawl even if authorities had nipped the bubble in the bud. Japan's two lost decades from this angle are best interpreted as a structural, rather than a business cycle phenomenon. However, on the other hand, it can be counterargued that the trauma transformed Japan from a risk-taking to a risk-adverse society with severe growth retarding consequences. If the trauma had been avoided, the structural factors would have been subsidiary. Most observers have preferred the latter theory, but as time elapses without a cyclical reversal, it seems prudent to give substantial weight to both explanations.

The East Asian story is untidy. The Washington consensus solution was excruciatingly painful for several years, but then induced a pro-competitive resurgence that significantly benefited the region. East Asia also weathered the 2008 final crisis better than most. Further liberalization could pay similar dividends, but a new epoch might call for novel crisis management tools, and better defenses against protracted collateral damage.

References

Akiyoshi, Fumio and Keiichi Kobayashi (2008) "Banking Crisis and Productivity of Borrowing Firms: Evidence from Japan," REITI Discussion Paper.

Aoki, Masahiko and Gary Saxonhouse (2000) *Finance, Governance and Competitiveness in Japan*, London: Oxford University Press.

Aoki, Masahiko (1988) *Information, Incentives and Bargaining in the Japanese Economy*, Cambridge: Cambridge University Press.

Aslund, Anders (1995) *How Russia Became a Market Economy*, Washington DC, Brookings Institution.

Benedict, Ruth (1946) *The Chrysanthemum and the Sword: Patterns of Japanese Culture*, Cambridge: Houghton Mifflin.

Bloomberg, Real Estate Economic Institute, Japan, Home Price Indices, March 18, 2009.

Blustein, Paul (2001) *The Chastening: Inside the Crisis that Rocked the Global Financial System and Humbled the IMF*, New York: Public Affairs.

Caballero, Ricardo J., Takeo Hoshi and Anil K. Kashyap (2006) "Zombie Lending and Depressed Restructuring in Japan," NBER Working paper No.12129.

Dallago, Bruno and Chiara Guglielmetti (2011) "The EZ in the Prospects of Global Imbalances: Two Europes?" in Steven Rosefielde, Masaaki Kuboniwa and Satoshi Mizobata, *Two Asias: The Emerging Postcrisis Divide*, Singapore: World Scientific.

Eberstadt, Nicholas (2007) "China's One-Child Mistake," *Wall Street Journal*, September 17.

Eberstadt, Nicholas (2010) "What Population Growth — and Decline — Means for the Global Economy," *Foreign Affairs*, November/December, Vol. 89, No. 6, pp. 54–64.

Ferguson, Niall (2008) *The Ascent of Money: A Financial History of the World*, New York: Penguin, 2008.

Ferguson, Niall (2010) "Complexity and Collapse," *Foreign Affairs*, March/April, Vol. 89, No. 2, pp. 18–32.

Fosberg, Aaron (2000) *America and the Japanese Miracle*, Chapel Hill, NC: University of North Carolina Press.

Fratzscher, Marcel (1998) "Why Are Currency Crises Contagious? A Comparison of the Latin America Crisis 1994–1995 and the Asian Crisis 1997–1998," *Review of World Economics*, Vol. 134, No. 4, pp. 664–691.

Goldman, Marshall (2003) *The Piratization of Russia: Russian Reform Goes Awry*, London: Routledge.

Hilferding, Rudolf (1910) *Das Finanzkapital. Eine Studie über die jüngste Entwicklung des Kapitalismus*, Vienna, Wiener Volksbuchhandlung.

Johnson, Chalmers (1982) *MITI and the Japanese Miracle: The Growth of Industrial Policy 1925–1975*, Stanford: Stanford University Press.

Kanaya, Akihiro and David Woo (2000) "The Japanese Banking Crisis of the 1990s: Sources and Lessons," International Monetary Fund Working paper No. 00/7.

Krugman, Paul (1994) "The Myth of Asia Miracle," *Foreign Affairs*, November/ December, Vol. 73, No. 6, pp. 62–79.

Krugman, Paul (1998) "It's Back: Japan's Slump and the Return of the Liquidity Trap," *Brookings Papers on Economic Activity*, Vol. 2, pp. 137–205.

Krugman, Paul (2010) "How Much of the World is in a Liquidity Trap," *New York Times*, March 17.

Lee, Sook-Jong and Hoon Jang (2010) *Toward Managed Globalization: The Korean Experience*, Seoul: East Asia Institute.

Leigh, Daniel (2009) "Monetary Policy and the Lost Decade: Lessons from Japan," IMF Working Paper WP/09/232.

Lummis, C. Douglas (2007) "Ruth Benedict's Obituary for Japanese Culture." Available at: http://www.japanfocus.org/-C__Douglas-Lummis/2474.

Maddison, Angus (2003) *The World Economy: Historical Statistics*, Geneva: OECD, Table C3–b, p. 298.

Mishkin, Frederic (1999) "Lessons from the Asian Crisis," *Journal of International Money and Finance*, Vol. 18, pp. 703–723.

Miyajima, Hideaki and Yishay Yafeh (2007) "Japan's Banking Crisis: An Event-Study Perspective," *Journal of Banking and Finance*, Vol. 31, No. 9, pp. 2866–2885.

Montes, Manuel (1998) "Lessons from the Economic Crisis in Asia," *Asia Pacific Issues*, No. 35, March, pp. 1–8.

Patrick, Hugh and Meissner, Larry (1986) *Japan's High Technology Industries: Lessons for Industrial Policy and its Limitations*, Seattle: University of Washington Press.

Pempel, T. J. ed. (2009) *The Politics of the Asian Economic Crisis*, Ithaca: Cornell University Press.

Radelet, Steven and Jeffrey Sachs (1998) "The East Asian Financial Crisis: Diagnosis, Remedies, Prospects," *Brookings Papers on Economic Activity*, Vol. 29, No. 1, pp. 1–90.

Rajan, Raghuram and Luigi Zingales (1998) "Which Capitalism: Lessons from the East Asian Crisis," *Journal of Applied Corporate Finance*, Vol. 11, No. 3, pp. 40–48.

Rosefielde, Steven and Stefan Hedlund (2009) *Russia Since 1980: Wrestling with Westernization*, Cambridge: Cambridge University Press.

Rosefielde, Steven (2002) *Comparative Economic Systems*, Oxford: Blackwell.

Rosefielde, Steven (2005) "Russia: An Abnormal Country," *European Journal of Comparative Economics*, Vol. 2, No. 1, pp. 3–16.

Rosefielde, Steven (2011) "China's Perplexing Foreign Trade Policy: Causes, Consequences, and a Tit for Tat Solution," *American Foreign Policy Interests.* Vol. 33, No. 1, pp. 10–16.

Rosefielde, Steven (2011) "East-West Convergence and Intra-Asian Stratification," in Steven Rosefielde, Masaaki Kuboniwa and Satoshi Mizobata, *Two Asias: The Emerging Postcrisis Divide*, Singapore: World Scientific.

Rosefielde, Steven (2011) "Review of Vavilov's The Russian Public Debt and Financial Meltdown," *Slavic Review.*

Rosefielde, Seven (2013) *Asian Economic Systems*, Singapore: World Scientific Publishing

Sawada, Yasuyuki, Kazumitsu Kawata, Masako Ii and Mark Lee (2010) "Did the Financial Crisis in Japan Affect Household Welfare Seriously," Towson University Working Paper 2010–11.

Scheinkman, Jose and Xiong Wei (2003) "Overconfidence and Speculative Bubbles," *Journal of Political Economy*, Vol. 111, pp. 1183–1219.

Shigatsuka, Shigenori (2005) The Asset Price Bubble in Japan in the 1980s: Lessons for Financial and Macroeconomic Stability, in Real Estate Inidicators and Financial Stability, BIS Papers No. 21, International Monetary Fund, pp. 42–62.

Shleifer, Andrei and Daniel Treisman (2004) "A Normal Country," *Foreign Affairs*, March/April, Vol. 84, No. 2, pp. 20–38.

Steinhauser, Gabriele and Greg Keller (2011) "Fuzzy Compromise Threatens Relevance of G–20," Yahoo!News, February 19.

Stiglitz, Joseph (1996) "Some Lessons from the East Asian Miracle," *World Bank Observer*, Vol. 11, No. 2, pp. 151–177.

Stiglitz, Joseph (2011) "Contagion, Liberalization and the Optimal Structure of Globalization," *Journal of Globalization and Development*, Vol. 1, No. 2.

Tatsuno, Sheridan (1986) *The Technopolis Strategy: Japan, High Technology, and the Control of the Twenty-First Century*, New York: Prentice Hall.

Ueda, Kazuo (2011) "Japan's Bubble, The USA's Bubble and China's Bubble," *China and World Economy*, Vol. 19, No. 1, pp. 47–62.

Vavilov, Andrey (2010) *The Russian Public Debt and Financial Meltdowns*, Basingstoke: Palgrave Macmillan.

Williamson, John (2002) "What Washington Means by Policy Reform," in Williamson, *Latin American Adjustment: How Much Has Happened?* Washington DC: Institute of International Economics.

Xiong, Wei and Yu Jialin (2011) "The Chinese Warrants Bubble," *American Economic Review*. Vol. 101, No. 6, pp. 2723–2753.

CHAPTER 2

THE 2008–2009 GLOBAL CRISIS

STEVEN ROSEFIELDE AND ASSAF RAZIN

Asia was victimized by the 2008–2010 global financial crisis spawned on Wall Street, but the East's beggar-thy-neighbor foreign trade practices, particularly China's dollar reserve hoarding, exacerbated U.S. unemployment, and impeded recovery.[1] This suggests that, while preventing a repeat performance of the 2008 crisis is primarily Washington's responsibility, Asia has a stake in repairing global monetary imbalances. The U.S., the European Union (EU), Asia, the World Bank, International Monetary Fund (IMF), and World Trade Organization (WTO) have done a shabby job managing the 2008 crisis's aftermath, and its leaders do not seem anxious to learn the essential lessons. This chapter recounts the story of the 2008 financial crisis, evaluates whether it could have been handled better, assesses the adequacy of reforms designed to prevent and mitigate recurrences, and considers what steps if any Asians should take to eliminate global imbalances and restore financial discipline.

2.1. Prevention

American policymakers not only failed to prevent the 2008 financial meltdown, they were complicit (unintentionally or otherwise) in creating the bubble that overwhelmed them. This failure to prevent cannot be

---

[1] Eric Fisher, "The Asian Dollar Surplus," Chapter 10 in this volume. If Keynesian multiplier effects are disregarded, the Chinese dollar reserve hoarding may be compatible with optimal Samuelson intergenerational equilibrium, or any harm done could be limited to global overtrading. Ben Bernanke, however, would dispute the link between Chinese dollar reserve hoarding and American unemployment because Beijing's holdings of American treasury bonds facilitate monetary ease and low interest rates.

attributed to an absence of early warning signs or a faulty understanding of the rudiments of economic stabilization.

Washington had ample warning throughout the 1980s, 1990s, and the early 2000s that its push for deficit spending and financial deregulation put the nation at risk for a hyper bubble, concentrated in the financial, commodities, and real estate sectors. The 160-billion-dollar savings and loan debacle, the 1998 collapse of Long-Term Capital Management hedge fund debacle, the 2000–2002 dot-com bubble, the 2001 stock market crash, the natural resource price bubble triggered by 9/11, the subprime mortgage fiasco, the 2006 American housing bust toxifying mortgage and derivative financial instruments, Chinese dollar hoarding, and the emergence of "institutional" bank runs should have signaled caution, but instead were read as precursors to a financial revolution that would permanently turbocharge the economy and provide politicians with a goose laying an inexhaustible supply of golden eggs.

This imprudence was easily rationalized because consumer prices were tame, employment was under 5% (the instantaneous rate defined as "full employment"), and GDP was expanding in line with the long-term post-war mean of 3.3% per annum. Likewise, pundits touted "divine coincidence" and belittled bubble talk, focusing instead on transient issues and forecasting blue skies forever. Watchdogs wanted to believe and did, ignoring their duty to protect. They could have easily curtailed subprime mortgages, curbed mortgage-backed derivative trading, slowed money creation, and trimmed the federal deficit, but they never seriously considered braking excess aggregate effective demand or proscribing financial adventurism.

American policymakers, unlike their Japanese counterparts two decades earlier, were not euphoric. They were purblind and self-serving, eclectically pressing pet programs and remain unchastened, confirming Reinhart's and Rogoff's findings in *This Time is Different: Eight Centuries of Financial Folly*.[2] The Federal Reserve and regulators have taken the

---

[2] Carmen Reinhart and Kenneth Rogoff, *This Time is Different: Eight Centuries of Financial Folly*, Princeton, NJ: Princeton University Press, 2009. It is worth noting that the failure to learn does not depend on the particular economic belief system since the study spans eight centuries. There always appear to be rationales for doing the wrong thing.

position that America's disequilibrium macroeconomic governance, including *laissez-faire* financial management and one-way street "state-private partnerships" are optimal except for a few refinements like "stress tests" and circuit breakers that now make the system failsafe.

Their attitude is revealingly illustrated by the absence of any watchdog institution tasked to alert policymakers to impending bubbles. The Council of Economic Advisors and the Joint Economic Committee of Congress could take on the role, but their primary loyalties are to perpetuating "divine coincidence" myths, assuring everyone that everything is under control. These organizations are prepared to debate issues of fine tuning but seldom start from the premise that the present system is prone to recurrent crises.[3]

There are occasional voices in the wind fretting about "irrational exuberance,"[4] and predicting bubbles and crises. The media notes the warnings; however, American policymakers historically have not responded in timely fashion (recurrent crises have been the norm), and are invariably taken off guard when bubbles burst. Washington today shrugs off its colossal federal deficit (more than 100% of GDP),[5] refusing to connect the dots between excess spending and bubble risk in the name of this or that greater good. Policymakers preoccupy themselves with "optimal" fine tuning, rather than preempting meltdowns. The Congressional Budget Office, for example, recently warned that the national debt is on pace to exceed GDP by 160% within a decade, a level on a par with contemporary Greece that could provoke an European-style debt crisis with catastrophic global implications unless policymakers in Washington can slam the brakes on spiraling deficits.[6] The report elicited yawns.

---

[3] Steven Rosefielde and Quinn Mills, *Democracy and Its Elected Enemies: American Political Capture and Economic Decline*, Cambridge: Cambridge University Press, 2013.

[4] Alan Greenspan, "The Challenge of Central Banking in a Democratic Society," December 5, 1996.

[5] As of May 18, 2012 America's national debt exceeded its GDP by 700 billion dollars: 15.7 versus 15.0 trillion dollars. The debt/GDP ratio is 105%. Available at: http://www.usdebtclock.org/

[6] Andrew Taylor, "CBO: Debt Crisis Looms Absent Major Policy Changes," *Yahoo!Finance*, June 22, 2011.

The reaction is unsurprising. The last thing American political authorities want to hear is that they should curb destabilizing deficit spending, "loose money," and indulgent financial regulation. Indeed, calls for substantially increasing the budget deficit without explicit limit are routinely heard from prominent public economists.[7] Witness the recent call of Larry Summers, one of President Obama's former chief economic advisors for 200 billion dollars of additional payroll tax cuts, and untold billions more spending on construction in order to avert a Japanese type "lost decade."[8]

There is no reason to expect constructive change soon,[9] nonetheless, a sound crisis prevention initiative can be crafted by recognizing the lacunae and calling for the establishment of an independent government agency with a duty to protect against bubbles and crises that not only monitors but also accurately diagnoses disorders and intervenes surgically. Stakeholders, including foreign governments, need not be direct participants, however, they should familiarize themselves with the crisis prevention effort, offer counsel and coordinate policies.

Reinhart and Rogoff's historical study of financial crises demonstrates that the creation of an independent government bubble monitoring and interdiction agency always was appropriate. Careful analysis of the origins of the 2008 global financial crisis confirms their finding and reveals, moreover, that prevention today is more urgent than ever before. Post "New Deal" deregulation coupled with a full employment imperative

---

[7] Paul Krugman, "Nobody Understands Debt," Op Ed, *New York Times*, January 1, 2012. "So yes, debt matters. But right now, other things matter more. We need more, not less, government spending to get us out of our unemployment trap. And the wrongheaded, ill-informed obsession with debt is standing in the way."

[8] Summers: More Stimulus Required to Avoid a "Lost Decade," *Yahoo!Finance*, June 13, 2011. Western governments also have become prone to lying about the scale of their deficit spending. For example, the European Commission is now insisting that an increase of 100 billion Euros on its programs does not increase its budget! *London Daily Mail*, July 1, 2011.

[9] The U.S. government for the first time is poised to become the largest source of outstanding loans for home mortgage and consumer credit loans, eclipsing the private sector. Government-financed borrowing for these purposes now runs at $6.3 trillion per year (up from $4.4 trillion in 2006) in the first quarter of 2011. Private mortgage and consumer credit by contrast was $6.6 trillion, down from $8.5 trillion in 2006. Gillian Tett, "The State is Now the Dominant Force in US Capital Markets," *Financial Times*, July 1, 2011.

(honored in name, but not the breech) have skewed macroeconomic policy toward a perpetual excess aggregate effective demand regime that fans the flames of "irrational exuberance" with all its attendant risks. The same basic story holds for the EU, modified to take account of democratic socialist influences and the supranational character of the organization. The EU is not a unitary state; it is a transnational entity with elements of shared governance that make it even more crisis prone than America.

2.2. The 2008 Financial Crisis and Subsequent Great Recession

The origins of the 2008 financial crisis can be traced to various milestones in the construction of the post-World War American economy. During the 1950s, Keynesianism became orthodox, at the same time, momentum built to rescind sundry New Deal and wartime restrictions on free enterprise, including wage-price controls, and fair trade retail pricing (Miller–Tydings Act 1937; McGuire Act 1952, both rescinded in 1975 by the Consumer Goods Price Act). Deregulation in rail, truck, and air transportation during the 1970s; ocean transport in the 1980s, natural gas, and petroleum sectors during 1970–2000; and telecommunications in the 1990s created opportunities for asset value speculation, soon facilitated by complementary deregulation initiatives in the financial sector. The Depository Institutions Deregulation and Monetary Control Act of 1980 (DIDMCA), and Garn-St. Germain Depository Institutions Act (1982) both increased the scope of permissible bank services, fostered mergers, facilitated collusive pricing, and relaxed accounting rules (Moody's, for example, is permitted to accept fees from the insurers it rates). Beginning in the early 1990s, banks shifted from the direct loan business to packaging and marketing novel debt instruments like mortgage-backed securities (ultimately including subprime loans) to other financial institutions, and shortly thereafter President William Jefferson Clinton approved the Gramm–Leach–Bliley Act (1999) enhancing business flexibility. The Glass–Steagall Act (Banking Act of 1933) had compartmentalized banks, prohibiting those engaged in stable businesses like mortgages and consumer loans from participating in riskier stock brokerage, insurance, commercial, and industrial activities with the intention of building a firewall against speculative contagion. The repeal of provisions banning holding companies from owning other financial companies ushered in an era of financial merger mania across old divisional lines, allowing companies like Citicorp and Travelers Group to unite.

These developments, replicated across much of the globe, were all positive from the standpoint of neoclassical microeconomic theory because they enhanced competitive efficiency, with the proviso that moral hazards and speculative abuses were optimally contained by residual regulations ("liberalization"). However, if residual *laissez-faire* (do whatever you want) regulations were inadequate, then ensuing financial crisis costs could easily outweigh deregulatory efficiency gains.

Clearly, there are legitimate grounds for conjecturing deregulatory involvement in the 2008 global financial crisis, but deregulation is not the only suspect. The financial environment also was placed in jeopardy by revisionist Keynesianism. John Maynard Keynes was an apostate monetarist who devised and spread the counter-depressionary gospel of deficit fiscal spending in his *General Theory of Employment, Interest and Money* (Keynes, 1936).

He contended that the Great Depression had been caused by deficient aggregate effective demand brought about by negative income effects, prolonged by a liquidity trap and claimed that full employment could be easily restored by offsetting private hoarding (speculative idle cash balances) with government expenditure programs (deficit financed state procurements and programs). Other things equal, Keynes insisted competitive markets could and would achieve perpetual full employment, if it were not for income (multiplier) effects, and this destabilizing force could be overcome without inflation through countercyclical government deficit spending and countervailing surpluses. There was no place in Keynes's universe for continuously mounting "structural deficits," sovereign debt and/or "managed" inflation that could feed speculation and cause financial crises.

Nonetheless, immediately after World War II, the U.S. government passed the Employment Act of 1946, prioritizing the attainment and maintenance of full employment (further codified and expanded in the Humphrey–Hawkins Full Employment Act, 1978). The law did not fix quantitative targets, but marked the Truman administration's expansion of federal powers to include macroeconomic administration, management and regulation, without explicit constitutional sanction, and established the Council of Economic Advisors to aid presidential policymaking, as well as the Joint Economic Committee of Congressmen and Senators to review executive policies.

These actions enabled Washington to go beyond the perimeters of Keynesian orthodoxy, whenever full employment could not be sustained with transcyclically balanced federal budgets. The exclusion remained moot throughout much of the 1950s, until William Phillips (1958) discovered and Paul Samuelson popularized the notion that full employment could only be maintained with "excess" monetary and/or fiscal stimulation accompanied by inflationary side-effects (Phillip's Curve). Keynes, many concluded, was almost right. Deficit spending was essential but it also should be applied no matter how much inflation it generates to secure the higher goal of full employment. Full employment zealots like Paul Krugman and Larry Summers insist that governments are "morally" obliged to deficit spend forever,[10] a position still widely maintained despite Milton Friedman's and Edmund Phelps' demonstrations that Phillips was wrong in the medium and long runs by omitting inflationary expectations.

The orthodox Keynesian straitjacket was loosened further by Walter Heller, Chairman of President John Kennedy's Council of Economic Advisors from 1961 to 1964, who introduced across the board tax cuts as a counter-recessionary stimulus, even though this meant creating credit not just for investment, but for consumption as well. Keynes's employment and income multiplier theory required stimulating investment as the only legitimate method for combating deficient aggregate effective demand [Works Projects Administration 1932 (WPA) providing 8 million jobs, and later investment tax credits]. He argued that new investment creates new jobs and wages and derivatively increases consumption, whereas deficit consumption spending via diminished marginal propensities to consume merely transfers purchasing power from one recipient to another, without increasing employment. Heller's revisionism brushed Keynes's concerns aside, making it possible for politicians to claim that any deficit spending which benefited them and their constituents would stimulate aggregate economic activity and employment, including

---

[10]There may be a political aspect to this advocacy because unemployment is believed to turn voter sentiment against the incumbent party.

inter-temporal income transfers from one consumer's pocket tomorrow to the other's today.

This logic was extended by falsely contending that deficit spending and expansionary monetary policy accelerate long-term economic growth. Although, there are no grounds for claiming that structural deficits and lax monetary policy accelerate scientific and technological progress (the ultimate source of sustainable economic growth), policymakers could not resist the temptation to assert that deficit spending and inflation are indispensable for maximizing current and future prosperity. The ploy has been successful as a political tactic, making deficits and inflation seem more palatable, but also has widened the door to compounding past abuses by upping the ante whenever the economy sours. Policymakers' reflex is not to retrench, but to do more of what caused problems in the first place.

Academic macroeconomists likewise succumbed to wishful thinking, brushing aside the speculative momentum embedded in postwar institutional liberalization and fiscal indiscipline. Influenced by Robert Lucas (1972), and Phil Kydland and Edward Prescott (1982), the conventional wisdom of 2000–2008 came to hold that business cycle oscillations were primarily caused by productivity shocks that lasted until price- and wage-setters disentangled real from nominal effects. These shocks sometimes generated inflation believed to be best addressed with monetary policy. Accordingly, central bankers were tasked with the mission of maintaining slow and stable, Phillips Curve compatible inflation. Although central bankers were supposed to be less concerned with real economic activity, many became convinced that full employment and 2% inflation could be sustained indefinitely by "divine coincidence."[11] This miracle was said to be made all the better by the discovery that real economic performance could be regulated with a single monetary instrument, the short-term interest rate. Happily, arbitrage across time meant that central bankers could control all temporal interest rates, and arbitrage across asset classes implied that the U.S. Federal Reserve could similarly influence risk adjusted rates for diverse securities. Fiscal policy, which had ruled the roost under the influence of orthodox Keynesianism from 1950–1980 in

---

[11] The term refers to situations where stabilizing inflation is the same as stabilizing output.

this way, was relegated to a subsidiary role aided by theorists' faith in the empirical validity of Ricardian equivalence arguments, and skepticism about lags and political priorities.[12] The financial sector likewise was given short shrift, but this still left room for other kinds of nonmonetary intervention. The consensus view held that automatic stabilizers like unemployment insurance should be retained to share risks in case there were any unpredictable shocks. Commercial bank credit similarly continued to be regulated, and federal deposit insurance preserved to deter bank runs, but otherwise finance was lightly supervised; especially "shadow banks", hedge funds and derivatives.

A similar myopia blinded many to the destabilizing potential of Chinese state-controlled foreign trading. As postwar free trade gained momentum, liberalizers not only grew increasingly confident that competitive commerce was globally beneficial, but that trade expansion of any kind increased planetary welfare. Consequently, few were perturbed after China's admission to the WTO in 2001 either by the conspicuous undervaluation of the renminbi (RMB) fixed to support export-led development, or by Beijing's ever mounting dollar reserves. It was assumed that even if China overexported (at the expense of foreign importables jobs), this would be offset by employment gains in the exportables sector as China increased its import purchases. "Overtrading" as theory teaches is suboptimal, but not seriously harmful to aggregate employment and has the compensatory virtue of expanding international commerce.

However, there was a fly in the ointment. The Chinese (and some others like Brazil) chose to hold idle dollar reserve balances (hoard), instead of importing as much as they exported, compounding a "saving glut" caused by a broad preference for relatively safe American financial assets.[13]

---

[12] See De Grauwe (2010).

[13] Ben Bernanke, Carol Bertaut, Laurie Pounder DeMarco, and Steven Kamin have provided convincing evidence that foreign investors during the 2000s preferred what they perceived to be safe American financial assets, particularly U.S. treasuries and Agency-sponsored collateralized debt obligations. Although, European foreign trade surpluses were smaller than China's, they leveraged their balance sheets, issuing large volumes of external dollar liabilities to finance purchases of U.S. mortgage-based securities, stoking the American housing bubble. See Bernanke *et al.* (2011).

Beijing's dollar reserves grew from 250 billion in 2001 to 2.6 trillion in 2010. In a perfectly competitive universe this would not matter because others would borrow these unused funds, but not so in a Keynesian world where rigidities of diverse sorts transform idle cash balances into deficient aggregate effective demand, and simultaneously serve as a vehicle for financial hard asset speculation. For reasons that probably involve the Chinese Communist Party's desire to protect privileged producers in both its domestic importables and exportables sectors (implicit, stealth "beggar-thy-neighbor" tactics), Beijing became an immense source of global real and financial sector disequilibrium, contributing both to the 2008 financial crisis and its aftermath. Chinese leaders in its state-controlled foreign trade system had and have the power to reset the renminbi exchange rate, and increase import purchases, but they chose and are still choosing to do little.[14]

The cornerstones of 2008 financial crisis in summary are: (1) an evolving deregulatory consensus; (2) a mounting predilection for excess deficit spending; (3) a penchant for imposing political mandates on the private sector like subprime mortgage, student loan lending, and excess automobile industry health benefits which drove GM and Chrysler into bankruptcy in 2009; (4) waning concern for labor protection manifest in stagnant real wages and therefore flagging mass consumption demand, (shift towards promoting the security of other social elements); (5) a proclivity to prioritize full employment over inflation; (6) the erroneous belief that structural deficits promote accelerated economic growth; (7) the notion that government insurance guarantees, off budget unfunded obligations like social security, and mandated preferences to savings and loans banks were innocuous, despite the 160-billion-dollar savings and loans debacle of the late 1980s–1990s; (8) deregulatory myopia, and activist social policy, including the encouragement of subprime loans, adjustable rate mortgages (ARM),

---

[14]The G-20 is trying to pressure China into curtailing its dollar surpluses without conspicuous success. The parties are still quibbling over technical measurement indicators. Rosefielde (2011), "China's Perplexing Foreign Trade Policy: Causes, Consequences, and a Tit for Tat Solution," *American Foreign Policy Interests*, Steinhauser and Keller, "Fuzzy Compromise Threatens Relevance of G-20," *Yahoo!News*, February 19, 2011. The renminbi appreciated 4.7% in 2011, less than the Japanese yen, which increased 6.3%.

and tolerance of finance-based credit expansion which flooded the globe with credit[15]; (9) lax regulation of post-Bretton Woods international capital flows (early 1970); (10) the "shareholder primacy" movement of the 1980s partnered Wall Street with CEOs to increase management's ability to enrich itself at shareholder expense, widening the gap between ownership and control first brought to light by Adolf Berle and Gardner Means in 1932[16]; (11) an indulgent attitude toward destructive financial innovation apparent in the 1987 "program trading," and 2000–2002 "dot-com bubble" stock market crashes[17]; as well as the 1998 Long-Term Capital Management hedge fund collapse[18]; (12) a permissive approach to financial auditing,[19] including mark to face valuation for illiquid

---

[15] Subprime mortgages involved loans to people likely to encounter difficulty maintaining their repayment schedules. ARMS allowed homeowners to borrow inexpensively, but obligated them to pay more if interest rates rose. Additionally, during the new millennium, it was common for banks to waive down payments, enabling "owners" to walk away from their properties when housing prices (and values) fell, leaving banks with an huge inventory of bankruptcy repossessions and distressed sales. The Clinton Administration pushed subprime lending. The value of U.S. subprime mortgages in 2007 was 1.3 trillion dollars. In an inflationary environment, driven in part by people borrowing from their home's inflationary premium, home buying was transformed into a speculative game. The ratio of global liquidity to global GDP quadrupled during 1980–2007, doubling in 2000–2007. Cross-border capital flows decupled during 1990–2007 from 1.1 to 11.2 trillion dollars. Derivatives rose from virtually zero in 1990 to 684 trillion dollars in 2007. American nonfinancial debt outpaced GDP growth since 2007 by 8 trillion dollars. See Mills (2009), p. 51.

[16] Berle and Means (1932). *The Modern Corporations and Private Property.*

[17] The dot-com bubble began shortly after Federal Reserve Chair Alan Greenspan's "irrational exuberance" speech on December 5, 1996. For proof that dot-com stocks were grossly overvalued, see Delong and Magin (2006). The Nasdaq composite index peaked at 5,132.52 on March 10, 2000, and bottomed at 1,108.49 on October 10, 2002. The Enron accounting scam, tied to energy deregulation and lax accounting by Arthur Anderson, also contributed to the slaughter.

[18] Nobel Prize laureate Myron Scholes and Robert Merton famous for devising a new method for valuing derivatives were members of LTCMs board of directors.

[19] Richard Bowen, III testified to the Financial Crisis Inquiry Commission that mortgage underwriting standards collapsed in the final years of the U.S. housing bubble (2006–2007). About 60% of mortgages purchased by Citicorp from some 1,600 mortgage companies were defective. Clayton Holdings reported in parallel testimony that only 54% of mortgage loans met their originators' underwriting standards.

securities; (13) the creation of a one-way-street, too big to fail mentality that transformed prudent business activity into a venal speculative game on Wall Street, main street and in Washington; (14) the 2001 Wall Street stock crash, which shifted speculative exuberance from stocks to hard assets (commodities, land, natural resources, precious metals, art, antiques, jewelry), and paved the way for the subordination of individual stock market investment to institutional speculation[20]; (15) credit easing in the wake of the dot-com bust, orchestrated by the Federal Reserve, which started a consumer credit binge, reflected in high consumption and low savings rates, adding fuel to the inflationary fires; (16) 9/11 and the Iraq war, which swelled America's federal budget deficit and triggered a petro bubble (and broadbased commodity inflation); (17) an epochal surge in global economic growth led by Brazil, India, Russia, and China (BRICs) wrought by technology transfer, outsourcing and foreign direct investment, which induced a wave of speculative euphoria; (18) Chinese stealth "beggar-thy-neighbor" renminbi undervaluation and dollar reserve hoarding, reflected in Chinese under importing, a burgeoning American current account deficit and an overseas "savings glut" which exacerbated inflationary pressures, raised prices for American treasuries and lowered interest rates, (widely mischaracterized as "financing imports"); (19) the 2006 American housing bust which toxified mortgage and derivative financial instruments[21]; (20) the emergence of "institutional" bank runs, where

---

[20] Jack Bogle, Founder of Vanguard Group, privately estimated that 40 trillion of the 41 trillion traded on world stock exchanges in 2009 year is speculative. The institutional share of American stock market investment has risen in the last two decades from 8% to 70%.

[21] American housing prices peaked in early 2005 and the Case–Shiller home price index began falling in 2006. Prices plunged 34% thereafter, bottoming in 2009, and are expected to continue declining in 2011 despite more than a trillion dollars of government support. On December 24, 2009, the Treasury Department pledged unlimited support for the next three years to Fannie Mae and Freddie Mac, despite 400 billion dollars in losses. The bubble was predicted by Robert Shiller in 2000. See Shiller (2000), *Irrational Exuberance* and Shiller (2008), *The Subprime Solution: How Today's the Global Financial Crisis Happened, and What to Do About It.* As early as 1997, the Federal Reserve Chairman Alan Greenspan fought to keep derivates unregulated, a goal codified in the Commodity Futures Modernization Act of 2000. Derivative like credit default swaps (CDS) were used to hedge or speculate against particular credit risks. Their volume increased 100-fold during 1998–2008, with estimates of the debt ranging as high as 47 trillion dollars. Total

financial and nonfinancial companies flee repurchase (repo) agreements, (21) rapidly mounting sovereign debt in Iceland, several EU states,[22] as well as similarly onerous debt obligations in California and Illinois; (22) a naive faith in "divine coincidence"; (23) a colossal regulatory blunder

---

over-the-counter derivative notional value rose to 683 trillion dollars by June 2008. Warren Buffet described the phenomenon as "financial weapons of mass destruction." *The Economist*, September 18, 2008.

[22] Debt obligations issued by nation states are called sovereign debt. Superficially, it might be supposed that sovereign bonds are more secure than their corporate equivalents, but the reverse often is the case because under the doctrine of sovereign immunity, countries cannot be forced to honor their obligations. Creditors only recourse is to passively accept rescheduling, interest reductions or even repudiation, see Eaton and Fernandez (1995). Sovereign debt initially played a subsidiary role in the 2008 financial crisis. The collapse of Iceland's main banks, and 77% stock plunge in September 2008, prompted rating agencies to drastically cut Iceland's sovereign debt rating from A+ to BBB–. The IMF arranged a rescue package November 19, 2008, but the cat was out of the bag. Suddenly, investors became aware that the global financial crisis's scope might be much wider than earlier supposed, raising the specter of a worldwide financial collapse that was not reversed until March 2009. Nonetheless, sovereign debt fears re-emerged in 2010 due to credit rating reductions for Greek, Irish, Portuguese, and Spanish sovereign debt that forced an EU to intervene in defense of these members. The rescue involved loans for conditionality, where credit impaired sovereigns were compelled to pledge the adoption of austerity measures reducing their "structural deficits." The problem which could easily expand to include Italy, and others, does not appear to jeopardize the international financial system immediately, but is a bad omen for the future. Additionally, many worry that if rating cuts contingent on budgetary debt reductions do not cease, it could force the EU to abandon the Euro as a common currency, and even result in the EU's dissolution. The root cause of the EU's problem is not excessive debt per se, but the ability of less productive members to run EU threatening deficits in a common currency regime, without the option of individual country currency devaluation. See Dallago and Guglielmetti (2011). As we know from the theory of optimum currency areas, there are benefits and costs to currency integration. Benefits are the reduced costs of doing business. If they are large, forming currency areas lead to large increases in trade. This is not what happened in the Eurozone after the monetary union was established. The key problem is building a consensus on how best to restore price equilibrium after asymmetric shocks, booms, and slumps that disparately affect individual member states. Labor mobility (Robert Mundell), fiscal integration (Peter Kenen), a strong central bank serving as lender of last recourse, and a fiscal unit to bail out sovereign debts lubricate equilibration, but do not automatically resolve conflicting member interests. The EU sovereign debt issue is tutoring members about the trade-offs that must be made, if the monetary union is to survive.

in imposing "mark to market" valuation (Fair Accounting Standard: FAS 157) of illiquid assets from November 15, 2007[23]; (24) increased separation of ownership from corporate control enabling top executives to excessively compensate themselves, including golden parachute perks. CEOs were institutionally encouraged to gamble with shareholders' money at negligible personal risk. (Bogle, 2011: p. 488) The 2008 global financial crisis thus was not just a garden variety White Swan business cyclical event. It was a long time coming, and prospects for a repetition depend on whether underlying structural disequilibria, including political indiscipline, are redressed.[24]

2.3. The Shock Wave

The defining event of the 2008 global financial crisis was a "hemorrhagic stroke"; a paralytic implosion of the loanable funds market that seemingly brought the global monetary and credit system to the brink of Armageddon. The September 2008 emergency was caused by the terrifying realization that major financial institutions, especially those connected with hedge funds, could not cover their current obligations either with asset sales or short-term bank credit because confidence had been lost in the value of their assets, and short-term lending suddenly ceased. People everywhere panicked at the prospect of cascading financial bankruptcies, where the securities of failed companies contaminated the value of other assets, triggering margin calls, shuttered credit access, lost savings, bank runs, stock market crashes, liquidity crises, universal insolvency, economic collapse, and global ruination. All crises are ominous, but this one seemed as if it just might degenerate into a Black Swan debacle (Taleb, 2007), equal to or greater than the Great Depression of 1929. After all, the U.S.

---

[23] FDIC chairman William Issac places much of the blame for the subprime mortgage crisis on the SEC for its fair-value accounting rules, misapplied in times of crisis. The Emergency Stabilization Act of 2008, signed on October 7, suspended mark to market asset pricing during crises. The new regulation is FAS 157-d.

[24] Morici (2010) "Down Grade U.S. Treasury's to Junk". Peter Morici contends that Congress and the White House made no compromise whatsoever in extending and expanding the Bush tax cuts, including a temporary 33% cut in poor and middle class social security taxes, ballooning the federal deficit to 1.5 trillion dollars in 2011; to say nothing of off-budget deficits ten times as large.

Treasury and Federal Reserve Bank had reassured the public that the forced sale of the "risk management" investment banking firm Bear Stearns to JP Morgan Chase on March 24, 2008, for 5.8% of its prior high value had fully solved the subprime loan, mortgage, and derivative securitization threat, but subsequent events revealed that Bear Stearns was just the tip of a potentially Titanic sinking iceberg, with American and European banking losses during 2007–2010 forecast by the IMF to reach 1 trillion, and 1.6 trillion dollars, respectively.[25] An additional 4 to 5 trillion dollars are expected to be lost through 2011, and although the Dow Jones Industrial Average fully recovered from the September 2008 highs by December 2010, 42% of its value was wiped out at the stock market crash's trough.[26]

The other shoe began falling on September 7, 2008, when the Federal National Mortgage Association (Fannie Mae), and the Federal Home Loan Mortgage Corporation (Freddie Mac) (specializing in creating a secondary mortgage market) were placed into conservatorship by the Federal Housing Financing Agency after new mark to market accounting regulations (FAS 157) created havoc in the mortgage industry.[27] At the

---

[25] Bear Stearns, founded in 1923 had survived the 1929 Wall Street crash, and achieved celebrity status in the new millennium because of Lewis Ranieri's pioneering innovation of the mortgage-backed securitization business. Its problems became public in June 2007 when the company pledged a 3.2-billion-dollar collateralized loan (collateralized debt obligation: CDO) to rescue one of its hedge funds. The CDOs were thinly traded, and when Bear Stern encountered liquidity problems, Merrill Lynch seized 850 million dollars worth, but only realized 100 million in forced liquidation. During the week of July 16, 2007, Bear Stearns acknowledged that its two CDO-supported hedge funds had lost nearly all their value amid a rapid decline in the subprime mortgages market. On March 14, 2008, the Federal Reserve Bank of New York agreed to grant Bear Stearns a 25-billion-dollar loan collateralized by free and clear assets from Bear Stearn in order to provide liquidity for 28 days. The deal, however, was changed two days later into a forced bailout when the Federal Reserve decided that the loan would be given to Bear Stearn's shotgun bride, JP Morgan, enticed into the marriage by a 35 billion non-recourse Federal Reserve loan. The action approved by Ben Bernanke, putting public money at risk, was justified by the necessity of preventing systemic failure, and forestalling the need for further intervention.

[26] The Dow Jones Industrial Average peaked on October 9, 2007, at 14,164, and bottomed on March 9 at 6,470. In early September 2008, it traded around 11,500, just where it stood at the end of 2010. The DJIA rose 4.7% in 2011.

[27] Lending institutions were abruptly required to write their illiquid mortgage assets down to rapidly falling current values, forcing them to sell securities to raise capital, and generating a vicious downward credit spiral.

time, Fannie Mae and Freddie Mac held 12 trillion dollars worth of mortgages.[28] Three days later on September 10, 2008, the "risk management" investment bank Lehman Brothers declared bankruptcy after having failed to find a buyer or acquire a Federal bailout to cover a 4-billion-dollar loss. Merrill Lynch, finding itself in similar dire straits, was sold to the Bank of America on the same day. Six days later, the Federal Reserve announced an 85-billion-dollar rescue loan to the insurance giant American International Group (AIG), also heavily involved in "risk management" securitization activities. The news ignited a wave of Wall Street short selling, prompting the SEC to suspend short selling immediately thereafter. Then on September 20 and 21, 2008, the Secretary of the Treasury Henry Paulson and Federal Reserve Chairman Ben Bernanke appealed directly to the U.S. Congress for an endorsement of their 700-billion-dollar emergency loan package designed to purchase massive amounts of sour mortgages from distressed institutions. Forty-eight hours later, Warren Buffett bought 9% of Goldman Sachs, another "risk management" investment bank for 5 billion dollars to prop the company up. On September 24, Washington Mutual became America's largest bank failure ever, and was acquired by JP Morgan Chase for 1.9 billion dollars.

These cumulating disasters, exacerbated by parallel developments in Europe and many other parts of the globe addicted to structural deficits, Phillips Curve–justified inflation, financial deregulation, asset-backed mortgages, derivatives, electronic trading, and hard asset speculation, sent shock waves through the global financial system, including the withdrawal of hundreds of billions of dollars from money market mutual funds (an aspect of the shadow banking system), depriving corporations of an important source of short-term borrowing. The London Interbank Offered Rate (LIBOR), the reference interest rate at which banks borrow unsecured funds from other banks in the London wholesale money market soared, as did TED spreads (T Bills versus Eurodollar future contracts), spiking to 4.65% on October 10, 2008, both indicating that liquidity was being rapidly withdrawn from the world financial system. In what seemed like the blink of an eye, the global financial crisis not only triggered a

---

[28] Both firms were subsequently delisted from the New York Stock Exchange in June 2010 because their share prices fell below one dollar.

wave of worldwide bankruptcies, plunging production, curtailed international trade, and resulting in mass unemployment, but morphed into a sovereign debt crisis. Countries like Iceland, Ireland, Greece, Portugal, Italy, and Spain found themselves mired in domestic and foreign debt that dampened aggregate effective demand, spawned double-digit unemployment and even raised the specter of EU dissolution (Dallago and Guglielmetti, 2011).

These overwhelming events, together with collapsing global equity, bond, and commodity markets, unleashed a frenzy of advice and emergency policy intervention aimed at staunching the hemorrhaging, bolstering aggregate effective demand, and repairing regulatory lapses to restore business confidence. FAS 157-d (suspension of mark to mark financial asset pricing) broke the free fall of illiquid, mortgage-backed asset valuations, offering some eventual support in resale markets. The Emergency Stabilization Relief Act bailed out system threatening bankruptcy candidates through emergency loans and toxic asset purchases. FDIC savings deposits insurance was increased from 100,000 to 250,000 dollars per account to forestall bank runs. The SEC temporarily suspended short selling on Wall Street. The government pressured banks to postpone foreclosures invoking a voluntary foreclosure moratorium enacted in July 2008.[29] The Federal Reserve and Treasury resorted to quantitative easing (essentially printing money) to bolster liquidity and drive short-term government interest rates toward zero, effectively subsidizing financial institutions at depositors' expense. The federal government quadrupled its budgetary deficit in accordance with Heller's neo-Keynesian aggregate demand management tactic, concentrating on unemployment and other social transfers, instead of the direct investment stimulation advocated by Keynes.[30] Committees were formed to devise bank capital "stress tests,"

---

[29] The moratorium was suspended in March 2009, but then applied again in 2010 by most states. Calls for further moratoria are still being heard in 2011.

[30] Alan Blinder and Mark Zandi (July 17, 2010) "How the Great Recession Was Brought to an End," the breakdown of the American one-trillion-dollar counter crisis fiscal stimulus package is divisible into two baskets: spending increases ($682 billion) and tax cuts ($383 billion). The Economic Stimulus Act of 2008 spent $170 billion. The American Recovery and Reinvestment Act of 2009 disbursed another $582 billion dollars on infrastructure ($147 billion; including $109 billion dollars of "nontraditional" infrastructure);

coordinate global banking reform, (Levinson, 2010) improve auditing and oversight, prosecute criminal wrong doing including Ponzi schemes (Bernard Madoff),[31] and investigate regulatory reform of derivatives and electronic trading (Dodd–Frank Wall Street Reform and Consumer Protection Act, July 2010).[32] In Europe, many imperiled banks were temporarily nationalized, and a series of intra-EU austerity and rescue programs launched. In the larger global arena, the IMF, World Bank, and others provided emergency assistance, and the deep problem of Chinese state-controlled trading was gingerly broached.

With the advantage of hindsight, it is evident the American government's Troubled Asset Relief Program (TARP), including the "cash for clunkers" program, other deficit spending and quantitative easing, passive acceptance of Chinese under-importing (dollar reserve hoarding), continued indulgence of destructive speculative practices(program trading, hedge funds, and derivatives), together with regulatory reforms and confidence building initiatives did not cause a Black Swan meltdown and the subsequent hyper-depression many justifiably feared.[33] Some of these

---

transfers to state and local governments($174 billion dollars: Medicaid $87 billion dollars, education $87 billion dollars), transfers to persons ($271 billion dollars: social security $13 billion dollars, unemployment assistance $224 billion dollars, food stamps $10 billion dollars and Cobra payments $24 billion dollars). Tax cuts under the 2009 act totaled $190 billion dollars, allocated to businesses ($40 billion dollars), making work pay ($64 billion dollars), first time homebuyer tax credit ($14 billion dollars), and individuals ($72 billion dollars). Subsequently, the government also provided $55 billion dollars of extended unemployment insurance benefits. See Table 10, p. 15. More than 90% of the stimulus was targeted at bolstering aggregate effective demand through transfers and tax rebates in the post 1960s Heller fashion, rather than in direct investment assistance (traditional infrastructure, business tax credits and first time home buyer credits) as Keynes himself recommended.
[31] Bernard Madoff, non-executive chairman of NASDAQ and founder of Bernard L. Madoff Investment Securities, LLC was sentenced to 150 years imprisonment and forfeiture of 17 billion dollars for a Ponzi scheme fraud costing investors 10–20 billion dollars, exposed by the 2008 financial crisis. Allen Stanford, Chairman of the Stanford Financial Group was charged with a similar fraud. Stanford was convicted March 6, 2012, and is serving a 110-year prison sentence.
[32] The Dodd–Frank Act contains 16 titles, strewn with prohibitions, rules, and rate fixing. It is difficult to render a summary judgment but has been criticized for not addressing the too big to fail issue, and indulging political at the expense of regulatory goals.
[33] Carmen Reinhart and Kenneth Rogoff have discovered startling qualitative and quantitative parallels across a number of standard financial crisis indicators in 18 post-war banking

same policies may deserve credit for fostering a recovery, tepid as it is,[34] but also can be blamed for persistent, near double-digit unemployment, a resurgence of commodity, stock, and foreign currency speculation, and the creation of conditions for a sovereign debt crisis of biblical proportions in the years ahead when the globe is eventually confronted with tens of trillions of dollars of unfunded, and un-repayable obligations.[35]

At the end of the day, it should not be surprising that the institutionalized excess demand disequilibrium of the American and European macroeconomic management systems would produce some relief, even though their policies were inefficient and unjust. Financial stability is being gradually restored, and output is increasing for the moment, but the adjustment burden has been borne disproportionately by the unemployed, would-be job entrants, small businesses, savers, pensioners, the next generation (impending national debt crisis), and a myriad of random victims, while malefactors, including politicians and policymakers, were bailed out.[36] Moreover, the mentality and institutions which created the crisis in the first place remain firmly in command. Incredibly, the Obama administration under cover of the Frank–Dodd Act already has begun mandating a massive expansion of the very same subprime loans largely

---

crises. They found that banking crises were protracted (output declining on average for two years); asset prices fell steeply, with housing plunging 35% on average, and equity prices declining by 55% over 3.5 years. Unemployment rises by 7 percentage points over four years, while output falls by 9%. Two important common denominators were reduced consumption caused by diminished wealth effects, and impaired balance sheets resistant to monetary expansion (liquidity trap). These regularities indicate that forecasts of a swift V-shaped recovery after the 2008 financial crisis were never justified based on historical precedent, although, it appears that this time a double dip recession, and a Black Swan catastrophe have been averted. See Reinhart and Rogoff (2009).

[34] America's real GDP as of January 1, 2012, remained below the end year 2008 level, but up from the 2009 bottom. Recovery is conventionally measured from the trough.

[35] The figure includes unfunded social security obligations, but excludes mortgage insurance guarantees.

[36] "The Perfect Bailout: Fannie and Freddie Now Directly to Wall Street," *Yahoo!Finance*, February 2, 2011. Treasury Secretary Tim Geithner is providing Fannie Mae and Freddie Mac with as much credit as they need to purchase toxic mortgages held by banks at prices that will not produce book losses. This amounts to a stealthy taxpayer payer funded bailout, giving a green light to all parties to repeat the reckless lending that caused the 2008 financial crisis confident that they will reap the gains, and taxpayer will eat the losses.

responsible for the 2006 housing crisis and the 2008 financial debacle that swiftly ensued (Rosefielde and Mills, 2013).[37] This action and others like it will continue putting the global economy squarely at Black Swan risk until academics and policymakers prioritize financial stability over parochial, partisan, ideological, and venal advantage (Wedel, 2009).

The 2008 financial crisis also has placed macroeconomic theory in a quandary. The "divine coincidence" is now seen for the pipedream that it was, but there is no new consensus to replace it other than the pious hope that structural deficits, loose monetary policy, and better financial regulation (aggregate demand management) will foster prosperity no matter how irresponsibly politicians, policymakers, businessmen, financial institutions, special interests, and speculators behave (White, 2010). Worse still, there seems to be little prospect that a constructive consensus soon will emerge capable of disciplining contemporary societies for the greater good by promoting optimal efficiency, growth, and economic stability. The global economy is flying blind, propelled by an intransigent mentality that spells trouble ahead with scant hope for learning by doing. Most players seem to believe that contemporary monetary and fiscal management,

---

[37] Wallison and Pinto (December 27, 2010), "How the Government is Creating another Bubble," *AEI Articles and Commentary*. Wallison and Pinto contend that the Dodd–Frank Act allows the administration to substitute the Federal Housing Administration (FHA) for Fannie Mae and Freddie Mac as the principal and essentially unlimited provider of subprime mortgage, at taxpayers' expense. Since the 2008 government takeover of Fannie Mae and Freddie Mac, the government-sponsored enterprises' regulator has restricted them to purchasing high-quality mortgages, with affordable housing requirements mandated in 1992 relaxed. This reduces the future risk, but the good is entirely negated by shunting the old destructive practices to the FHA on the pretext of supporting the soundness of the entire mortgage industry. The gambit in the usual way, allows the administration to present a prudent face with regard to Fannie Mae and Freddie Mac, while diverting attention from the 400-billion-dollar loss previously racked up by Fannie Mae and Freddie Mac, and recklessly reprising the Housing and Urban Development Administration's (HUD) prior destructive policies. Wallison, Pollock, and Pinto (January 20, 2011) "Taking the Government Out of Housing Finance: Principles for Reforming the Housing Finance Market, AEI Online. Peter Wallison, Alex Pollock, and Edward Pinto report that the U.S. government sponsored 27 million subprime and Alt-policies. To correct the situation, they recommend that the government get out of the housing finance business. Government regulation should be restricted to ensuring mortgage credit quality. Assistance to low-income families should be on-budget. Fannie Mae and Freddie Mac should be privatized.

combined with better financial regulation, will work well enough, but they appear to be conflating wishful thinking with economic science.

2.4. Duty to Prevent

The global financial crisis of 2008 and the PIIGS debacle were foreseeable and were foreseen. Both were preventable as will be the next episode already under construction. The record reveals a profound myopia, intransigence, and unwillingness to learn that is unlikely to be remedied by better theory and patchwork stress tests.

There are no panaceas, but establishing a government body dedicated exclusively to monitoring, diagnosing, and surgically remedying bubble phenomena well before any great rupture surely should be considered a constructive first step. The Bubble Prevention Authority (BPA) cannot supersede other regulatory and advisory agencies, but it could prove a counterweight to wishful thinking by putting the government formally on notice that cumulative disequilibria are getting out of hand. This can be easily accomplished by requiring the BPA to submit seminal annual reports to Congress detailing risks and proposing concrete action, both in the short and intermediate term.

References

Berle, Adolf and Gardner Means (1932) *The Modern Corporations and Private Property*, New York: Macmillan.

Bernanke, Ben (2004) *Essays on the Great Depression*, Princeton, NJ: Princeton University Press.

Bernanke, Ben, Carol Bertaut, Laurie Pounder DeMarco and Steven Kamin (2011) "International Capital Flows and Returns to Safe Assets in the United States, 2003–2007," Federal Reserve System International Financial Discussion Paper No.1014.

Blinder, Alan and Mark Zandi (2010) "How the Great Recession Was Brought to an End," Blinder-Zandi Report, July 27. Available at: www.economy.com/mark-zandi/documents/End-of-Great-Recession.pdf.

Bogle, John (2011) *Don't Count on It*, New York: John Wiley, p. 488.

Dallago, Bruno and Chiara Guglielmetti (2011) "The Eurozone and Global Imbalances: Two Europes?" in Steven Rosefielde, Masaaki Kuboniwa and

Satoshi Mizobata, *Two Asias: The Emerging Postcrisis Divide*, Singapore: World Scientific.

De Grauwe, Paul (2010) "Top-Down Versus Bottom-Up Macroeconomics," *CESifo Economic Studies*, Vol. 56, No. 4, pp. 465–497.

Delong, J. Bradford and Konstatine Magin (2006) "A Short Note on the Size of the Dot-Com Bubble," National Bureau of Economic Research Working Paper 12011.

Dooley, Michael P., David Folkerts-Landau and Peter Garber (2004) "The Revived Bretton Woods System," NBER Working Paper No. 10332.

Eaton, Jonathan and Raquel Fernandez (1995) "Sovereign Debt," in G. Grossman and K. Rogoff, *Handbook of International Economics*, Chapter 39, Vol. III, Amsterdam: Elsevier Science B.V.

The Economist (2008) "A Nuclear Winter?" September 18.

Eichengreen, Barry (2004) "Global imbalances and the lessons of Bretton Woods," NBER Working Paper No. 10497.

Greenspan, Alan (1996) "The Challenge of Central Banking in a Democratic Society," Speech, December 5.

Keynes, John Maynard (1936) *The General Theory of Employment, Interest and Money*, London: Macmillan.

Krugman, Paul (2012) "Nobody Understands Debt," *New York Times*, January 1.

Kydland, Phil and Edward Prescott (1982), "Time to Build and Aggregate Fluctuations," *Econometrica*, Vol. 50, No. 6, pp. 1345–1370.

Levinson, Mark (2010) "Faulty Basel: Why More Diplomacy Won't Keep the Financial System Safe," *Foreign Affairs*, May/June, Vol. 89, No. 3, pp. 76–88.

Lucas, Robert Jr (1972) "Expectations and the Neutrality of Money," *Journal of Economic Theory*, Vol. 4, No. 2, pp. 103–124.

Lucas, Robert Jr. (2003), "Macroeconomic Priorities," *American Economic Review*, Vol. 93, No. 1, pp. 1–14.

Mills, Quinn (2009) *World Financial Crisis 2008–2010: What Happened, Who is to Blame and How to Protect Your Money*, Create Space.

Morici, Peter (2010) "Down Grade US Treasury's to Junk" Yahoo!Finance, December 20.

Phillips, William (1958) "The Relationship between Unemployment and the Rate of Change of Money Wages in the United Kingdom 1861–1957," *Economica*, Vol. 25, No. 100, pp. 283–299.

Reinhart, Carmen and Kenneth Rogoff (2009) *This Time is Different: Eight Centuries of Financial Folly*, Princeton, NJ: Princeton University Press.

Rosefielde, Steven (2011) "East-West Convergence and Intra-Asian Leveling," in Steven Rosefielde, Masaaki Kuboniwa and Satoshi Mizobata, *Two Asias: The Emerging Postcrisis Divide*, Singapore: World Scientific.

Rosefielde, Steven and Quinn Mills (2013) *Democracy and Its Elected Enemies: American Political Capture and Economic Decline*, Cambridge: Cambridge University Press.

Shiller, Robert (2000) *Irrational Exuberance*, Princeton NJ: Princeton University Press.

Shiller, Robert (2008) *The Subprime Solution: How Today's the Global Financial Crisis Happened, and What to Do About It*, Princeton, NJ: Princeton University Press.

Stiglitz, Joseph (2010) "New 600B Stimulus Fuels Fears of US Currency Wars," *Democracy Now*, November 5.

Stiglitz, Joseph (2011) "Contagion, Liberalization and the Optimal Structure of Globalization," *Journal of Globalization and Development*, Vol. 1, No. 2.

Taleb, Nassim (2007) *The Black Swan: The Impact of the Highly Improbable*, New York: Random House.

Tett, Gillian (2011) "The State is Now the Dominant force in US Capital Markets," *Financial Times*, July 1.

Wagner, Daniel (2011) "Watchdog: Gov't pay rules had few lasting effects" *Associated Press Online*, February 10.

Wallison, Peter J. and Edward Pinto (2010) "How the Government is Creating another Bubble," *AEI Articles and Commentary*, December 27.

Wallison, Peter J., Alex Pollock and Edward Pinto (2011) "Taking the Government Out of Housing Finance: Principles for Reforming the Housing Finance Market," *AEI Online*, January 20.

Wedel, Janine (2009) *Shadow Elites: How the World's New Power Brokers Undermine Democracy, Government and the Free Market*, New York: Basic Books.

White, William (2010) "Some Alternative Perspectives on Macroeconomic Theory and Some Policy Implications," Federal Reserve Bank of Dallas Globalization and Monetary Policy Institute, Working Paper No. 54.

Yahoo!Finance (2011) "The Perfect Bailout: Fannie and Freddie Now Directly to Wall Street," February 2.

The Atlantic (2011) "Why Bank of America Must be Thrilled to Pay a 3 Billion Dollar Penalty," January 4.

CHAPTER 3

CRISIS IN TRANSITIONING COUNTRIES

YOJI KOYAMA

3.1. Introduction

A group of countries consisting of Albania and successor countries of
the former Yugoslavia, excluding Slovenia, has been called the "Western
Balkans" by the European Union (EU). All these were previously socialist countries, although their governing systems were quite different (self-
managed in the former Yugoslavia versus extreme Stalinist in Albania).
There was system change in the former Yugoslavia in 1989–1990 and
also in Albania in 1992. The process of the transition to a market economy proceeded afterward. In the case of the former Yugoslavia, the
systems change resulted in the breakup of the former Yugoslav
Federation. It is still fresh in our memory that there were severe ethnic
conflicts in 1991–1995 and the Kosovo war in 1999. These events caused
turbulence, economic stagnation, and a delay in EU accession. As the
Balkans has been historically called "Europe's powder keg," the region
has been unstable. If it is neglected it might threaten the security of the
EU. In order to solve the problem, the Stabilization and Association
Process was initiated by the EU in 1999, which created brighter prospects for their EU accession.

The European Council, held in June 2011, decided that Croatia would
be admitted to the EU in July 2013. Now Macedonia, Serbia and
Montenegro are candidates while the rest of the Western Balkan countries
are potential candidates.

The countries of the Western Balkans are located on the periphery
of Europe and, generally speaking, are poor. Among them, Croatia is

comparatively rich. Its GDP per capita in 2009 is €10,100 the highest in the Western Balkans, far higher than in Bulgaria (€4,500) and Romania (€5,500), which joined the EU in 2007 (Gligorov *et al.*, 2010). The Western Balkan economy steadily developed after 2000 and was expected to continue growing. However, the global financial crisis, culminating in the Lehman Shock on September 15, 2008, crushed this expectation. The shock's intensity varied among these countries. Croatia was hit hardest by the global financial crisis.

This chapter investigates why the Balkan economies are vulnerable, using Croatia as an example.[1] It begins by describing the economies of the West Balkans, and the global financial crisis's impact on them. Second, Croatia's crisis management is reviewed. Third, Croatia's economic development after the 1990 regime change is traced to provide a better understanding of why it was so vulnerable to external shocks. Fourth, Croatia's chronic current account deficit is discussed. Fifth, Croatia's "Economic Recovery Program" announced in April 2010 is evaluated. Finally the chapter offers some conclusions.

3.2. Characteristics of the Economies of the Western Balkans and Impact of the Global Financial Crisis on them

3.2.1. *Characteristics of the economies of the Western Balkans*

West Balkan economies have been greatly dependent on the EU economy. Their main foreign trade partners are EU member countries. 60%–80% of their exports went to the EU markets, and a similar percentage of imports came from the EU. All West Balkan countries have a common structural

---

[1] For description of this chapter I am indebted to the following researchers: Dr. Radmila Jovancevic, Dr. Ivo Bicanic, Dr. Ivo Druzic, Dr. Vladimir Stipetic, Dr. Tihomir Domazet, Dr. Matko Mestrovic, Dr.Sandra Svaljek, Dr. Dubravko Radosevic, Dr. Ivan Teodorovic, Dr. Maruska Vizek, Dr. Paul Stubbs and Dr. Zoran Aralica. I would like to express special thanks to Dr. Denis Redzepagic (Researcher at the Economics Institute Zagreb) and Dr. Branka Mraovic (Professor at the University of Zagreb, Faculty of Geodesy), both of whom gave me precious comments and a lot of information in response to my repeated inquiries. However, all possible errors should be ascribed solely to the author.

weakness: high unemployment rates, ranging from 8.4% in Croatia to 33.8% in Macedonia, partly mitigated by unrecorded employment in the informal economy (which constitutes more than 30% of GDP throughout the Western Balkans). All of the countries have low saving rates (in 2005 gross domestic saving as a percentage of GDP ranged from −2.2% in Bosnia and Herzegovina to 23.3% in Croatia). Aggregate investment rates (in 2005 gross domestic investment rate ranged from 15.9% in Bosnia and Herzegovina to 29.9% in Croatia) exceeded the saving rates, causing chronic current account deficits (Kathuria, 2008, pp. 19, 20).

Therefore, their economic development has relied heavily on foreign savings, i.e. FDI inflow, borrowing from abroad and foreign remittances. Dependence on remittance from abroad has been high, especially in

Table 3.1. Basic West Balkan economic indicators.

	Population (thousands)	Per capita GDP in 2008 (Euro)	Unemployment rate in 2008 (%)	Remittance from abroad in 2006 (% of GDP)	National currency	Exchange rate regime*
Croatia	4,435	10,700	8.4	2.9	Kuna	Managed floating
Macedonia	2,047	3,200	33.8	4.3	Denar	Hard peg
Albania	3,177	2,800	13.1	14.9	Lek	Floating exchange rate
Bosnia and Herzegovina	3,842	3,300	23.4	17.6	Convertible Mark (KM)	Currency board
Montenegro	629	4,900	17.2	13.6	Euro	Unilateral euro adoption
Serbia	7,350	4,600	13.6		Dinar	Managed floating
Kosovo	2,200	1,726**	42.2***	n.a.	Euro	Unilateral euro adoption

Source: Astrov (2010).

* Bartlett and Monastiriotis (2010), ** Gashi (2010), p. 81. ***European Commission.

Table 3.2.   FDI inflow in Southeastern Europe.

	FDI inflow (million EUR)							Per capita inflow (EUR)	Per capita stock (EUR)
	2001	2002	2003	2004	2005	2006	2007	2008	2008	2008
Albania	232	143	157	278	213	259	481	682	215	935
Bosnia	133	282	338	567	493	572	1546	690	179	1,400
Croatia	1,468	1,138	1,762	950	1,468	2,765	3,667	2,930	661	4,930
Macedonia	499	112	100	261	77	345	506	413	201	1,600
Montenegro	5	76	44	53	393	644	1,008	832	1,325	4,864
Serbia	184	504	1,204	777	1,265	3,516	2,272	1,879	256	1,586

Source: Hunya (2008), p. 8; Hunya (2009), p. 8.

Bosnia and Herzegovina, Albania, and Serbia and Montenegro (in 2006 the remittance from abroad as a percentage of GDP was 17.6%, 14.9% and 13.6% respectively).

After 2000, especially after 2005 the amount of FDI inflow in this region increased remarkably (Table 3.2). The following reasons can be mentioned: West Balkan wages are lower than in Central Europe; West Balkans enjoy preferential EU access, and have liberalized intra-regional trade (Kekic, 2005: p. 6). Moreover, Croatia and Macedonia were granted a status of candidate by the EU in 2005. It seems that this fact favors both countries.

As Table 3.3 shows, inward FDI flowed mostly into services, especially banking, telecommunications and real estate rather than manufacturing. Apparently, conditions in the manufacturing sector were not sufficiently attractive to foreign investors, contrary to local expectations. Greenfield investment has been small because inward FDI has favored opportunities associated with the privatization of existing assets.

The presence of foreign banks in the region is remarkable. As of early 2010 the share of banks controlled by foreign-capital in total assets ranges from 75.3% in Serbia to 95.0% in Bosnia and Herzegovina (Table 3.4). Why have foreign banks entered this region? In the 1990s, many enterprises found themselves in financial straits due to the post-communist transformational recession and turbulent situations in the region. State banks suffered from high percentages of nonperforming loans previously

Table 3.3. Inward FDI: Sectoral distribution in Albania, Bosnia, Croatia, and Macedonia.

	ALB	BOSNIA	CRO	MAC	WB-4
(as of December 2007, share in %)					
Manufacturing	36.3	19.0	23.0	35.6	23.5
Electricity, gas and water supply	0.2	—	0.6	6.4	0.9
Construction	5.6	0.7	0.4	3.4	0.7
Wholesale, retail trade, repair of veh. etc.	9.6	8.1	5.3	10.4	6.1
Hotels and restaurants	3.0	—	2.7	2.1	2.3
Transport, storage and communication	36.9	16.4	10.9	21.3	12.6
Financial intermediation	2.4	39.1	53.2	12.6	47.9
Real estate, renting and business activities	3.3	1.3	1.8	4.2	1.9
Others	2.9	15.5	2.1	4.1	4.1
Total	100.0	100.0	100.0	100.0	100.0

Source: Hunya (2009), p. 44.

provided to these enterprises by the state. Governments in the region could not afford to recapitalize these domestic banks. In addition, domestic banks lacked contemporary managerial know-how, loan assessment experience and professional competence. Therefore, they welcomed the entry of foreign banks. At the same time, foreign banks were bullish about West Balkan growth potential, and sought to incorporate local banks into their own network. Foreign-owned banks soon came to possess the lion's share of banking assets. Greek banks are predominant in the southern part of the Western Balkans, while Austrian and Italian banks are predominant in Croatia.

In this region, use of foreign currencies (currency substitution) is prevalent in people's daily lives, a pattern that was also observable during the socialist period in Yugoslavia. Working abroad has been permissible since the second half of the 1960s. Hundreds of thousands of Yugoslavians migrated to West Europe and remitted foreign currencies to their families and relatives back home. Although foreign currencies were not openly used as the medium of exchange at that time (they were used informally), they were often used as medium of value preservation.[2]

In the late 1980s, when inflation turned to hyperinflation in Croatia, it became common to use credit with the *"devizna klauzla"* (foreign exchange clause) as a hedge. A credit with the *devizna klauzla*, in other words, a Kuna credit indexed to foreign currency effectively means that the credit is in a foreign currency, even though the beneficiary is paid in domestic currency. Therefore, "Kuna credits indexed to foreign currency" are close substitutes for foreign currency insofar as they serve as common stores of value. The situation was similar in rest of the former Yugoslavia, and remains unaltered to this day. Interest rates on Kuna loans are comparatively low. These credits typically have been indexed to euro, but in recent years the Swiss Franc also was widely used because lending rates were lower.[3] The use of foreign currency deposits too has been widespread, accounting for almost a half of Monetary aggregate M4 (M4 is the broadest money which comprises Money (M1), savings and time deposits, foreign currency deposits as well as money market instruments) (see Fig. 3.1). This is why people consider the Croatian economy euro-ized.

As shown in Table 3.4, foreign-owned banks account for 90% of the total assets of the Croatian banking system. Domestic banks including foreign-owned banks have been relying heavily on funding from foreign banks. Several years ago, the Croatian National Bank took measures aimed at limiting bank external borrowings, and correspondingly the share of loans granted to domestic banks in the total foreign bank loans, declined from 70.0% in 2003 to 57.3%. By contrast, foreign banks, supported by their domestic affiliates, reconfigured their lending toward direct loans to private enterprises in Croatia. As a result, the

---

[2]In the late 1970s, when I studied in the Republic of Serbia of the Socialist Federal Republic of Yugoslavia I found an advertisement "Deposit your foreign currencies with the Belgrade Bank" on a side-body of buses which run on streets in Belgrade.

[3]The share of Swiss franc–indexed claims in total claims on other domestic sectors increased from 3.1% at end-2004 to 16.9% at end-2009. Most Swiss franc-indexed loans are loans to households. At end-August 2010, these loans accounted for almost one fourth of total credit liabilities of households (*CNB Bulletin*, No. 163, pp. 19–20).

MONETARY AGGREGATE M4

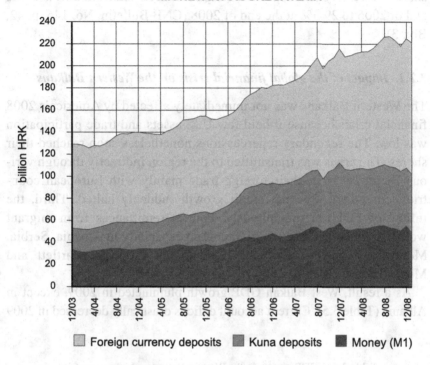

Legend: ▢ Foreign currency deposits ▪ Kuna deposits ■ Money (M1)

Figure 3.1. Croatian monetary aggregates.

Source: CNB *Bulletin*, No. 146, p. 26.
Note: Kuna *deposits* include bonds and money marketing instruments.

Table 3.4. Banking sector in the Western Balkans.

	Domestic credit to private sector (of GDP)	Domestic credit to households (of GDP)	Banking sector assets (of GDP)	Foreign-owned banks share of assets (%)	Loan/deposits ratio
Albania	35.3	13.2	91.0	93.6	65.1
Bosnia	53.5	27.2	87.2	95.0	118.3
Croatia	67.4	37.1	122	90	129.1
Macedonia	43.9	15.5	77.8	93.1	98.4
Montenegro	87.2	31.5	113.8	84.5	122.6
Serbia	39.7	13.9	67.9	75.3	130.6

Source: Country Report, 8 February 2010, UniCredit Group, p. 4 and CNB, Bulletin, No. 146.

share of foreign banks loans to enterprises increased from 20.9% at the end of 2006 to 29.5% at the end of 2008 (CNB Bulletin, No. 146, p. 42, Box 3).

3.2.2. Impact of the global financial crisis on the Western Balkans

The Western Balkans was not immediately affected by America's 2008 financial crisis because it held few U.S. assets and trade participation was low. The secondary repercussions nonetheless soon reached their shores. The crisis was transmitted to the region indirectly through various channels. First, their foreign trade mainly with European countries, contracted. Second, credit growth suddenly halted. Third, the inflow of FDI fell precipitously. Fourth, remittances from migrant workers, which had been very important especially in Albania, Serbia, Montenegro and Bosnia and Herzegovina dropped (Bartlett and Monastiriotis, 2010: p. 3).

As a result, West Balkan GDP growth plummeted in 2009, except in Albania (Table 3.5). Current account deficits drastically decreased in 2009

Table 3.5.   GDP growth in the Western Balkan and other countries.

Country	2007	2008	2009	2010	2011
Croatia	5.1	2.4	−5.8	−1.2	1.0
Macedonia	6.1	5.0	−0.9	0.7	2.0
Albania	5.9	7.7	3.3	4.0	4.1
Bosnia and Herzegovina	6.2	5.7	−3.0	0.9	2.2
Montenegro	10.7	6.9	−5.7	0.5	2.0
Serbia	6.9	5.5	−3.1	1.8	2.5
Reference					
Hungary	0.7	0.9	−6.7	1.2	2.5
Estonia	6.9	−5.0	−13.9	3.1	5.7
Latvia	10.0	−4.2	−18.0	0.0	3.6
Lithuania	9.8	2.9	−14.7	1.3	5.0

Source: Podkaminer *et al.* (2011).

Table 3.6. Changes in current accounts.

	2007	2008	2009	2010*	2011**
Croatia	−7.5	−9.1	−5.5	−1.4	−2.5
Macedonia	−7.1	−12.8	−6.7	−2.8	−6
Albania	−10.6	−15.5	−15.5	−11.9	−11.8
Bosnia and Herzegovina	−10.7	−14.2	−6.2	−5.5	−6.7
Montenegro	−40.2	−51.3	−30.1	−25.7	−21.9
Serbia	−17.7	−21.6	−7.2	−6.9	−8.0

*preliminary.
**forecast.
Source: Podkaminer *et al.* (2011).

in most of the countries because their imports decreased more quickly than exports. Albania was an exception. Its GDP did not decrease in 2009, and its ratio of foreign trade to GDP is small.

Looking at the Western Balkans as a whole, the impact of the crisis has been less drastic than the Baltic States and Hungary (see Table 3.5). The impact varies among countries. Albania managed to maintain positive economic growth, even in 2009. For about 45 years after World War II, it was under Stalinist-style communist rule that isolated it from rest of the world. After the systems change in 1992, the country started the transition to a market economy and simultaneously opened its doors to the outside world. Despite its small size, the ratio of foreign trade to GDP in Albania is still low. Macedonia was less damaged by the global financial crisis. Both countries have points in common. First, their economies have not been export driven. Second, the weight of the financial sector is small, and has been less scathed than most Central and Eastern countries due to their relative insularity (until recently) from international financial markets. However, their dependence on the Greek economy makes them vulnerable to Athen's unfolding mega-crisis.[4]

In Serbia the GDP growth rate decreased from 5.5% in 2008 to −3.1% in 2009, but it recovered to 1.8% in 2010. In the case of Croatia the

---

[4] See Chapter 4 of this book.

situation remains serious. Its GDP growth rate decreased from 2.4% to −5.8%, and the negative growth continued in 2010. The difference in their economic performance may partly be ascribed to their exchange rate regime. Officially both use managed floats. In the case of Serbia, however, the regime is closer to the flexible exchanged rate.[5] After capital inflows suddenly stopped, the domestic currency (dinar) depreciated by 23% in the five months starting in October 2008, and then stabilized throughout 2009. This mitigated the decline in output. In the case of Croatia, its exchange rate regime is, in fact, closer to a Euro peg system. The Croatia exchange rate fluctuated between 7.3 HRK/EUR and 7.5 HRK/EUR during the observed period.[6] It is known that flexible exchange rate regime countries are better than fixed exchange rate regimes in mitigating the negative output effects of demand shocks (Richter, 2009).

Croatia and Central and Eastern Europe countries that have acceded to the EU share many common characteristics. Their incomes level is much higher than the West Balkan average (Albania and Macedonia are the region's poorest members). Their ratio of foreign trade to GDP is high. The weight of their financial sector in the economy is larger, and the dependence on remittances from migrant workers abroad is low. Nonetheless, as mentioned above, Croatia also has important affinities with other countries in the Western Balkans. Its economy is structurally weak, and development depends heavily on foreign capital.

In order to finance their external deficit, Bosnia and Herzegovina and Serbia concluded a Stand-by Agreement with the IMF in 2009 and received $1.6 billion and $4 billion in support, respectively (CEE Quarterly, 2009: p. 24). It is noteworthy that the Vienna Initiative also played a role in mitigating the crisis. The program was initiated in January 2009 by public and private sector stakeholders of EU-based cross-border bank groups active in emerging Europe. The primary

---

[5] "This was a controlled depreciation with the central bank intervening heavily by selling its foreign currency reserves to limit the extent of depreciation" (Petrovic, 2010: p. 115).
[6] Petrovic (2010) says, "Croatia, which is also a highly euroized economy, opted for a much stronger defense of her currency and consequently experienced only a minor depreciation, but also a far larger output decline" (p. 116).

founder was the EBRD. The initiative has been mainly targeted at countries that urgently need IMF/EC macroeconomic support (Hungary, Romania, Serbia, Bosnia and Herzegovina, and Latvia). The main aims are (1) to prevent a large-scale and uncoordinated withdrawal of cross-border bank groups from the region, (2) to ensure that parent bank groups publicly commit to maintain their exposures and recapitalize their subsidiaries, (3) to guarantee that national support packages of cross-border bank groups benefit their subsidiaries in emerging Europe and avoid a home-bias in dealing with Europe's banks, (4) to agree on basic crisis management and crisis resolution principles. Host country authorities are responsible for appropriate macroeconomic policies; liquidity support in local currency irrespective of bank ownership, and supporting their deposit insurance schemes. Parent bank groups — and the home country authorities behind them — are responsible for providing funding in foreign exchange and recapitalizing subsidiaries, and (5) to strengthen cross-border regulatory cooperation and information sharing. Thanks to this initiative, capital outflows were stabilized from Q1 2009, and are the smallest in relative terms in emerging Europe compared with other emerging markets[7] (EBRD, 2010). The Vienna Initiative did not increase loans in the Western Balkans, but it did prevent a full-scale regional banking crisis.

3.3. Impact of the Global Financial Crisis on Croatia

3.3.1. *Impact of the global financial crisis*

The global financial crisis hit Croatia indirectly (mainly through the EU countries) through three channels. First, external demand fell. Demand in the EU countries decreased, causing a decrease in Croatian exports to EU markets. Clothing, furniture, automobile parts and shipbuilding were severely damaged, discouraging domestic investment and weakening aggregate demand.

---

[7] On average during the period Q4 2008–Q1 2009, BIS reporting banks reduced their assets in emerging Europe by less than 4% in contrast to 8%–12% in Russia, Ukraine, Latin America, and other Emerging Asia (EBRD, 2010).

Second, the international financial market tightened. According to Quarterly Report of the Croatian National Bank (*Bulletin*, No. 146), foreign banks played a significant role in financing Croatia's domestic sectors. Croatian banks and nonbanking financial institutions accounted for 57.3% of total foreign bank loans, currency and deposits in 2008, whereas, mostly private owned enterprises accounted for 29.5%, and the public sector 13.2%.[8] As external conditions deteriorated, rollover of debts became much more difficult. Money supply (M1) decreased consecutively for three months from September 2008 (the rate of its growth in September, October and November was −3.55%, −1.83% and −3.11%, respectively). Similarly, the broadest money (M4) decreased for two consecutive months from October (the rates of its growth in October and November were −1.50% and −2.39%,

---

[8] Domestic banks increased their foreign liabilities by as much as EUR 2.1 billion in 4Q 2008 mostly in order to compensate for the withdrawal of household foreign currency deposits and to finance the needs of the central government whose access to direct foreign financing was impeded at that time (*CNB Bulletin*, No. 146, p. 43). The *Bulletin* explains that the withdrawals of household foreign currency deposits in October "were triggered by a temporary decrease in confidence in the banking system" (*CNB Bulletin*, No. 146, p. 25). Banks offset this outflow by increasing their foreign liabilities or more precisely by increasing their borrowings from parent banks abroad (short-term loans, currency and deposits) (Ibid, p. 41). Here it puzzles us outside observers that households withdrew foreign currency deposits, which was nearly bank run. Foreign currency deposits are usually considered to be the most secure instruments for value preservation in transition countries. Why did Croatian people withdraw their deposits? This phenomenon should be interpreted in the institutional context. First, banks worldwide were in trouble at that time. Second, in Croatia there has been a tradition of mistrust in the banking system, even in foreign-capital banks. People had a bitter experience. Many Croatian citizens lost their foreign currency deposits after the collapse of Ljubljanska banka in the early 1990s, and also lost their savings during the banking sector crisis in the 1990s prior to the privatization (Glumina banka, Rijecka banka, etc.). Of course, people use banks' service, but in a pessimistic atmosphere during the global financial crisis, bank run was more likely to occur. I owe Dr. Denis Redzepagic for this interpretation. In addition, there seemed to be a political factor. Some rich individuals with large amounts of money panicked due to some political ongoings in Croatia at that time and withdrew their foreign currency deposits. However, as the situation calmed down very soon they returned their deposits back to the banks and approximately two-thirds of previously withdrawn deposits were returned in two to three months. I owe Dr. Branka Mraovic for this information.

respectively). Banks' lending interest rates rose.[9] The Croatian National Bank cut bank reserve rate requirements from 17% to 14% in December 2008, and slashed it further to 13% in February in 2009. Nevertheless, bank lending to enterprises and households decelerated, resulting in a further decline in economic activity. Financing through the interbank market increased and the overnight interest rate reached 17.14% in November 2008. In order to finance the budget deficit, the Central Government secured essential funds through short-term bank loans as well as Treasury-bill issuance. The yield on Treasury-bills reached 8.50% in November 2008.[10] Domestic banks had to struggle with this liquidity problem throughout 2009.

Third, FDI inflows decreased. In Q3 2009, FDI outflows exceeded inflows. On annual basis, the amount of FDI, which stood at €3,483 (8.1% of GDP) in 2007, suddenly plummeted by nearly 70% from €3,226 million (6.8% of GDP) in 2008 to € 989 million (2.2% of GDP) in 2009. These precipitous movements harmed the economy.

In 2009 household consumption and gross fixed capital formation decreased by 9% and 12%, respectively. Also industrial production and construction decreased by 9.2% and 6%, respectively. Of this the biggest decline was recorded by basic pharmaceutics (−43%). In the shipbuilding industry, Croatia's major export, production plunged by 13%. In addition, due to a decline in the number of tourists from foreign countries, especially from EU countries, revenues from services drastically decreased. In Q4 2008 illiquidity and low turnover in the domestic capital market sparked a sharp fall in the value of most shares listed on the

---

[9] As for banks' interest rates on Kuna credits not indexed to foreign currency, the interest rate on short-term credits to enterprises increased from 7.84% in September to 9.45% in November 2008 while the interest rate on short-term credits to households increased from 12.20% to 12.41% during the same period. As for banks' interest rates on Kuna credits indexed to foreign currency, the interest rate on short-term credits to enterprises increased from 7.57% in September to 8.38% in November 2008 while the interest rate on short-term credits to households increased from 8.69% to 9.0% during the same period (*CNB Bulletin*, No. 146, pp. 70–71).

[10] The spreads between required yields on Croatian Eurobonds and those on benchmark German bonds exceeded 500 basis points at the end of March 2009 (*CNB Bulletin*, No. 152, p. 4).

Zagreb Stock Exchange. The domestic share index (CROBEX), declined by 42.4% from the previous quarter. The fall was steeper than in Central and Eastern Europe.[11] Employment began to decline in Q2 2009, one quarter after the major drop in economic growth, with no signs of recovery as of Q2 2010. It remains 5% below the level of the previous year (ILO, 2011, p. 38). On annual basis, the unemployment rate, reported in the Labor Force Survey (LFS) increased from 8.4% in 2008 to 9.3% in 2009 (Table 3.8).

As Table 3.5 shows, in 2009 the GDP growth rate is −5.8% in Croatia and −6.7% in Hungary. However Hungary enjoyed positive growth rate in 2010 (1.2%), while Croatia's GDP continued to contract (−1.2%). According to the EBRD, among 28 transition countries, only 4 countries (Croatia, Latvia, Romania and the Kyrgyz Republic) recorded negative GDP growth in 2010. Croatia on balance appears to have fared more poorly than in Hungary.

3.3.2. *Responses by the government*

The government adopted three budget revisions in 2009. In July, Croatia decided to raise the VAT by one percentage point to 23% and introduced a Crisis Tax (effective from August 1, 2009). The tax takes 2% of all pensions, salaries and other incomes higher than HRK 3,000 (EUR 409) monthly and 4% of all amounts higher than HRK 6,000 (EUR 819). Taking into account that the average wage was HRK 7,700 in 2009, the new tax hurt most Croatian households. They became more pessimistic and decreased their consumption. This slowed economic growth, reduced expected VAT and excise tax revenue, lowering their contribution to the national budget.

In late April 2010, the government announced its "Economic Recovery Program", which abolished the 2% tax on monthly income between more

---

[11] The second biggest fall during Q4 2008 in Central and Eastern European countries was recorded by Ljubljana (−40.3%), followed by Budapest (−35.1%), Prague (−28.85%), Warsaw (−27.1%) and Bratislava (−20.8%) stock exchange indices (*CNB Bulletin*, No. 146, p. 33).

than HRK 3,000 and less than 6,000 on July 1. The 4% crisis tax on monthly income over HRK 6,000 was phased out on October 31, 2010.

There have been heated discussions among Croatian economists about how the 2008 global financial crisis's aftermath should be dealt with best. Croatia's two most prominent economists argued at the annual Quo Vadis Croatia conference that the government's crisis response was hampered by the country's defective post-communist transition regime (Ljubo Jurcic and Vojnic (2009)).

Let us therefore review the post-crisis experience.

3.4. The Croatian Economy after the Regimes Change

3.4.1. *Developments in politics*

After the collapse of Yugoslav self-managed socialism in 1990, the first free election based on a multi-party system was won by the Croatian Democratic Alliance (HDZ), led by Franjo Tudjman. This party was populist and included supporters from across the political spectrum from fascism to anti-fascism supporting the higher nationalist cause of forming an Independent Republic of Croatia (Jurcic and Vojnic, 2009: p. 763). The HDZ government ruled the country for about 10 years. While fighting the "Independence War" (from autumn 1991 through November 1995), the government pressed for market transition. Western countries initially responded warmly to Croatia at the time of independence, but had a change of heart. They were repelled by Tudjman's ultra nationalist course, and consequently opposed Croatia's EU accession as long as the HDZ remained in power.

A center–left coalition led by Social Democratic Party, however, brought about a fundamental shift in early 2000. The new government promoted the democratization of the political system and repudiated nationalist self-sufficiency in favor of international cooperation. In the process, the HDZ which won the parliamentary elections in both 2003 and 2007 transformed itself into a moderate, externally oriented, center-right party.

3.4.2. Dominance of neo-liberal doctrines

According to Jurcic and Vojnic (2009), for the most of the 1990s except for a very short time, cooperation between economic sciences and economic policies was unsatisfactory (p. 753). They wrote:

> For many years before signs of a great crisis, which was similar to that of the 1930s, appeared on the world sphere our economic sciences warned that only based on a combination of an invisible hand of Adam Smith and a very visible hand of John Maynard Keynes useful economic policies can be carried out. On the contrary to recommendations of our economic sciences, economic policies in the 1990s gave themselves to the domination of the doctrines of neo-liberalism more than other countries in transition (Jurcic and Vojnic, 2009, p. 770).

The privatization in Croatia did not achieve the expected result because the process was marred by politics. Using expressions such as the classical appearance of "mafiocracy", "savage capitalism" and "primitive accumulation", Dragomir Vojnic criticized Croatia's privatization program (Vojnic, 1999: pp. 17–18). Big-scale and profitable enterprises went into the hands of members or supporters of the HDZ, the ruling party at that time. According to Bartlett (2003), the new owners were not dynamic risk takers, but all too often political "place-men," whose connections to the ruling party were more important than their abilities as managers or entrepreneurs. Most were more interested in short-term profit taking and asset stripping than in long-term investment and strategic restructuring of the enterprises. The cash sucked out of what once were sound enterprises was then divided among them and the HDZ. These managers were called "tycoon capitalists." Other beneficiaries were managers of socially owned firms who borrowed funds privately to purchase company shares on a leveraged basis using special government loans as collateral (Bartlett, 2003: pp. 110–111).

It is said that the managerial buyouts played the dominant role in Croatian privatization. The most frequently reported way that managers attempted to buy majority positions in companies were "managerial loans", "manager's insurance schemes", and "ghost buyers on one side, and by undervaluing assets on the other" (Bicanic, 1993: p. 435). "Managerial loans" are part of an opaque system that allowed top managers to receive large and favorable loans from banks (whose managers are their established business partners and often friends) up to ten thousand DM (Deutsche Mark). Sometimes the banks accepted management shares, overvalued real estate or frozen "foreign currency savings deposits" as collateral (Bicanic, 1993: p. 435; Kalogjera, 1993: p. 81). The second method involved enterprises paying large insurance premiums for their managers which were then cashed for a discount at banks and the cash was used by managers to buy shares. The third tactic was to pay workers to act as ghost buyers of shares with large discounts and then sell them on the black market or cede them to a manager (Bicanic, 1993: p. 436).

Free issue of shares up to the value of DM 20,000 was provided to war invalids and families of war victims by amendments to the privatization law in December 1993. In March 1994, a measure was passed which allowed people to buy shares with frozen foreign currency savings. Bartlett severely criticizes these ploys, condemning them as cosmetic, designed only to disguise the fact that the principal new owners of the formerly socialized industries were now the state, and a narrow elite of tycoon capitalists (Bartlett, 2003: p. 100). This degenerate privatization they insisted impaired Croatia's modernization and competitiveness.

3.4.3. *Program for economic stabilization*

Post-communist Croatia was beset by recession. The country lost its markets in the former Yugoslav Republics and was ravaged by its war of independence. Manufacturing was especially hard hit, with about a third of its capacity damaged. GDP in 1993 was lower than the 1990 level by nearly 40%. Industrial production declined by 42.5% in 1993 compared with 1990. Inflation under these conditions was inevitable. Prices galloped with inflation exceeding 1,500 % in 1993. The Program for Economic Stabilization was announced in October 1993 to grapple with the situation. It had two phases. First, it sought to suppress inflation swiftly, and then afterward introduce structural reforms to assure long-term economic stability. Its key points were fiscal reform, acceleration of privatization, restructuring loss-making public sector enterprises, restructuring of the banking system and developing the financial system (Jovancevic, 1999: pp. 240–241).

The following measures were adopted to suppress the hyperinflation: (a) devaluation of the domestic currency, subsequently fixed to a hard currency (German mark, later to the Euro), (b) reduction of the money supply, (c) termination of price and wage indexing, (d) curtailed public consumption, and (e) enhancement of Central Bank independence (Obadic, 2010). In May 1994 a new currency, the Kuna, was introduced replacing the Dinar. Inflation was suppressed within the year. Inflation has been less than 5% thereafter, except in 2008. The central bank's reserves increased. The first phase of the Stabilization Program was successfully completed, but second phase structural reforms have gone badly.

The program was neo-liberal. Jurcic and Vojnic (2009) contend that, "Not only was there no conception and strategy of development which economic policies could rely on, but also terms such as industrial policy, regional policy and similar have been almost completely forgotten" (p. 764). In order to suppress inflation, the exchange rate has been used as an anchor, with the Kuna pegged at first to German Mark and later the Euro. The exchange rate regime has been a managed float but the rate was pegged too high,[12] generating a tidal wave of cheap imports. Jurcic says that stable exchange rates and zero budget deficits sometimes must be employed to promote full employment, balanced international payments, etc., but they are not all weather policies. (Okrugli Stol, 2010: p. 495). Jurcic (2009) points out that "stability of exchange rate" and "zero budget deficit" have been fetishized to the nation's detriment (p. 747).

---

[12] Jurcic and Vojnic (2009) argue that the exchange rate has been too high for the Croatian economy, using indices of deviation of an exchange rate from a rate based on purchasing power parity (pp. 766–767). The extent of overevaluation of Croatia' real effective exchange rate differs depending on methods of its measurement. According to the macroeconomic balance approach, downward adjustment of the real effective exchange rate of 5%–6% would be required to close the gap between the sustainable level of the current account balance and the underlying current account balance. According to the external sustainability approach, Croatia's real effective exchange rate is overvalued by about 5%–11% (IMF 2010, Annex I. Assessing Croatia's Real Exchange Rate).

The Dayton Accord in November 1995 initiated a construction boom that caused the international payments deficit to unsustainably soar from 4.3% of GDP in 1996 to 12.2% in 1997. The government responded by tightening credit and curtailing deficit spending, which together brought about a recession, with GDP growth declining to −0.9% in 1999. The economy then promptly deteriorated further due to increased enterprise debt, mounting non-performing loans and financial difficulties in the banking sector. Many domestic banks were sold to foreigners.

As of 2008, of the ten largest banks, which account for 87.9% of the market share, nine banks are foreign. Two Italian banks account for 41% of the market share, five Austrian banks comprise 35.9%, a French bank accounts for 7.5% and a Hungarian bank has 3.5% and a Croatian (state) bank 4.2% (CEE Banking — Still the right bet, UniCredit Group, July 2008).

3.4.4. *Escape from the recession in 1999*

The new center-left coalition government tried to escape this recession in 2000 with ambitious public infrastructure projects, especially road construction. The policy was effective (Jurcic and Vojnic, 2009, p. 768). After having experienced negative growth in 1999, Croatian GDP grew at moderate pace until the recent global financial crisis. GDP recovered the 1989 level in 2005 and exceeded 115% in 2008 (1989 level =100). The unemployment rate (LFS) decreased from about 15% in 2002 to 8.4% in 2008 (Table 3.7). Nonetheless, the quality of this growth was problematic. It has both de-agrarianized and de-industrialized the nation in favor of services (Jurcic and Vojnic, 2009: p. 770).

3.4.5. *Changes in industrial structure, agriculture and de-industrialization*

Table 3.8 illustrates the troublesome development. Employment in agriculture, forestry, and fishing almost halved, from 10.5% to 5.4%, during 1998–2006. It decreased from 24.6% to 22.3% in industry. Outputs in agriculture and manufacturing only have regained three-fourths (76.7% and 75.4%, respectively) of the levels recorded in 1989. By contrast, other activities, especially services, have remarkably increased.

Table 3.7. Macroeconomic indicators of croatia.

	2002	2003	2004	2005	2006	2007	2008	2009	2010
GDP growth rate (real)	5.2	4.3	3.8	4.2	4.7	5.5	2.4	−6	−1
GDP/capita (EUR at exchange rate)	5,451	5,747	6,224	8,000	8,800	9,700	10,700	10,100	10,300
GDP/capita (EUR at PPP)	9,260	9,680	10,290	12,700	13,800	15,200	15,600	14,800	n.a.
Gross industrial production annual change in % (real)	5.4	4.1	3.2	4.6	4.2	4.9	1.2	−9.2	1
Gross agricultural production annual change in % (real)	7.7	−15.9	11.9	−8.7	4.4	−3.9	8	n.a.	n.a.
Construction industry, hours worked annual change in % (real)	12.8	22.8	1.9	−0.7	9.4	2.4	11.8	−6	n.a.
Consumption of households, annual change in % (real)	7.6	4.1	4.3	4.4	3.5	6.2	0.8	−9	0
Gross fixed capital form., annual change in % (real)	12	16.8	5	4.8	10.9	6.5	8.2	−12	1
Unemployment rate –LFS, in %, average	14.8	14.3	13.8	12.7	11.1	9.6	8.4	9.3	10

(Continued)

Table 3.7. (*Continued*)

	2002	2003	2004	2005	2006	2007	2008	2009	2010
Consumer prices,% p.a.	1.7	1.8	2.1	3.3	3.2	2.9	6.1	2.4	2.5
General gov. budget balance, in % of GDP	-4.8	-6.3	-4.2	-3.5	-2.6	-1.2	-1	-2.9	-3
Discount rate of NB, % p.a., end of period	4.5	4.5	4.5	4.5	4.5	9	9	9	n.a.
Current account in % of GDP	-8.7	-7.3	-4.4	-5.5	-6.9	-7.6	-9.2	-5.5	-6.5
Gross external debt in % of GDP	n.a.	n.a.	71.6	71.8	75.1	76.8	83.8	95	n.a.

Note: Data for 2010 are forecast.
Source: Vidovic and Gligorov (2006), p. 3; Vidovic (2010), p. 117.

Table 3.8.   Changes in employment structure.

Activity	1998	2006
Agriculture, forestry and fishing	10.8	5.4
Industry total	24.6	22.3
Construction	7.0	8.9
Wholesale, retail trade, hotels, etc.	20.0	23.0
Transport and telecommunications	7.1	6.7
Other activities	30.6	33.7
Total	100	100

Source: wiiw (2007), p. 126.

Agriculture has declined during the past 20 years. After the regime change, agriculture was left as it was without adequate government assistance. Many peasants abandoned farming. Most of the abandoned lands went unsold, and less and less land has been cultivated. Compared with the pre-war time (the year 1939), the total agricultural acreage decreased to only a third of its former size, and the total cultivated land decreased to almost half. The situation in stockbreeding is serious. The number of cattle halved. Although Croatia's livestock exports prospered after World War I and veal exports flourished after World War II, the country turned into a net importer of beef and pork due to the stockbreeding crisis (Stipetic, 2009).

Shipbuilding is Croatia's most important manufacturing industry. It held third place in world shipbuilding in the former Yugoslav period (Horvat, 1999; BCE, May 2000). After 1990, however, Croatian shipbuilding began to stagnate due to the loss of its COMECON market, and the retention of state ownership which impaired its competitiveness. Croatian shipbuilding today accounts only for around 1.5% of the global market and is in fourth place in Europe. Still shipbuilding remains a very important industry, generating 5% of GDP, and it accounts for more than 11% of total Croatian exports (Buturac *et al.*, 2009: p. 683). It employs 12,000 workers, and it is estimated that a further 35,000 jobs are directly linked to the industry. There are six shipyards, of which only one (Pula) is profitable. The remaining shipyards are loss-making and continue their operations with the aid of government's subsidy,[13] in violation of EU's regulations. The government also has a foreign investment focused privatization plan. It has invited public tenders, but buyers are scarce.[14]

Let us break down the composition of FDI to Croatia. Financial intermediary investment occupies first place (53.2%), followed by manufacturing (23.0%), transportation, storage and communication (10.9%), wholesale, retail trade, repair of vehicles, etc. (5.3%), hotels and restaurants (2.7%), real estate, renting and business activities (1.8%) (Hunya, 2009: p. 44). According to Vidovic and Gligorov (2004), this distribution was driven by privatization opportunities (two-thirds of the total), such as the sale of Croatian Telecom, banks or the pharmaceutical company Pliva, the takeover of breweries, cement industry, and other construction material industries. Greenfield investment has been negligible (only 16% of the total FDI stock), even though it was desired by the government and business circles. The export-oriented industries attracting FDI were pharmaceuticals (Pliva), other non-metallic products (i.e., cement industry), food and beverages (Coca Cola), rubber and plastics and electrical and optical equipment (Siemens).[15] The remaining branches are oriented toward the domestic markets. Foreign investment enterprises account for only 16% of the total Croatian exports. This situation is quite different from Hungary, the Czech Republic, and Poland, where foreign investment enterprises have been the driving force behind exports, with the share of foreign investment enterprises in exports being 89%, 60%, and 60%, respectively (Vidovic and Gligorov, 2004: p. 15). FDI improved Central European export competitiveness, but Croatia has been unable to duplicate Hungary's, the Czech Republic's and Poland's success.

---

[13] The shipbuilding industry is still very heavily supported by the state, with subsidies accounting for a massive 10% of any ship's contract prices. The accumulated losses were in excess of €719 million as of February 2006 (Croatian Online, Wednesday Column — Croatia Business 3: Shipbuilding Part One, http://croatiaonline.blogspot.com/2006/02/wednesday-column-croatia-business-3.html).

[14] The government announced a tender on August 1, 2009, for the sale of its six shipyards. Later there has been a little progress, but due to the global financial crisis the government has not succeeded in the sale yet (*EEM*, October, December 2009 and other issues).

[15] The data are from 2003.

External borrowing also increased rapidly with the intermediation by foreign-owned banks. Much of it went into consumption and nontradable sectors (construction, real estate, and wholesale and retail trade), feeding into higher imports (IMF, 2009: p. 6).

3.5. A Chronic Current Account Deficit

The Croatian economy has had a chronic macroeconomic imbalance, with the current account deficit averaging 6%–7% of GDP. About two-thirds of its total exports went to EU member countries, while roughly two-thirds of its imports came also from the same area. Croatia's exports have performed poorly, despite special treatment from the EU after 2001.

Table 3.9 provides the following insights. First, Croatia has continuously recorded deficits in goods trade with the export/import ratio hovering around 50%. Its trade balance deficit reached over 20% of the GDP (21.2% in 2007 and 22.7% in 2008). A large part of these deficits have been covered by service sector surpluses. Tourism dominates the service trade. Attractions like the Adriatic Coast generate enormous rents comparable to crude oil revenues from the Norwegian Northern Sea,[16] but demand can be volatile. For example, the number of tourists fell drastically during the ethnic conflicts in Bosnia and Herzegovina in the first half of the 1990s and the Kosovo war in 1999, and again during the recent global financial crisis. This makes export diversification imperative.

Second, a substantial amount of direct investment has been recorded every year. In 2007, net FDI inflow reached 8.1% of GDP, well above the current account deficit in that year. In 2009, however, due to the influence of the global financial crisis net FDI inflow fell to only 35% of the level recorded in 2007, and in 2010 plummeted further to 17%. An economy heavily dependent on FDI is precarious and its effects on international competitiveness uncertain.

According to Vidovic and Gligorov (2004), Croatian manufacturing exports to the EU increased only moderately between 1995 and 2002, and Croatia's market share of the EU market (excluding intra-EU trade) declined significantly from 0.42% to 0.29% (p. 30). This means that the

---

[16] Bartlett (2003), p. 120.

Table 3.9. Croatia's Current Account and Foreign Direct Investment in 2005–2010.

	2005	2006	2007	2008	2009	2010
(in million EUR)						
Current account	−1,975	−2,726	−3,236	4,371	−2,361	−2,505
(in % of GDP)	(−5.5%)	(−6.9%)	(−7.6%)	(−9.2%)	(−5.2%)	(−5.4%)
Trade balance in goods	−7,518	−8,344	−9,434	−10,794	−7,398	−7,475
(in % of GDP)	(−21.0%)	(−21.3%)	(−22.0%)	(−22.8%)	(−16.2%)	(−16.1%)
Export	7,220	8,464	9,193	9,814	7,691	8,449
Import	−14,738	−16,808	−18,626	−20,608	−15,089	−15,924
Service and income	4,359	4,511	5,154	5,387	4,002	3,881
Transportation	376	474	542	509	255	302
Travel	5,394	5,709	6,035	6,694	5,649	5,635
Other services	−453	−480	−310	−245	−237	−171
Compensation of employees	260	373	494	564	587	438
Interest and investment income	−1,219	−3,702	−1,606	−2,135	−2,251	−2,324
Current transfer	1,184	1,107	1,043	1,036	1,035	1,089
Capital and financial accounts	3,009	3,699	4,141	5,956	3,299	1,309
Direct investment	1,276	2,562	3,468	3,246	1,207	593
(in % of GDP)	(+3.6%)	(+6.6%)	(+8.1%)	(+6.9%)	(+2.6%)	(+1.3%)
Reserve assets	−822	−1,412	−722	330	−896	−83
Net Errors and Omissions	−1,003	−973	−904	−1,620	−793	−655
International reserve of CNB	7,438	8,725	9,307	9,121	10,376	10,660

Source: *CNB Bulletin*, No. 169, pp. 48–55 and IMF (2010), p. 27.

international competitiveness of Croatian manufacturing has fallen. Why? There are several contributory factors. First, due to insufficient investment in manufacturing its technology has been lagging behind that of other countries, especially East Asian countries. Second, due to ongoing globalization, products made in East Asian countries, especially China have been increasingly flowing into European markets (see Table 3.10). Gross

Table 3.10. Trends in EU27 market shares of apparel and clothing by SEE and other selected countries, 1996–2005.

Partner	1996	2000	2001	2004	2005
World ($ millions)	38,363	43,250	44,242	67,183	74,124
South Eastern Europe	7.71	9.93	11.93	11.80	10.52
Albania	0.19	0.21	0.27	0.21	0.19
Bosnia and Herzegovina	0.06	0.22	0.26	0.21	0.21
Croatia	1.54	1.05	1.14	0.87	0.74
Macedonia	0.54	0.55	0.57	0.52	0.51
Serbia and Montenegro	0.20	0.24	0.32	0.27	0.30
Bulgaria	1.04	1.70	2.10	2.17	2.06
Romania	4.15	5.96	7.26	7.55	6.51
CIS12	1.53	1.81	1.88	1.67	1.54
Middle East and North Africa	27.79	26.37	27.72	27.63	24.98
East Asia and South Asia	49.29	51.74	51.40	55.17	61.09
Bangladesh	3.97	5.74	6.16	7.64	6.61
China	16.48	21.23	22.16	27.67	35.86
Hong Kong	11.67	7.76	6.42	4.72	3.86
India	6.89	5.79	5.94	5.89	6.85
Indonesia	3.66	4.41	4.26	3.01	2.52
Pakistan	2.41	2.06	2.13	2.29	1.90

Source: Kathuria (2008), p. 50; The original is EU data from UN COMTRADE database.

labor costs in all countries in the Western Balkans increased during the period 2001–2005 (Table 3.11). It is noteworthy that labor costs in Croatia are not only the highest of all the countries in the Western Balkans but also higher than some new EU member states such as Bulgaria, Hungary, and Poland. Unit labor costs in Croatia soared (Fig. 3.2), from 2005 until Q2 2008, following the pattern exhibited by the PIIGS.[17] Looking at Table 3.12, the share of fuels in total exports was high and increased from 9.2%

---

[17] See Chapter 4 of this book.

Table 3.11.   Gross labor cost in the western balkans.

Country	2003	2004	2005
(All sectors, in Euros)			
Albania	134	148	161
Croatia	740	794	841
Bosnia and Herzegovina	395	402	420
Macedonia	322	335	343
Montenegro	271	303	326
Serbia	255	281	307
Reference			
Bulgaria	142	150	161
Hungary	541	578	638
Poland	497	501	586

Source: Kathuria, S. (ed.) (2008), pp. 52–53.

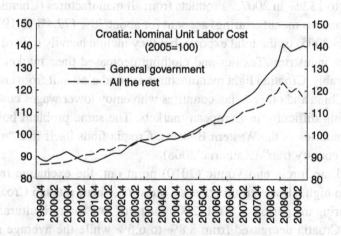

Figure 3.2.   Croatia: Nominal Unit Labor Cost (2005 = 100).

Source: IMF (2010), p. 5; Original: Croatian National Bank.

Table 3.12. Structure of Croatian exports by major product category, 1996 and 2005.

Share of total exports (%)	1996	2005
Food and feed	11.4	10.5
Agricultural raw materials	4.7	3.4
Ores and metals	2.2	3.8
Fuels	9.2	13.9
Chemicals	14.1	9.8
Leather and rubber	2.3	1.7
Wood and papers	2.7	3.0
Textiles and clothing	16.5	7.7
Machinery excluding auto	20.0	27.0
Motor vehicles and parts	1.4	2.0
Miscellaneous manufacturing	15.4	17.0

Source: World Bank (2008), p. 40.

in 1996 to 13.9% in 2007.[18] Products from all manufactures (Chemicals to Miscellaneous manufacturing) account for about 70% (72.4% in 1996 and 68.2% in 2005) of the total exports, but they incline heavily toward labor-intensive industries. Textiles and clothing decreased their market shares considerably. Croatian light manufactures are under assault from competitors in China and other Asian countries who enjoy lower wages costs, and are having difficulty in European markets. The same problem holds for other countries in the Western Balkans. Croatia finds itself in a "middle-income country trap" (Kathuria, 2008).

Third, as Jurcic and Vojnic (2010) point out, the exchange rate has been too high. However, this raises a question. Tariff rates in Croatia are low. During the period of 2001–2005 the tariff rate for agricultural products in Croatia decreased from 8.8% to 6.6% while the average rate in

---

[18] Croatia produces natural gas and crude petroleum but cannot satisfy domestic needs. The country has been importing them from foreign countries. However, as Croatia was placed as a basis for refining gas and petroleum during the former Yugoslavia it has more than enough refining capacity. Now the country imports natural gas and crude petroleum well over its domestic needs and exports refined gas and petroleum to neighboring countries.

the Western Balkans remained almost unchanged (slightly increased from 11.0% to 11.2%). The tariff rate for industrial products in Croatia decreased from 7.5% to 2.1% while the average rate in the Western Balkans decreased from 8.6% to 4.7%. The tariff rate for all goods in Croatia decreased from 7.6% to 2.4% while the average rate in the Western Balkans decreased from 8.8% to 5.3% (Kathuria, 2008: p. 38). The tariff rates in Croatia have been the lowest in the Western Balkans and are comparable to those in developed industrial countries. If transition countries such as Croatia are prohibited from to using tariffs to protect their own industries, then there seems to be no way for them to protect themselves other than devaluation. Croatia, however, has chosen to avoid the devaluation option, even though the Kuna is clearly over-valued. Presumably, Croatia's experiences with hyperinflation first in 1989 during the period of the former Yugoslavia, and then again in 1993 after independence, partly explain this reluctance. Croatian monetary authorities also may have been following the European Central Bank's (ECB) advice. Croatia is heavily euroized and attentive to the interplay of the EU's and its own interests.[19] The issue will be resolved by default when Croatia accedes to the eurozone, but as the PIIGS example shows, this may be a case of jumping out of the frying pan into the fire.

Croatia's external deficit as a percentage of GDP reached 85% in the end of 2003, a level that seems unsustainable. The World Bank Development Finance report of 2005 demoted Croatia to a "severely indebted middle-income country",[20] from a "moderately indebted middle-income country". This ratio reached almost 100% (98.5%) in 2009, on a par with the PIIGS.

A few years earlier some economists (e.g., Jovancevic, 2002), from anxiety about the country, argued for a new economic development model. The switch was not made, leaving Croatia especially vulnerable to the reverberations of the 2008 global financial crisis.

---

[19] Croatia's case presents a striking contrast to Serbia, where the monetary authorities allowed a bigger depreciation of the national currency after the onset of the financial crisis although the country had a similar situation.

[20] The World Bank criterion for a country being "severely indebted" is that either the debt to GDP ratio is above 80% or that the ratio of debt to exports of goods and services is above 220%. Either condition is sufficient. The case of Croatia corresponds to the former. (Vidovic and Gligorov, 2006: p. 23).

3.5.1. *Economic recovery program*

Croatia's current Economic Recovery Program contains short-term, mid-term, and long-term policy measures. It recognizes that the state cannot displace the private sector, and urges the public to change its concepts and habits.

As previously explained, devaluation is not a viable option for the fore-seeable future[21] and will become irrelevant when Croatia ultimately joins the eurozone sometime after 2013. Internal devaluation (wage and price compression) is mentioned elliptically, but not emphasized.[22] Conventional remedies, by default are the program's mainstay.

Fiscal policies are targeted at (1) fiscal consolidation, and (2) a gradual decrease of general government expenditure and revenue shares in GDP. All tax breaks are to be abolished, except the fiscal stimulation for R&D. Government expenditures will be cut. EU regulation will

---

[21] As mentioned above, already in the late 1960s, in the former Yugoslav Federation foreign currencies deposit was widespread owing to remittance by workers working abroad. As the economic crisis in the former Yugoslavia deepened, people lost their trust in their national currency (Dinar) and got into the habit of saving foreign currencies. Immediately before the breakup of the former Yugoslavia in 1991 household foreign currency savings deposits were frozen. In spite of such a bitter experience, it has become natural practice for Croatian people to save money in foreign currency and get loans in foreign currency. About 90% of loans to households and three-quarters of loans to enterprises are denominated in foreign currencies. What would happen if the Kuna is devalued? The value of foreign currency savings deposit would remain unchanged, but the burden of loan repayment would immediately become heavier. Because households and enterprises usually get their revenue in Kuna while the amount of their foreign currency loans calculated in national currency (Kuna) would increase. IMF (2010) shows its trial calculation. In the case of a 30 percent real depreciation, it could increase public debt from 44% to 58% of GDP and external debt from 99% to 142% of GDP (p. 12). In this regard, this option is similar to the dilemma which Latvia faced in 2009. Instead of (external) devaluation of the national currency (Lat), Latvia has chosen "internal devaluation," i.e., to curtail wages and pensions and decrease unit labor costs. For economic crisis in Latvia, see Koyama (2010).

[22] In an interview at the Economic Institute Zagreb on April 28, 2010, Dr. Dubravko Radosevic said, "Indeed, as adopted in Latvia, we will try the internal devaluation, namely, to curtail wages and decrease unit labor costs. This is a strategy that the Program of Economic Recovery proposes".

govern state support, that is, the government will not grant state subsidies to specific industries like shipbuilding.

As for public administration, (1) it will be rationalized and (2) its efficiency improved. Decentralization will be pursued by transferring part of the work at the middle level of the government to the lower level of the government and nongovernment bodies. The number of workers in the public sector shall be reduced by 5%, and the total payroll of workers in the public sector shall be cut by 10%. The government will prepare plans to privatize the remaining state-owned enterprises (big-scale enterprises such as Croatian Electric Power, Croatian Insurance, Croatian Railways, etc., are still in state hands).

As for revitalization, state intervention in the economy will be curtailed, and business start-ups encouraged. Investment projects will emphasize "green" options: (i) energy (renewable energy is attached importance), (ii) environmental protection, (iii) education and health, (iv) agriculture and irrigation, and (v) infrastructure. Projects will be financed primarily by private capital and financial resources from the EU funds, rather than through public enterprises. The government will promote technology transfer to improve competitiveness by reducing obstacles discouraging FDI. Economic diplomacy will be enlisted in a campaign to increase exports and FDI inflow. The HBOR (Croatian Bank for Export and Import) will be institutionally and financially strengthened.

"Flexecurity" will become the watchword for the labor sector. The concept, popular in Nordic countries, diminishes labor protection in order to increase labor demand. Retraining also will be stressed.

The government plans to address the problem posed by the graying of its population. It intends to reduce pensions and increase the labor participation rate. Croatia's population is aging and birth rate is declining,[23] making it essential to raise revenues and cut benefits. Croatia's pension system will collapse in the near future unless bold measures are taken soon.

---

[23] Life expectancy at birth is 75.35 years for total population, 71.72 years for males, and 79.18 years for females (2009 estimate). Birth rate is 1.42 children born/women (2009 estimate). Available at: http://www.economywatch.com/economic-statistics/Croatia/Life_Expectancy_Rate/

3.6. Conclusion

After the systems change in 1989–1990, similar to other countries of Central and Eastern Europe, the West Balkan countries liberalized foreign trade, capital mobility, and finance in accordance with the neo-liberal, Washington Consensus. Privatization of state-owned (or socially-owned in the case of successor countries of the former Yugoslavia) was implemented in the Western Balkan countries, but the process was opaque. Neither privatization nor FDI inflows have improved the international competitiveness of Croatia's manufacturing industries. FDI inflows in the Western Balkan countries, including Croatia, have been directed mostly to financial sectors, real estate, telecommunication, etc. Economic development has been consumption driven and dependent on foreign capital, making West Balkan economies increasingly vulnerable to external shocks. This above all else explains why the West Balkans were so severely hurt by the 2008 global financial crisis.

Croatia's external debts mounted to nearly 100% of GDP in 2008, a problem that cannot be easily resolved with its competitiveness impeding, consumption-driven development model. It is addicted to domestic consumption exceeding domestic production, imports exceeding exports, and investments exceeding savings.[24]

EU accession may compound Croatia's woes. Once inside the EU, it will not be able to subsidize the shipbuilding industry, which has been one of the economy's mainstays. Perhaps, it will find a white knight, or strategic partner, but if not, the entire industry may disappear.

The austerity measures required by neo-liberal policies also seem politically dangerous. It is not clear that the Croatian people will be willing to endure the pain. They might, if the employment scenario improves, but here too vigorous state intervention may be required beyond what neo-liberals consider acceptable.

Croatia's near-term economic outlook therefore is worrisome.

---

[24] Jurcic and Vojnic call this an "atypical model of economic development, which puts the cart before the horse."

References

Astrov, Mario, Kazimierz Laski and Leon Podkaminer *et al.* (2010) "Will Export Prevail over Austerity?" Current Analyses and Forecasts, July 2010, Vienna: wiiw (The Vienna Institute for International Economic Studies).

Bartlett, William (2003) *Croatia: Between Europe and the Balkans*, London and New York: Routledge.

Bartlett, Will and Vassilis Monastriotis (2010) *South Eastern Europe After the Crisis: A New Dawn or Back to Business as Usual?* LSEE at the London School of Economics and Political Science.

Bicanic, Ivo (1993) "Privatization in Croatia," *East European Policies and Societies*, Vol. 7, No. 3.

Buturac, Goran, Edo Rajh and Ivan Teodorovic (2009) "Hrvatsko Gosdarstvo u Svijetlu Globalne Recesije," Ekonomski Pregled, Godina 60, Broj 12.

Druzic, Ivo (2006) *A Journey Through Transition Time: With Special Reference to Croatia*, Zagreb: Political Culture.

EBRD (2010), Vienna Initiative Factsheet. Available at: http://www.ebrd.com/pages/research/publications/factsheets/vienna.shtml.

Gashi, Petrit (2010) "The Global Economic Crisis and Kosovo," in Bartlett and Monastiriotis (eds.), *South Eastern Europe after the Crisis*.

Gligorov, Vladimir, Josef Poeschl and Sandor Richter *et al.* (2009) Where Have All the Shooting Stars Gone? Current Analyses and Forecasts 4, July 2009, Vienna: wiiw.

Gligorov, Vladimir, Peter Havlik, Michael Landesmann, Josef Poeschl and Sandor Richter *et al.* (2010) Crisis Is Over, but Problems Loom Ahead, Current Analyses and Forecasts 5, Vienna: wiiw.

Horvat, Branko (1999) "The Results of Backward Transition in the Republic of Croatia," in Heuberger, Valeria *et al.*, *At the Crossroads: Disaster or Normalization? The Yugoslav Successor States in the 1990s*, Frankfurt am Main: Peter Lang.

Hunya, Gabor (2008) Decline to Follow Uneven FDI Inflow Growth: wiiw Database on Foreign Direct Investment in Central, East and Southeast Europe2008, Vienna: wiiw.

Hunya, Gabor (2009) FDI in the CEECs under the Impact of the Global Crisis: Sharp Declines. wiiw Database on Foreign Direct Investment in Central, East and Southeast Europe 2009, Vienna: wiiw.

ILO (2011) Global Employment Trends 2011: The Challenge of a Jobs Recovery, Report, 1 January.

IMF (2009) Republic of Croatia: 2009 Article IV Consultation — Staff Report; Public Information Notice on the Executive Board Discussion; and Statement by the Executive Director for the Republic of Croatia, June 2009, IMF Country Report No. 09/185.

IMF (2010), Republic of Croatia: 2010 Article IV Consultation — Staff Report; Public Information Notice on the Executive Board Discussion; and Statement by the Executive Director for the Republic of Croatia, June 2010, IMF Country Report No. 10/179.

Jovancevic, Radmila (1999) "Macroeconomic Environment and the Banking System of Croatia," in Sevic, Zeljko, *Banking Reform in South East European Transitional Economies*, London: University of Greenwich Business School.

Jovancevic, Radmila (2002) "Banking System in Croatia and Its Broader Macroeconomic Environment," in Sevic, Zeljko, *Banking Reforms in South-East Europe*, Edward Elgar: Cheltenham, UK and Northampton, MA, USA.

Jurcic, Ljubo (2009) "Hrvatska: Velika Transformacija (Uvodno izlaganje i poruke Savjetovanja), 17. Tradicionalno Opatijsko Savjetovanje Hrvatskih Ekonomista," *Ekonomski Pregled*, Godina 60, Broj 12.

Jurcic, Ljubo and Dragomir Vojnic (2009) "Quo Vadis Croatia — Neke karakteristike momenta razvoja u svijetlu turbulentnih dogadjana u zemlji i svijetu — Kako dalje? — Hrvatska na putu Europsku uniju," *Ekonomski Pregled*, Godina 60, Broj 12.

Kalogjera, Drazen (1993) "Privatizacija u Stabilizaciji i Razvoju Hrvatskog Gospodarstva," *Drustvena Istrazivanja 3*, God. 2, Broj 1, Zagreb.

Kathuria, Sanjay ed. (2008) *Western Balkan Integration and the EU: An Agenda for Trade and Growth*, World Bank.

Kekic, Laza (2005) "Foreign Direct Investment in the Balkans: Recent Trends and Prospects," *Journal of Southeast European and Black Sea Studies*, Vol. 5, No. 2, pp. 171–190.

Koyama, Yoji (2010) "Economic Crisis in the Baltic States: Focusing on Latvia," *Economic Annals*, No. 186, Faculty of Economics, the University of Belgrade.

Nikic, Gorazd (2004) "Gospodarski Aspekti Pristup Hrvatske Europskoj Uniji: Proteklih deset godina i deset godina ispred nas," *Ekonomski Pregled*, Vol. 55, No. 3–4.

Obadic, Alka (2010) Predavanje: Stabilizacija i Hrvatska Monetarna Politika, Studij "Ekonomika poduzetnistva" u Varazdinu Osnovne gospodarstva Hrvatske — ljetni seminar- sk.god. 2009/2010.

Okrugli Stol Hrvatskog (2010) "Drustva Ekonomista Odrzan Povodom 60 dana Vladinog Programa Gospodarskog Oporavka," *Ekonomski Pregled*, Godina 61, Broj 7–8.

Ott, Katarina (2010) "The Crisis in South East Europe — The Case of Croatia," in Bartlett and Monastiriotis (eds.), South Eastern Europe after the Crisis.

Petrovic, Pavle (2010) "Economic Crisis in Serbia: Impacts and Responses," in Bartlett and Monatiriotis (eds.), South Eastern Europe after the Crisis.

Podkaminer, Leon, Vladimir Gligorov, Mario Holzner, Michael Landesmann and Roman Roemisch *et al.* (2011) Recovery: Limp and Battered, Current Analyses and Forecasts 8, July 2011, Vienna: wiiw.

Richter, Sandor *et al.* (2009) "New EU Member States Facing Recession," in Gligorov, Vladimir, Josef Poeschl and Sandor Richter *et al.* (2009).

Stipetic, Vladimir (2009) *Kriza u poljoprivredi — prioritetnoj djelatnosti buduceg gospodarstva Hrvatske, Zbornik radova Kriza i Okviri Ekonomske Politike*, Zagreb: Razred za Drustvene Znanosti Hrvatske akademije znanosti i umjetnosti i Hrvatski institute za financije i racunovodstvo.

UNDP (2009) Human Development Reports 2009. Available at: http://www.hdrstats.undp.org/en/indicators/.

Uvalic, Milica (2010) "The Impact of the Global Economic Crisis on Southeast Europe," Paper presented at the 11th bi-annual EACES conference, held on August 26–28, in Tartu.

Vidovic, Hermine (2009) "Croatia: Servicing Foreign Debt Remains Major Weak Point," in Gligorov, Vladimir, Joseph Poeschl and Sandor Richter *et al.* (2009).

Vidovic, Hermine (2010) "Another critical year ahead," in Gligorov, Vladimir, Peter Havlik, Michael Landesmann, Joseph Poeschl and Sandor Richter *et al.* (2010).

Vidovic, Hermine and Vladimir Gligorov (2004) "Croatia's Delayed Transition: Competitiveness and Economic Challenges," wiiw Research Reports, No. 304.

Vidovic, Hermine and Vladimir Gligorov (2006) "Croatia: Growth Slowdown and Policy Alternatives," wiiw Research Reports, No. 324.

Vlada Republike Hrvatske (2010) "Program Gospodarskog Oporavka," An English summary of the Government's Economic Recovery Program

appeared in IMF 2010, Annex II. Available at: http://www.vlada.hr/en/
naslovnica/novosti_i_najave/2010/travanj/predsjednica_vlade_predstavila_
program_gospodarskog_oporavka.

Vojnic, Dragomir (1999) "Countries in Transition — Achievements, Problems
and Prospects," in Proceedings of the 3rd International Conference Enterprise
in Transition, University of Split, Faculty of Economics, Split, Croatia.

wiiw (2007) *wiiw Handbook of Statistics 2007*, Vienna: wiiw.

World Bank (1997) "Croatia Beyond Stabilization," Report No. 17261–HR.

World Bank (2001) "Croatia Regaining Fiscal Sustainability and Enhancing
Effectiveness," A Public Expenditure and Institutional Review.

World Bank (2010) "Enhancing Regional Trade: Integration in Southeast
Europe," World Bank Working Paper No. 185.

Periodicals

Business Central Europe (BCE), London: The Economist.

Bulletin (Quarterly Report and Annual Report), Croatian National Bank.

CEE Quarterly, UniCredit Group.

Emerging Europe Monitor (EEM): South East Europe, London: Business
Monitor International.

Transition Report, London: European Bank for Reconstruction and Development
(EBRD).

CHAPTER 4

PIIGS

STEVEN ROSEFIELDE AND ASSAF RAZIN

4.1. Supranationalism

The global financial crisis which erupted in the U.S. instantaneously swept across Europe. Like the U.S., the European Union (EU) was ripe for a crash. It had its own real estate bubble, indulged in excessive deficit spending, financially deregulated, and rapidly expanded credit (partly through derivatives).[1] Policy responses and recovery patterns for key EU members like Germany, France (within the Eurozone) and the U.K. (outside the Eurozone) were similar. However, after the bubble burst and the crisis began unfolding, it became clear that the Eurozone's plight differed from America's in one fundamental respect. There was no exact counterpart of Eurozone PIIGS (Portugal, Italy, Ireland, Greece, and Spain) in the U.S. Some U.S. states had overborrowed, but the sovereign debt crisis did not place individual states at deflationary risk or threaten the viability of the federal union. This was not so for some members within the Eurozone.

The disparity is easily traced to the EU's and Eurozone's special form of governance called "supranationality" (a partially sovereign transnational organization) that has been largely ignored in economic treatises about the costs and benefits of customs unions and economic communities.[2] Until now, it has been tacitly assumed either that supranational governance was as good, or better, than national economic mechanisms; that any policy

---

[1]"European Financial Stability and Integration Report 2010," European Commission, Economic Staff Working Paper, Brussels, April 11, 2011.
[2]Kaiser and Starie (2009).

regime accessible to nation states could be replicated without dysfunction by supranational communities.

Nation states before World War II never voluntarily surrendered their control over fiscal and monetary policy as part of a package to achieve political goals, even though they participated in international institutions like the League of Nations. The horrors of WWII, combined with cold war politics, the welfare state tide, and unreflected sympathy for World Governance,[3] however, propelled Europe along a novel supranational trajectory with unintended consequences. On September 19, 1946, Winston Churchill gave a speech in Zurich not only advocating Franco-German rapproachement, but the creation of a "United States of Europe," called a European "Third Way." He also advocated a "Council of Europe," formed soon thereafter with the assistance of the then French Foreign Minister Robert Schuman, mandating the establishment of supranational communities on the path to a fully democratic, integrated Union.[4] The Schuman Declaration on May 9, 1950, reaffirmed the concept in conjunction with the formation of the European Coal and Steel Community (ESCS). It proclaimed the European Community as the world's first supranational institution, marking the "birth of modern Europe," and initiating an epoch where intra-European wars were impossible. The Soviet Bloc formed a rival economic community, the CMEA (Council for Mutual Economic Cooperation) in 1949, but Comecon as it is sometimes called was more like the OECD (Organization for Economic Cooperation and Development), rather than a supranational economic governance mechanism superior to national authorities.[5]

Schuman's utopian vision which can be traced back to France's first socialist Claude Henri de Rouvroy, the Comte de Saint-Simon (1760–1825) (On the Reorganization of European Industry, 1814) was the prelude to a succession of developments culminating in today's European Union including the European Economic Community (EEC), known as the Common Market (1958), the European Community (1967) (together with

---

[3]Rosefielde and Mills (2012).
[4]The term supranational community was coined by Jean Monnett, Head of France's General Planning Commission.
[5]The members of CMEA were the Soviet Union, Poland, East Germany, Hungary, Czechoslovakia, Romania, Bulgaria, Cuba, Vietnam, and Mongolia.

the European Commission and the European Council of Ministers), the European Council (1974), the European Monetary System (1979), the European Parliament (1979), the Schengen Agreement (1985), The Single Market Act (1986), the Maastricht Treaty (1993) founding the European Union (EU), and European Monetary Union (2002), which inaugurated the euro.

Europeans are broadly pleased with the result. There has been no intra-member wars, a common European identity has emerged, members are democratic and socially progressive, there is free travel and capital mobility within the EU space, the economy has been liberalized, and living standards have risen. However, EU's economic performance has hardly matched Schuman's idealist claims for communal supranationalism. Growth has been anemic, unemployment high and moral hazard problems severe. Supranational governors have found it easier to agree on broad principles than to effectively implement them. Schuman felt sure that communitarians would be considerate, fair, self-restrained, and altruistic or could be tutored to act responsibly, but this judgment is now being called into question for being the triumph of hope over experience.[6] On one hand, the supranational deck was stacked in favor of overborrowing by the PIIGS and East Europeans. On the other hand, the PIIGS were misled into prematurely surrendering control over their monetary and foreign exchange rate policy without receiving fiscal *quid pro quos*. As a consequence, the EU finds itself in an idealistically incorrect position,

---

[6]Jakub Grygiel, "One Market, One Currency, One People" The Faulty Logic of Europe," Foreign Policy Research Institute, ENOTES, January 10, 2012. "Were the EU a term paper, a lenient professor would likely give it a D+... The project of a united Europe is based on the belief that economic unity (itself poorly defined) will lead to political unity. Such a line of causation demanded a technocratic approach. Missing the underlying national unity, the establishment of a common market and a common currency had to be pursued by a supra-national elite with a very tenuous electoral accountability. Absent a demos, the technocrats had to take over the decision-making process. The hope, based on the assumption that a common economy creates a unified people, was that at a certain point a European demos would arise allowing the functioning of a European democracy. But until then, technocracy would have to suffice, and indeed, it was the only way to manage European affairs. The "democratic deficit" of EU institutions is, therefore, a direct outcome of the faith in the transformative powers of economic structures."

where the gap between rich and poor members is widening, at a time when supranational institutional arrangements are forcing the PIIGS to extricate themselves from their predicament with painful and problematic deflationary tactics necessary to regain their competitive strength.

The contradictory social democratic mandate to bring ever more relatively poor countries into the fold, boosting their creditworthiness with implicit guarantees, pressuring them to adopt the euro and straitjacketing their fiscal options, while undermining fiscal discipline with sympathetic approval of entitlements and leveling has solutions within a nation state framework (a true United States of Europe) that could be simulated by a supranational organization. However, this is extraordinarily difficult to accomplish because Schuman's communitarian optimism was misplaced. The EU has yet to find a supranational architecture that reconciles his idealism with a political will for optimal transnational macroeconomic regulation.[7] It is in this sense that the 2008 financial crisis's aftermath is more a culturally conditioned supranational systemic dilemma than a relatively simple matter of conventional international macroeconomic policy, and as such an overlooked element in the half century long debate on optimal economic unions and communities. If the EU does eventually go the way of the CMEA, it will not be because economists failed to grasp the theory of unions and communities, but because they did not endogenize EU supranational theory in institutional and political practice.

4.2. Road to EU Monetary Union (EMU)

The road to the European monetary unification, the monetary centerpiece of a full European Economic Community and Union, went through the European Monetary System (EMS) in 1979–1998, where eight member countries tried to dampen fluctuations in their foreign exchange rate parities.[8] They pegged their currencies to the Deutsche Mark in what

---

[7]The supranational entitlement and moral hazard problem mirrors domestic disorders often said to cause Eurosclerosis, but is potentially more pernicious because governments can borrow more than individuals.

[8]Gros and Thygesen (1999). After the demise of the Bretton Woods system in 1971, most EEC members agreed to maintain stable foreign exchange rate parities. Fluctuations were restricted to no more than 2.25% (the European "currency snake"). The system was

turned out to be a futile effort to curb inflation and advance European Community integration. Nonetheless, 11 members of the European Union upped the ante by choosing a solution that required more, rather than less cooperation in forging the future Eurozone. On January 1, 1999, they created a common currency area (European Monetary Union: EMU) that effectively imposed a fixed exchange rate on all member countries. Participants surrendered their authority over national monetary policy and vested it in the supranational hands of the European Central Bank (ECB), forcing members to rely exclusively on fiscal and regulatory policy to manage macroeconomic disequilibria. The decision was an act of blind faith because many members failed to honor their Maastricht pledges to contain inflation and deficit spending prior to monetary union. Aspirants seeking EU accession were supposed to hold inflation to no more than 1.5% per annum; to maintain a stable exchange rate with the ERM without devaluation, to run public sector deficits less than 3% of GDP, with a public debt under 60% of GDP. Many established members and aspirants alike flunked the tests after they joined the EMU, setting a pernicious precedent for future PIIGS, and providing an early warning that even if an Eurozone satisfied the structural conditions for ideal customs union, the moral hazard might be significant.

4.3. Eurozone Trilemma

Was the decision to persevere in forging an Eurozone wise in the face of the EMU's failure? Few pondered the precedent, focusing instead on the first principles of customs and monetary union theory. Here too, however, there were grounds for concern. The theory of optimal currency areas clearly implied that monetary union was not a one-way-street. Its merit

---

replaced by the European Monetary System (EMS), and the European Currency Unit (ECU) was defined. It fixed parities, set an exchange rate mechanism (ERM), extended European credit facilities, and created a European Monetary Cooperation Fund that allocated ECU to member central banks in exchange for gold and U.S. dollar deposits. The German Deutsche Mark was the de facto anchor because of its relative strength and the country's low-inflation policies. In the early 1990s, the EMS was strained by conflicting macroeconomic policies in Germany and England. Britain and Italy withdrew in 1992. Speculative attacks on the French Franc led to widening the band to 15% in August 1993.

depended on various tradeoffs. Milton Friedman observed that nations can deal more deftly with disorders if they have their own currency, allowing them to vary prices and wages, but this requires them to accept high costs of doing business across national boundaries. Consequently, monetary unions are attractive where there is a high volume of intra-regional trade and labor mobility, and unattractive otherwise. The supranational fiscal regime likewise is a matter of concern. If it is strong, and tasked to assist members confronted with deficient aggregate effective demand, the risk members incur in surrendering the monetary option is partly compensated by pledges of supranational fiscal aid. If it is weak, nations place all their eggs in the supranational monetary basket, with no recourse other than accepting painful deflationary adjustments.

The U.S. provides a good example of an optimal currency area. It has a high volume of intra-national trade (McKinnon, 1963). American labor is mobile (Mundell, 1971), and Washington has the muscle to effectively use fiscal power in alleviating distress in vulnerable states (Kenen, 1967). Also, the Federal Reserve has the authority to act as a "lender of last resort" if Washington's fiscal policy is insufficient.[9]

The EU by contrast is a dubious candidate for an optimal currency area (Eurozone) because although it too trades intensively within the region, national work restrictions greatly impair intra-European labor mobility, and supranational fiscal power is feeble because rich members do not want to assume heavy financing burdens during turbulent times. The obverse also is true. Countries like Sweden and Norway which shunned the euro are thriving and appear to have benefited by retaining their monetary option.[10]

Robert Mundell (1963) and Marcus Fleming (1962) have succinctly formulated the theoretical problem facing the supranational Eurozone (setting aside the further issue of moral hazard), in the form of a two-not-three

---

[9]Mundell (1961); McKinnon (1963); Kenen (1967); and Paul De Grauwe, (2011). The structural problem in the Eurozone is created by the fact that the monetary union is not embedded in a political union (Eurointelligence 11.03.2010). See also Paul De Grauwe (2000).

[10]The same argument holds for North America. Canada's economy has performed well without forging a monetary union with the U.S.

trilemma.[11] Countries seeking to form a supranational monetary union can enjoy two, but only two desirable policy goals: (1) free international capital flows (connected with optimal fiscal policy), (2) potent monetary policy to stabilize output, employment, inflation and financial markets, and (3) exchange rate stability. The U.S. picked free capital mobility and monetary independence, letting its foreign exchange rate float. China decided to retain its monetary independence and control its exchange rate, abandoning free capital flows, while the European Union has selected a third way. It mimicked the U.S. at the supranational level, accepting floating exchange rates for the euro, but at the national level failed to complement the choice with a supportive fiscal regime for distressed economies and friction-free labor mobility, leaving vulnerable nations like the PIIGS in a lurch. When times are bad, the euro appreciates as investors shift to what they perceive as a German safe haven, reducing the PIIGS export competitiveness, while idle labor is prevented from migrating.

4.4. PIIGS Predicament

What works for America does not work for Schuman's supranational EU because of the omitted variables in optimal monetary union discourse (labor immobility and fiscal rigidities).[12] The optimal trilemma solution for an ideal customs union is unattainable for the PIIGS, and fellow current account deficit Eurozone members. Their option is not choosing two out of three virtuous "lemmas." Each finds itself instead in a pickle having to rely on domestic wage and price adjustment because members unwittingly relinquished their independent monetary, exchange rate, and fiscal policy (due to excessive debt) in an immobile labor regime, while

---

[11] There are two basic types of trilemma. The most common occurs where people are compelled to choose among three undesirable options. The economic usage is different. Trilemmas here all involve favorable options, but picking any two precludes acquiring the third.

[12] The ECB sets Eurozone-wide interest rates, but if these rates are inappropriate for distressed economies like Greece, Athens lacks an independent currency to remedy the problem. Likewise, it has no national central bank to act as "lender of last resort." THE ECB cannot act as a "lender of last resort" for Greek banks because it does not get easy mandate from its Board to do so for political reasons, as well as the fact that regulation of banks and deposit insurance is mostly in the hands of national authorities.

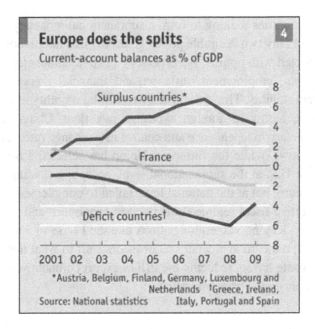

Figure 4.1.

Source: The Economist, 2010.

Germany and other current account surplus members retain free capital flows, a supranational monetary policy tailored to their needs, and the appreciating currency they desire. See Fig. 4.1 (*The Economist*, 2010) for the consequent divergencies within the EMU.

The PIIGS are not entirely straitjacketed. They can extricate themselves from depression and financial ruin with a "real depreciation" or "internal devaluation," but this is little consolation because it places an immense burden on prices, wages, and productivity growth in an adverse financial environment.[13]

4.5. Competitive Asymmetries

Superior German productivity growth, moreover, makes a bad situation for the PIIGS even worse. Fig. 4.2 (*The Economist*, 2011) reveals that PIIGS

---

[13]Not all "internal depreciations" are intolerable. The reunification of East and West Germany provides a relatively painless example. Germany held wages down and increased productivity to alleviate unemployment and cope with income transfers flowing to the former communist east.

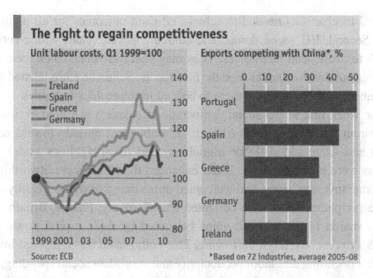

Figure 4.2.

Source: The Economist, 2011.

unit labor costs rose steadily during 2001–2010, while German unit labor costs fell reciprocally. *Ceteris paribus*, the incentive for Germany to outsource and invest in PIIGS diminished at the same time foreigners were coaxed into diverting their purchases of EU exports from the PIIGS to Germany. Given the EU's supranational straitjacket, there does not appear to any compelling reason to anticipate a swift reversal of the PIIGS's ill-fortune. A utopian welfare-state vision intended to ameliorate transnational income inequality, thus may perversely aggravate the problem.

4.6. Social Democratic Culture

Needless to say, this outcome was unintended, and indeed would not have occurred if PIIGS acted like virtuous Germans. They would not have assumed unmanageable debt obligations, and EU fiscal, monetary and foreign exchange rate policies would have been appropriate for them. These requirements however underscore two fundamental defects in the EMU (Eurozone) supranationalism. First, the systems architecture is too rigid. A meritorious regime should provide good solutions across a wide spectrum of initial conditions. For the moment at least, the EU has not devised the supplementary internal mechanisms needed to achieve efficient outcomes for all its members. Second, EU social democratic culture fostered values which enticed PIIGS to overextend themselves. They may well have done so on their own volition, but this does not change the fact that the Schuman ethos abetted their delinquency by encouraging them to believe in miraculous free rides.

The weak link in EU social democratic utopianism is a predilection for egalitarian outcomes combined with an ambivalent attitude toward equal effort and value added (labor immobility and fiscal rigidities aside). EU leaders were pleased that the EMU enhanced the PIIGS's creditworthiness in private investors' eyes, and welcomed outsourcing from the wealthy core to the periphery. They were delighted that Germany, France, Britain, and others shared in the windfall gains generated by these capital flows, and PIIGS's excess sovereign borrowing. This enthusiasm was tempered by the PIIGS's declining unit labor productivity and exorbitant social spending, but not enough to outweigh the satisfaction derived from narrowing the intra-union per capita income gap. Moreover by raising the prospect of "haircuts" (debt forgiveness), the European Council and parliament telegraphed the message that financial indiscipline and extravagant social programming ultimately may prove to be winning strategies. This double think, expecting responsible behavior, and doing little to encourage it makes it unlikely that European leaders can construct a well-functioning Eurozone anytime soon.

4.7. PIIGS in Crisis

Speculative bubbles like the one sparked by EU's contradictory welfare state political goals often end in crises. Investors panic when they discover that sand castles are crumbling, and debts may never be fully repaid even if they are restructured. This is what has been transpiring in fits and starts after the Autumn of 2010. Ireland was the first victim. Its toxic debt had been accumulating for a decade fueled by Irish bank borrowing in the international wholesale market to finance a property development bubble. When real estate crashed, private bank balance sheets melted down, panicking the government into plugging the hole with a 50 billion euro commitment, equivalent to a third of Ireland's GDP. This dubious pledge was swiftly followed in 2008 by an equally ill-advised 100% guarantee of all bank deposits and most debt. The ECB joined the party allocating a quarter of its Eurozone lending to Irish banks by September–October 2010, all to no avail. Ireland ultimately managed to staunch runs on its private banks by borrowing approximately 145 billion dollars (70% of GDP), but this raised its debt-to-GDP ratio to stratospheric Greek levels, effectively bankrupting the nation. The Irish government saved its banks and their creditors by forcing the Irish people to shoulder an unbearable burden. A 10% drop in GDP slashed jobs, driving the unemployment rate to 14%.

Spain's experience followed a similar script, but its real estate bubble which began in 1985 was home grown, with the government providing incentives for owning rather than renting, including 40- and even 50-year mortgages. Speculation accelerated after Spain adopted the euro driven by huge capital inflows until 2008, when the global financial crisis took the wind out of the real estate market's sails, throwing the country into deep recession. The national budget plummeted into deficit. It was 9.2% in 2010, and even if pared the debt-to-GDP ratio is expected to rise to 90%. On balance, Spain appears stronger than other PIIGS because of its conservative banking philosophy. However, Madrid is not out of the woods yet. Further deterioration in housing prices in adverse times could threaten mortgage-dependent private bank solvency, and intensify the decline in housing demand because under Spanish law evicted owners remain liable for their mortgage debt.

Greece's version of the supranational EU melodrama has a different plot. The principal culprit in Hellas was unrestrained government welfare expenditures financed with overseas borrowing. Greek governments customarily have run large public deficits to fund government sector jobs, pensions and other social benefits since democracy was restored in 1974. Its debt-to-GDP ratio has exceeded 100% since 1993. The burden was softened before 2001 by drachma devaluation, but this option was foreclosed in 2001 when Greece adopted the euro. At first this did not seem to matter because euro accession allowed Athens to finance debt on favorable terms, an advantage leveraged by persistently falsifying official data on the country's financial condition. The chickens however finally came home to roost. On April 27, 2010, the Greek debt rating was cut to "junk" status by Standard & Poor. The ECB has tried to help by suspending its prohibition on buying junk collateral, but the situation continues deteriorating despite new austerity measures approved by parliament in July 2011 in part because the fear of default raises interest costs that cannot be paid.

The best current estimates of the PIIGS's budgetary deficits and cumulative debt forecast that Greece's debt-to-GDP ratio will reach 180 in 2014.

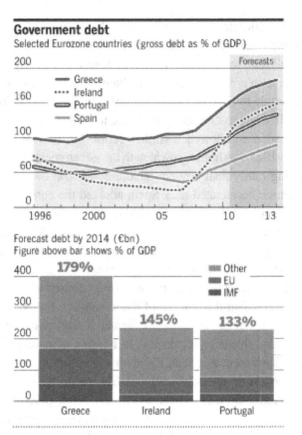

Figure 4.3.

Source: The Economist, 2011.

Ireland's plight will be nearly as dire with a debt-to-GDP ratio of 145, followed by Portugal at 135 and Spain 90 [see Fig. 4.3 (Martin Wolf, *Financial Times*, June 2011)].

Obviously, while Europe's sovereign debt crisis can go from bad to worse as Germany and France permit, the longer PIIGS delay getting their houses in order, the direr the consequences will be.

4.8. What Can Be Done?

Schuman would have known what to do. The EU rich should pay. The people should be protected and EU bad boys should be admonished to grow up (to forswear levering and resist moral hazards). This is the social democratic way that inspired supranationalism, and is the formula that will be applied, rhetoric to the contrary notwithstanding. The exact prescription is up for continuous negotiation.

The maxim that the rich should pay at the supranational level means that the ECB, perhaps supplemented with new institutions will grudgingly provide loans to prevent PIIGS from defaulting on their sovereign debt. They also could provide "solidarity" grants by analogy with foreign catastrophe aid. If these tactics prove insufficient, wealthy EU members like Germany and France can consent to partial "haircuts." This could be done in diverse ways, but the details are not matters of high principle. What matters is that creditors will be transformed into limited liability partners sharing the cost of past transgressions so that debtors can have a fresh start without being formally cast into permanent default.

Paul De Grauwe (2011) recently called for the ECB to be even more ambitious, serving as lender of last resort both to Eurozone member banks and those facing sovereign debt crises, stressing how easily liquidity crises can degenerate into system-wide insolvency. His argument is that sovereign debt in a single currency area is denominated in "foreign" money (money that cannot be issued by the governor of the individual central bank), because the individual central bank cannot perform as "lender of last resort" by printing money. Only the ECB can do it, and this requires complex coordination with other ECB governors. Therefore, De Grauwe argues that it is wrong to restrict ECB monetary policy to inflation fighting, ignoring contagion of sovereign debt crises from one country to another as financial perils develop. Inflation fighting he insists, contrary to Goodfriend's advice (Goodfriend,

2011), must be integrated with a war against insolvency because the catastrophic potential of insolvency dominates the moral hazard risk.

4.9. What Will Be Done?

De Grauwe does not downplay the moral hazard problem, but claims reassuringly that it can be managed by imposing rules that constrain government debt issuance. He is right in principle, but glosses the problems of national entitlements and supranationality. The sovereign debt crisis besetting the EU today has not arisen because European Council encouraged PIIGS to misbehave, or because the Germans are fixated on inflation fighting. It erupted because the PIIGS refuse to curb domestic entitlements, and the EU cannot compel them to desist regardless of whether the ECB adopts a conservative or liberal monetary regime.[14] The Eurozone debt crisis thus is not really about "optimal debt."[15] It is driven by the domestic and supranational politics of social entitlement that depend little on short term ECB monetary accommodation.

Being good little PIIGS means promising Brussels to try curbing entitlements, probing the envelope of toleration, and biding ones time for the right moment for another spending spree. There are limits, but they are soft because supranational social democracies usually acquiesce to recidivism.

It is highly unlikely therefore that the European Union will confront a moment of truth in the foreseeable future when members seriously contemplate secession, tough talk to the contrary notwithstanding.[16]

Winners in the daily trench wars (as distinct from attaining the competitive ideal) like Germany which enjoy current account surpluses, high national savings, rising productivity and moderate per capita GDP growth, risk losing more than they gain from exiting the EU, even if they have to pay for partial haircuts. Germany still carries the baggage of distrust from the Nazi era, and is able to pursue its business and foreign policy agenda

---

[14]De Grauwe (2011) and Goodfriend (2011).

[15]Greece paid Goldman $300 million to help it hide its ballooning debts, according to http:www.businessinsider.com/henry-blodget, 2010–2012. cf. Feldstein (2012).

[16]Social democracy in Europe is not only good politics, it is good business for insiders. The commitment of EU leaders to supranationalism consequently runs deeper than idealism. See Rosefielde and Mills (2013).

much more effectively under EU cover than if it tried to prize similar concessions by other means. The French value the EU relationship for other reasons, but like Germany are far from the threshold of secession.

The EU's bailout of Greece on July 21, 2011, confirms this surmise. The Eurozone countries and the International Monetary Fund (IMF) will give Greece a second bailout worth euro 109 billion (155 billion dollars), on top of the euro 110 billion granted a year ago. Banks and other private investors will add euro 50 billion (71 billion dollars) more to the rescue package until 2014 by either rolling over Greek bonds that they hold, swapping them for new ones with lower interest rates or selling the bonds back to Greece cheaply. The deal involving private creditors may well be deemed a "selective default" by rating agencies, making Greece the first euro country to ever be in default, but this is not expected to have drastic consequences given the other positive aspects of the rescue package. To dampen adverse effects, the Eurozone will back new Greek bonds issued to banks with guarantees. This is essential because Greek banks use Greek government debt as collateral for emergency support from the European Central Bank. Those bonds would no longer qualify as collateral if hit with a default rating, meaning Greek banks would lose ECB support and quickly collapse. Bond rollovers, or swaps will give Greece more time to recover and cut approximately 21% of its future debt burden.[17] Authorities agreed to provide the new Eurozone rescue loans to Greece at a 3.5% interest rate, with maturities between 15 and 30 years, plus an additional 10 year grace period. Moreover, EU bailout overseers were given the power to intervene in countries before they are beset with full blown crises, an institutional reform opposed by Germany.[18]

4.10. Survival

PIIGS, for their part, regret having to pay the piper (creditors, reduced government spending, depression, and mass unemployment), but the

---

[17]The new Greek bonds issued to the banks would have long maturities of up to 30 years and low interest rates according to the Institute of International Finance, the group representing private sector creditors. French President Nicolas Sarkozy estimated that the rates would average 4.5%.

[18]Economists often pretend that public programs Pareto efficiently maximize social welfare, but Kenneth Arrow long ago showed that the claim is misleading, due to information-based market failures in the context of medical care, finance, etc.

political and economic benefits of EU membership still lopsidedly exceed costs, even in a worst case scenario where defaults trigger a decade of suffering. They might contemplate exiting the Eurozone in order to increase the number of instruments for dealing with problems largely of their own making, but not the EU which provides valuable customs union benefits, enhanced creditworthiness and the possibility of compassionate transfers when the going gets tough. Moreover, rich members seeking to rid themselves of noisome PIIGS cannot compel them to exit the Eurozone by treaty, and practical difficulties will likely dissuade PIIGS from attempting to resurrect national currencies on their own.

The same principles apply for new entrants. Costs and benefits of EU and Eurozone accession will depend on each individual case more than generic economic considerations. It follows directly not only that talk of Eurozone, and or EU dissolution is premature, but EU enlargement considered the partnership's greatest foreign policy success, remains on track. Croatia is acceding, Montenegro and Macedonia are official candidates, and negotiations are in process for Turkey and Iceland. Preliminary discussions have been conducted with Russia.

The substantive issue moving forward therefore is whether members are sufficiently dissatisfied with muddling that they are willing to reform or ditch supranationality. Inertia favors doing nothing fundamental. Resistance to replacing member governance with unified federal rule is likely to be insurmountable now that the bloom is off the rose, while German and French authorities will be charier than ever of ceding ultimate control over the purse to supranational bodies. The EU's inflexible supranational architecture is the patchwork result of contradictory social democratic goals, not a failure of intellect. Any changes made therefore only are apt to improve flexibility at the margin rather than functioning as a viable surrogate for a unified state. As such reform may deter or mitigate crises in some instances, but should not prevent them. Politics has been in command from the beginning, and continue to take precedence over economic potential and performance.

Nonetheless, this judgment should not be construed to mean that a default, should it occur, would be innocuous. The inflexibility of the EU's supranational architecture raises the specter of hyper-deleveraging. For example, if the EU's latest rescue plan for Greece proves inadequate and its sovereign debt goes into full default despite Eurozone guarantees, Greek bank lending capacity will plummet placing extraordinary downward pressure on wages, prices and aggregate effective demand because Athens does not control its interest rate (equivalently, its money supply) or foreign exchange rate. Argentina's experience in 2001 under less rigid conditions suggests that EU supranationality could make PIIGS pain and suffering a protracted ordeal.[19]

4.11. EU Supranationality: Net Assessment

It therefore can be reasonably concluded that the political and economic benefits of EU supranationality as they are currently constituted are asymmetric. The EU has wrought substantial political benefits including the democratization of new members and intra-European major war avoidance, but eurozone architecture is economically inefficient, bubble prone and subject to serious systemic risk. This package may be good enough for supporters of the welfare state, but prospective Asian emulators should weigh the evidence more judiciously.

---

[19]Kiguel (2011). Argentina, like Greece was confronted with a conundrum. It sought to restore access to the international capital market (sovereign debt problem) by raising taxes and cutting public expenditures to pay down its indebtedness. But, in doing so it risked making repayment more difficult by plunging the economy into deep depression. Kiguel argues that Argentina's budget cutting had precisely this adverse effect, and cautions the EU accordingly. His preferred solution is to hold the line on deficit spending insofar as possible, and promote productivity and competition with nondeflationary tactics. Another complementary approach that he fails to consider is steamrolling vested political interests, streamlining government services and earmarking savings for debt repayment. The structural similarities between Argentina and Greece that guide Kiguel's recommendation are: (1) loss of devaluation option (currency board and dollarization in the Argentinean case; replacement of the drachma with the euro in the Greek case), (2) loss of access to the international capital market (excess sovereign debt), (3) and loss of monetary options due to dollar/euroization. On the policy front, both Argentina and Greece tried to acquire external assistance and ultimately failed to obtain enough. They also resorted to deflation to spur competitiveness, but here too were unsuccessful.

References

De Grauwe, Paul (2000) *Economics of Monetary Union*, New York: Oxford University Press.

De Grauwe, Paul (2011) "The European Central Bank as a Lender of Last Resort," 19 August.

Feldstein, Martin (2012) "The Failure of the Eurs," *Foreign affairs*, Vol. 91, issue 1, pp. 105–116.

Fleming, Marcus (1962) "Domestic Financial Policies Under Fixed and Flexible Exchange Rates," IMF Staff Papers 9, pp. 369–379.

Goodfriend, Marvin (2011) "Central Banking in the Credit Turmoil: An Assessment of Federal Reserve Practice," *Journal of Monetary Economics*.

Gros, Daniel and Niels Thygesen (1999) *European Monetary Integration*, London: Longman.

Kenen, Peter B (1967) "Toward a Supranational Monetary System," In: G. Pontecorvo, R. P. Shay and A. G. Hart, (eds.), *Issues in Banking and Monetary Analysis*, New York: Holt, Reinhart, and Winston.

Kiguel, Miguel (2011) "Argentina and Greece: More Similarities than Differences in the Initial Conditions" 16 August.

McKinnon, Ronald I (September 1963) "Optimum Currency Areas," *The American Economic Review*, Vol. 53, No. 4, pp. 717–725.

Mundell, Robert A (1961) "A Theory of Optimum Currency Areas," *The American Economic Review*, Vol. 51, pp. 657–664.

Mundell, Robert A (1963) "Capital Mobility and Stabilization Policy Under Fixed and Flexible Exchange Rates," *Canadian Journal of Economic and Political Science*, Vol. 29, No. 4, pp. 475–485.

Rosefielde, Steven and Quinn Mills (2013) *Democracy and its Elected Enemies: American Political Capture and Economic Decline*, Cambridge: Cambridge University Press.

Wolfram, Kaiser and Peter Starie (eds.), (2009) *Transnational European Union: Towards a Common Political Space*, London: Routledge.

CHAPTER 5

GLOBAL DEFAULT

STEVEN ROSEFIELDE AND DANIEL QUINN MILLS

When PIIGS (Portugal, Ireland, Italy, Greece and Spain) cannot pay their sovereign debt, the EU bails them out, and in the worst case, creditors take hair cuts that are painful, but bearable. Is an American default "thinkable"? If it is, would it be more destructive than the PIIGS debacle?

An American default until recently was considered unthinkable. U.S. did not seem capable of acting like an irresponsible third world country. It was thought to be immune from running ruinous debts, and if difficulties arose, it was firmly believed that politicians would always take bitter medicine before repudiating solemn obligations. The U.S. behavior during the deficit ceiling debate in July 2011 and thereafter suggests that this supposition was complacent. Most U.S. presidents, senators, and congressmen, like their Greek counterparts, do not seek to defraud creditors with malice aforethought; they simply cannot grasp that they can spend too much, and that there could be a day of reckoning on their watch. They have always kicked the can down the road and expect to keep doing so assuming that the size of the national debt will never be a hard constraint.[1]

This wishful thinking is conspicuous in the self-congratulations and lamentations prompted by the Obama administration's 2.4 trillion dollar "compromise" framework agreement (August 2, 2011) which merely

---

[1] Paul Krugman, "Nobody Understands Debt," Op Ed, *New York Times*, January 1, 2012.

reduces projected cumulative deficits over the next decade by 20%,[2] without a word about when the debt will be paid down, what constitutes an optimal debt/GDP ratio, or how an American default could wreck havoc on the global economy.

The public, professional economists, the business community, and vulnerable interest groups are similarly myopic despite a sharp stock market drop precipitated by Standard and Poor's downgrading American creditworthiness from AAA to AA+ (August 4, 2011) for the first time since Moody's awarded the coveted AAA rating in 1917. The government, businessmen, and investors fret, but continue to believe that no serious harm can befall them at the end of the day from a consume now, pay later mentality because rational policymakers will ultimately put public welfare ahead of partisan advantage or, as Warren Buffett likes to say, U.S. has infinite hidden strengthens allowing it to thrive amid almost any adversity.

Until the 2008 financial crisis, adequate GDP growth, inflation, dollar devaluation and foreign demand for U.S. treasury bonds and bills (primarily China and Japan) kept a lid on debt financing costs and the debt/GDP ratio. The Troubled Asset Relief Program (TARP) and the spending explosion that replaced it (not part of the original deal),[3] however, fundamentally changed the game. Deficit spending bolted upward but failed to generate rapid growth or inflation sufficient to diminish the real debt burden. GDP still had not recovered the 2007 peak in mid 2012 according to revised government data.[4] (GDP fell 5.1% peak to trough 2007–2009.) There has been no growth dividend, or internal dollar depreciation to

---

[2]The American deficit spending and national debt situation as of 2011 is:
- U.S. income (tax revenue): $2,170,000,000,000
- Federal budget: $3,820,000,000,000
- New debt: $,650,000,000,000
- National debt: $14,271,000,000,000
- August 2011 cut: $ 38,500,000,000(about 1% of budget).

[3]Alan Blinder and Mark Zandi, *"How the Great Recession Was Brought to an End"*. Available at: www.economy.com/mark-zandi/documents/End-of-Great-Recession.pdf, July 2010.

[4]GDP fell 5.1% peak to trough 2007–2009. U.S. Department of Commerce, Bureau of Economic Analysis, BEA 11–38, National Income and Product Accounts, Revised Estimates: 2003 Through the First Quarter of 2011, July 29, 2011.

significantly reduce the debt load, placing the adjustment burden squarely on program cuts and tax increases.

One and a half trillion dollars of annual fiscal stimulus 2008–2012, more than 4 trillion dollars cumulatively; trillions of newly printed dollars (QE1 and QE2 quantitative easing), and a 20% trade weighted dollar devaluation, have not triggered the GDP growth required to repay borrowed funds. Instead, debt has mounted, and purchasing power over foreign imports eroded, leaving future generations to deal with Washington's wishful thinking. Somehow amid this adversity, the Obama administration and other proponents of "spend now, pay later" have failed to come to grips with the counter-productiveness of piling on debt for short-term political and venal gain.[5] They are unfazed by the prospect of projected trillion dollar annual deficits 2011–2020 ballooning the national debt toward 160% of GDP.[6] They shrug when warned that Fannie Mae (Federal National Mortgage Association), Freddie Mac (Federal Home Loan Mortgage Corporation) and the FHA (Federal Housing Administration) are on track to generate trillions in further losses,[7] and that cumulative OASDI (Old Age, Survivors and Disability Insurance Act) deficits 2016–2040 are projected to add trillions more to the national debt.[8]

They are committed to deficit spending, printing money, and devaluing the dollar until vindicated. They are not considering paring stultifying mandates, regulations, and dubious entitlements, exchange traded funds (ETF) and speculative derivatives. Their blase attitude is apt to prevail. However, suppose that the growth and inflation leaders still are counting on does not materialize, and the foreign appetite for U.S. debt is satiated. What will happen then?

There are many scenarios, but a few elements are critical. First, and foremost is the danger of sovereign (China, Japan, and Germany, and private) capital flight. Foreign holders of U.S. liquid assets and the domestic

---

[5] Larry Summers, *"On the Economy,"* Available at: www.Ohiomm.com/blogs/da.../larry-summers-on-the-economy/.

[6] "CBO: Obama Understates Deficits by 2.3 Trillion", *Yahoo!Finance*, March 18, 2011.

[7] Peter Wallison and Ed Pinto (December 27, 2010), "How the Government is Creating Another Bubble," (AEI Articles and Commentary).

[8] Status of Social Security and Medicare Programs, Summary of the 2010 Annual Reports. Available at: www.socialsecurity.gov.

hot money crowd may throw in the towel, driving down stock, bond, and real estate prices, and further devaluing the dollar. Capital losses and rising interest rates will depress aggregate effective demand, unemployment will rise into the high double digits, and there will be powerful, negative global multiplier effects as U.S. depression spreads rapidly across the globe.

Ben Bernanke will press forward with QE-infinity, but no one may borrow the newly minted funds. Deflation could become intense, raising the real cost of the national debt that will not vanish of its own accord. The International Monetary Fund (IMF) and the European Union (EU) may try to help, but they do not have deep enough pockets to succeed. They failed to prevent the PIIGS's technical default, and cannot possibly tide U.S. over for more than a few months.

The scale of carnage likewise will make the PIIGS case child's play. The entire global economy will experience colossal de-levering, not the nick caused by the PIIGS zone failure, causing havoc everywhere. Prevention and crisis management are possible. There are many options, all distasteful: slash entitlements, drastically increase taxes, and partially default on debt.[9] However, it is unrealistic to expect prompt, effective action. Restoring equilibrium will not be swift or kind, and the politicians' capacity for making bad situations worse should not be underestimated.

The bright spot is devaluation. Theory teaches that as the dollar cheapens, export and asset demand should rise. This will mitigate some negatives, but will not be a panacea because foreign beggar-thy-neighbor protectionism (particularly China) will blunt the effect, and exports are a relatively small part of aggregate U.S. economic activity. The U.S. and the world therefore will be at risk once again to a 1930s scale depression, but this time around the cause will not be private financial speculation and faulty monetary policy. The culprit will be preventable, but nonetheless runaway U.S. deficit spending and sovereign debt.

---

[9]The debt problematic can be treated as a trilemma where the nation can have a (1) sustainable national debt, (2) under-tax, and (3) overspend. It is possible to achieve any two goals, but not all. If nations under-tax (overspend), they must underspend (overtax) to achieve sustainable national debts. The approach suggests a political divide with Democrats preferring 2 and 3, and Republicans 1 and 2, but the reality is that neither wants a fundamental change because the status quo facilitates politocracy (trafficking in public services).

The U.S. debt crisis is not written in the stars but is being driven by pathologies that are difficult to reverse because of the government's unwillingness to limit spending to current revenue or increase taxes to cover shortfalls. It can borrow funds in the open market and compel households to purchase state bonds. Or it can print money hoping to stay a step ahead of inflation.

Postwar U.S. political culture has developed a pronounced preference for deficit spending and moderate inflation as joint forms of indirect taxation on induced GDP growth and consumer purchasing power. The strategy works if growth dividends are sufficiently large and inflation rates are politically tolerable. These conditions are likely to be satisfied where deficit spending is small, but will be increasingly violated as borrowing increases. The risk of a U.S. debt crisis is rising beyond anything that Standard and Poor's envisions because Washington's appetite for deficit spending is growing unabated at a time when the growth dividend and politically tolerable inflation not only are not raising sufficient indirect taxes, but high unemployment, sluggish economic activity and devaluation are causing intense public disgruntlement. These economic conditions perversely encourage politicians to borrow more rather than reduce programs or increase taxes, aggravating the cumulative disequilibrium, and increasing the temptation to default.

The problem is compounded by asymmetric assessments of costs and benefits. Some powerful politicians seem to believe that their priorities take precedence over the short-term wellbeing of others. They demand drastic increases in deficit spending and urge increased taxes on corporations and the wealthy to pay for still more public programming, forgetting that the same ploy was responsible for the longevity of the Great Depression from 1929 to 1941. Others seem anxious to wage war on every flimsy pretext. Whatever the merit of these positions, the demands greatly raise default risk.

The attitudes are not new but are more perilous today because the excess social security (FICA) collections that once defrayed other social spending will vanish, forcing politicians to borrow just to preserve existing programs. Trillions more will be needed to subsidize social security, medicare, and medicaid as FICA revenues shortfall benefit commitments. Although annual social security account statements have long cautioned that current FICA revenues only partially cover promised benefits, politicians find it preferable to pile on debt than slash promises, increase the retirement age, or increase FICA taxes on a population that is already stressed.

On the surface, most Americans do not have grounds for complaint because 47% of households pay no federal tax. Raising revenues from some of these households and others earning more than $50,000 per year, it would seem to follow should be easy. However, the "tax free household" statistic is misleading. It conceals a shift from federal income taxation to fees, other state, local, property, and sales taxes as well as skyrocketing health insurance costs resulting from various government medical mandate and transfer schemes. Real personal disposable household income adjusted for all these factors is falling, making it harder to squeeze blood from stones.

Moreover, as few seem to appreciate government reach is vastly greater than official federal spending because of grants-in-aid, mandates, and unfunded insurance guarantees to Fannie Mae and Freddic Mac. Politicians of most persuasions do not want to relinquish the power that comes with grants-in-aid (freeing up tax transfer monies for deficit reduction and debt repayment) or acknowledge that as debt ratings fall, contingent mortgage, educational, and other guarantees become ticking time bombs.

The propensity for American politicians to kick the can down the road is reinforced by the transformation of government into a "privatized" state service business that takes precedence over their traditional job of representing constituencies and pressing partisan agendas.[10] It can be argued that the governance the American people get is precisely what the majority wants. It is naive to believe that political agents are angels, and savvy to suppose that the sophisticated majority approve their representatives pragmatism. The surmise is misleading. While the U.S. government does provide the information needed to sort out much of what is happening, government spokesmen and the media selectively disseminate data and frame issues in ways that conceal most of what is really important. People are coached into conceptualizing the debt issue through stereotyped

---

[10]Steven Rosefielde and Quinn Mills, *Democracy and its Elected Enemies: American Political Capture and Economic Decline*, Cambridge: Cambridge University Press, 2013.

partisan filters instead of the lens of optimal financial management. They are encouraged to judge whether the government should pare the growth of deficit spending or use the opportunity to promote egalitarianism (soak the rich), shielding the deeper question of public economic efficiency and welfare.

The U.S. consequently still does not see that it cannot have its cake and eat it,[11] even though the mechanism for the fire next time is staring it in the face, making it probable that the U.S. will follow the PIIGS with devastating consequences. The refusal of politicians to appreciate that money really does not grow on trees is the triumph of human folly over rational expectations. Crises cannot be prevented if critical actors are willing to jump off cliffs to prove that men can fly.

---

[11]Downsizing and rationalizing governance at this juncture would go a long way toward mitigating the contractive effects of fiscal and monetary restraint, but the possibility is seldom raised by macroeconomic policymakers.

PART II

PREVENTION

CHAPTER 6

PREVENTION AND COUNTER-MEASURES

TORBJÖRN BECKER

6.1. Introduction

This chapter discusses prevention and crisis management strategies that have developed over several decades before the crisis of 2008–2009. It then provides a detailed empirical examination of how key economic indicators identified after previous crises correlate with economic performance in the 2008–2009 crisis. This examination is closely related to long-running efforts to develop early warning indicators of crises and more recent discussion of macro-prudential indicators as ways to prevent crises.[1] As will be evident in the chapter, the cost of crises is in many cases very substantial, and ways to prevent or limit the impact of crises should be a top priority among economists and policy makers. However, the chapter illustrates the weaknesses of many of the current early warning indicators, which suggests that more research efforts in this area are called for. The empirical part also details the geographic impact of the crisis and offers some perspective on its global scope.

Economic crises are not new phenomena. Policy makers have pondered how to prevent and deal with them for centuries. The definition of "crisis" has differed over time and across countries and has been used to describe a wide range of diverse phenomena, including for example, debt, banking, currency, oil, and food-related events. The crisis label is also used extensively to describe economic problems at the regional and country level,

---

[1]Kaminsky, Lizondo and Reinhart (1998) present a first early warning model of currency crises, later enhanced by Berg and Pattillio (1999), while for example Kaminsky and Reinhart (1999) focus on banking crises and Manasse and Roubini (2005) on debt crises.

e.g., the Latin American, Asian, Russian, ERM (European Exchange Rate Mechanism), or Nordic crisis.

Becker and Mauro (2006) focus on economic crises defined as episodes with substantial losses of GDP and document the frequency of these events over the last century for the countries included in the Maddison (2003) dataset. GDP was selected as the key crisis indicator because it is closely related to consumption and welfare. The authors show that output crises occurred throughout the 20th century, but the number of countries entering a crisis has varied substantially over time. The peak was the great depression, when 45% of the countries in the sample experienced the onset of a crisis. In the post-war period, the frequency varies between 2%–10%, and at the end of the century, only 2%–5% of countries entered into crisis.

If countries want to prevent output losses, a first step is to investigate their triggers or correlates. Becker and Mauro accomplish this by relating the onset of a GDP crisis to a large number of shocks, or sub-crises such as the debt, banking, currency and oil crises. The list of shocks or component crises also includes sudden capital flow stoppages, drastic changes in terms of trade, sharp international interest rate movements, political crises, armed conflicts and natural disasters. The authors then use shock frequency data, together with information on output losses and conditional probabilities that link output losses to shocks to compute the expected value of losses for different types of countries. It turns out that sudden stops in capital flows are particularly harmful to emerging markets, while terms-of-trade shocks are correlated with extreme income losses in developing countries. Other shocks, such as political, currency and debt crises also carry substantial costs.

In the current crisis (the 2008–2009 crisis and its lingering aftermath), a variety of shocks hit many countries at the same time. Around half the 183 countries in the International Monetary Fund (IMF)'s World Economic Outlook database experienced a decline in GDP. It is premature to make a final account of how many countries will experience output collapses as defined in Becker and Mauro (2006) because most have not yet returned to pre-crisis GDP levels, but the figure surely will be the highest since the great depression. It is also clear that banking problems, overvalued currencies, sudden stops in capital flows and massive swings in terms-of-trade all occurring simultaneously have contributed to this crisis's global scale, in line with the correlates identified by Becker and Mauro.

The remainder of this chapter is organized in four sections. First, we look at regional economic performance, followed by an extensive section on crisis prevention detailing how early warning indicators and prevention measures correlate with economic performance. A section on crisis management discussing domestic and international responses to the crisis is provided next, before drawing lessons in the conclusion.

6.2. Economic Performance in the Crisis

The 2008–2009 crisis was global, but its impact was uneven across countries and regions. This section documents the phenomenon. It reveals that the 2008–2009 was atypically concentrated in advanced countries, unlike much of the postwar period where emerging markets crises were more prevalent.[2]

Compared to 2004–2007, the growth rates during the current crisis receded in all country groups. However, it was only in advanced countries and the nations of Central and Eastern Europe that growth rates turned negative on average in 2008–2009. Furthermore, in developing Asia, Latin America and the Caribbean, Middle East and North Africa, and Sub-Saharan Africa, crisis growth rates were comparable to growth in 2000–2003, and it is pre-crisis growth rates that look abnormally high. This is also true for the BRIC (Brazil, Russia, India, and China) countries except Russia, which suffered a significant drop in growth rates in the crisis, well below pre-crisis rates (Fig. 6.1).

The projected rebound in growth rates follows a similar pattern across country groups, with advanced countries and the CEE (Central and East European) region showing the slowest recovery, suggesting that the global

---

[2]There are now a number of studies that have looked at the economic impact of the crisis and its correlates, see for example, Berkmen *et al.* (2009), Lane and Milesi-Feretti (2010), Frankel and Saravelos (2010), Barrell *et al.* (2010). All these papers differ from the current analysis in either how the crisis impact is measured, the variables that are correlated with the crisis, the geographical coverage or regional breakdown and/or sample period. For a more extensive discussion focused on Central and Eastern Europe, see Becker *et al.* (2010).

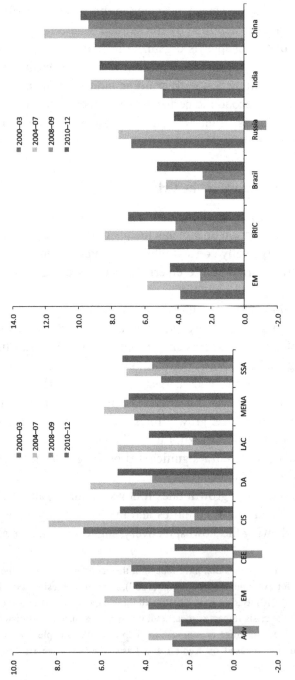

Figure 6.1. GDP growth pre- and post-crisis around the world.

Note: IMF data and *World Economic Outlook* October 2010 forecast. Country labels are: Adv: Advanced economies; EM: Emerging markets; CEE: Central and Eastern Europe (including the Baltic countries); CIS: Commonwealth of Independent States; DA: Developing countries in Asia; LAC: Latin America and the Caribbean; MENA: Middle East and North Africa; SSA: Sub-Saharan Africa; BRIC: Brazil, Russia, India and China.

crisis may be less global than commonly portrayed. It is really a crisis among advanced countries and the CEE region and to some lesser extent the Commonwealth of Independent States (CIS). Other parts of the world have not experienced the same dramatic growth slowdown or output losses. This is not only true for developing Asian, including India and China, but also for other emerging market countries outside the CEE and CIS regions.

Given the regional impact of the crisis to date, the following presentation will focus on two particularly hard hit groups: advanced countries and the CEE region. Their experience is contrasted separately with developing Asia, and a basket of other regions, including Latin America and the Caribbean, Middle East and North Africa, Sub-Saharan Africa, and the CIS countries, including the former CIS country Georgia (Fig. 6.2).

The crisis was a very significant negative event for world output and growth because many of the world's wealthiest nations were particularly hard hit. It also had a pronounced impact on regional composition of global GDP due to developing Asia's relatively strong performance.

The share of world GDP contributed by advanced countries fell three percentage points from 2007 to 2009, and is projected to fall almost as

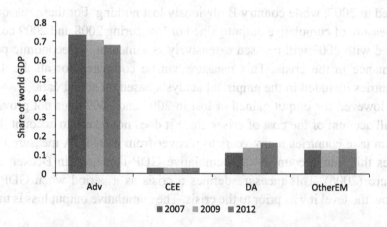

Figure 6.2. Share of world GDP for different country groups.

Note: Based on IMF data on GDP in nominal USD and IMF forecasts. Country labels are: Adv: Advanced countries, CEE: Central and Eastern Europe including the Baltic countries, DA: Developing countries in Asia, Other EM: Latin America and the Caribbean, Middle East and North Africa, Sub-Saharan Africa and the Commonwealth of Independent States (including ex-CIS country Georgia).

much thereafter to end-2012.[3] Developing Asia increased its share of world GDP by the same amount, and is expected to make similar gains in 2010–2012, reducing global income disparities.

6.2.1. *Income levels rather than growth rates matter*

When it comes to assessing economic performance, researchers often use growth rates exclusively. However, in crisis times, there is reason to consider income levels rather than growth rates, since this is more closely linked to welfare. The distinction between growth rates and income levels is more important in crisis times because growth rates during these intervals are often negative, sizeable, and unusually volatile. When average growth performance is used to compare countries in a crisis, significant differences in income levels (and thus welfare) can get lost. For example, compare two countries A and B that both start with an income level of 100 in 2007. Country A then experiences a negative growth rate of 10% in 2008 and in 2009 "recovers" by growing by 10%. In contrast, country B has zero growth in both years. Both countries will have a zero average growth rate, but after the second year, country A's income level will only be 99 and the country will have lost a cumulative 11% of its income compared to 2007, while country B obviously lost nothing. For these reasons, a measure of cumulative output gained or lost during 2008 and 2009 compared with 2007 will be used extensively as a measure of economic performance in the crisis. This measure can be computed for all the 153 countries included in the empirical analysis based on actual data.

However, the output gained or lost in 2008 and 2009 does not provide a full account of the cost of crises since it does not take into account that it can take countries many years to recover from a crisis. A measure that takes this into account is the cumulative GDP loss used in Becker and Mauro (2006). This measure defines a crisis as a period when GDP is below the level it was prior to the crisis. The cumulative output loss is then

---

[3]The calculation is based on the 153 countries included in the empirical section, see Appendix for the full list of countries included. This does not correspond to the shares presented in the IMF's World economic outlook that uses PPP adjusted dollars, where advanced countries account for roughly half of global GDP.

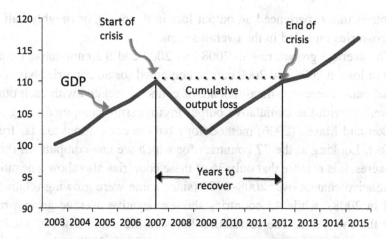

Figure 6.3. Definition of cumulative output loss and years to recover.
Note: Definitions based on the methodology in Becker and Mauro (2006).

the sum of output lost in each year compared to the pre-crisis GDP level until GDP has recovered back to its pre-crisis level. This is illustrated in Fig. 6.3, where a crisis starts at the end of 2007 and last until 2012. In this example, the cumulative output loss is 18% of pre-crisis GDP and the time to recover back to its pre-crisis GDP level is five years. This can be compared with cumulative output in 2008 and 2009 of 11% of pre-crisis GDP, or average growth in 2008 and 2009 (which is a measure used extensively in other papers) of minus 3.7%.

The Becker and Mauro (2006) methodology is applied to all of the countries that had a negative growth rate in at least one of the years 2008 and 2009, which then defines the start of the crisis for that country. The return to the pre-crisis GDP level is estimated by using the IMF World Economic Outlook forecasts for the period 2010–2012.[4] Since some countries will not have returned to their pre-crisis GDP level in 2012 (the last year of this IMF forecast) the growth rate thereafter is assumed to be the projected 2012 growth rate. This measure is generated for all of the 77

---

[4]The IMF forecast of course changes over time and the forecast used here is the October 2010 World Economic Outlook that was available when the main drafting of this chapter was done. The outlook has obviously changed for individual countries since then but the main messages of this chapter do not change because of this.

countries that experienced an output loss in the crisis, or roughly half of the countries included in the overall sample.[5]

The average growth rate in 2008 and 2009 and the cumulative output gain or loss in 2008 and 2009 can be computed for all countries based on actual data. These two measures are of course correlated with each other as well as with the cumulative output loss measure computed using the Becker and Mauro (2006) methodology but the correlations are far from perfect. Looking at the 77 countries for which we can compute all three measures, it is notable that only 36 of these countries also show a negative cumulative change over 2008–2009 (since some were growing relatively well in 2008), while 45 countries show a negative average growth rate over the two years. The correlation between the cumulative output loss measure and the two others — average growth 2008–2009 and cumulative output 2008–2009 — are 82% and 69%, respectively. In short, if income levels rather than growth rates matter, using growth rates to compare crisis performance can be misleading. Furthermore, since the duration of a crisis can differ between countries, just looking at the immediate impact and not the full path to recovery can also lead to the wrong conclusions.

Figure 6.4 shows three variables for each country group: first, the diamonds indicate the share of countries in a country group that lost GDP in the crisis (measured on the right hand scale); second, the darker bars indicate the average cumulative loss of output during the crisis episode (computed for the countries in a country group that actually lost output in the crisis and using the method described above in Fig. 6.3, measured on the left hand scale); finally, the lighter bars indicate the average number of years it is expected to take for countries to return to their pre-crisis GDP level (as defined in Fig. 6.3, measured on the left-hand scale).

The diamonds in Fig. 6.4 display significant differences between advanced countries and emerging markets as well as between different emerging market regions when it comes to the share of countries that lost

---

[5]Becker and Mauro seeks to identify major output collapses and use two filters that remove output drops that last for less than two years and are smaller than 5% of pre-crisis GDP. In this chapter, the focus is more generally on economic performance and the output loss measure is competed for all countries that had negative growth in at least one of the years 2008 and 2009, and the additional conditions that declines have to be at least 5% or last for at least two years have not been imposed here.

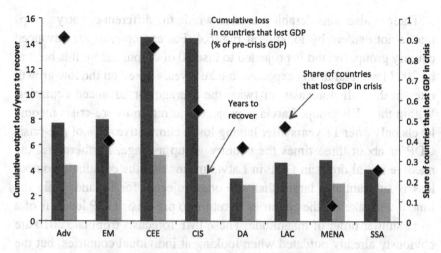

Figure 6.4. Regional comparison of crisis impact on GDP.

Note: Author's calculation based on IMF data and forecasts. Years to recover: The number of years it will take for countries that experienced an output loss in the crisis to return to its pre-crisis GDP level shown as average for the countries in a country group. Cumulative loss: How much GDP a country has cumulatively lost compared to its pre-crisis GDP level during the years before it returned to its pre-crisis GDP level computed as in Becker and Mauro (2006), but using IMF growth forecasts to predict GDP path. Adv: Advanced economies, EM: Emerging markets, CEE: Central and Eastern Europe (including the Baltic countries), CIS: Commonwealth of Independent States, Dev.Asia: Developing countries in Asia, LAC: Latin America and the Caribbean, MENA: Middle East and North Africa, SSA: Sub-Saharan Africa.

GDP during the crisis. A staggering 90% of advanced countries lost income during the crisis compared to pre-crisis income levels, whereas "only" 40% of emerging market countries suffered income losses. Differences among emerging market countries in various parts of the world are also notable, with 85% of countries in Central and Eastern Europe (CEE) suffering losses, while less than 1 in 10 countries in the MENA (Middle East and North Africa) region lost income in the crisis.

In terms of cumulative output lost and years to recover to pre-crisis GDP, advanced and emerging market countries are more alike, with average cumulative GDP losses of around 8% of pre-crisis GDP (darker bars) and 4 years to return pre-crisis GDP levels (lighter bars). The regional picture is more diverse, with CEE and CIS losing on average close to 15% while average losses in Asia are estimated at only 3% of pre-crisis GDP (darker bars).

There is also considerable variation within the different country groups that is not evident by looking at Fig. 6.4. For example, in the advanced country group, Ireland is projected to lose 20 of output before it is back at its 2007 level and this is expected to take 8 years based on the low growth rates in the IMF forecasts, or twice the average for advanced countries. Within the CEE group, Latvia is projected to return to pre-crisis income levels only after 11 years after having lost a cumulative 42% of pre-crisis GDP or about three times the country group average. Furthermore, the massive initial drops in GDP in Latvia means that the cumulative output loss is substantially larger than the one projected for Ireland while the time it will take for the countries to return to pre-crisis GDP levels is of a more similar order of magnitude. These IMF forecasts from late 2010 are obviously already outdated when looking at individual countries, but the numbers on output losses and crisis duration illustrate the general point that the economic impact of crises can be massive and long-lived and just comparing initial changes in growth rates between countries can be misleading.

6.3. Crisis Prevention Strategies

This section provides an overview of the lessons learned from previous crises, and the early warning indicators and strategies devised in various countries before 2008 to prevent recurrences.[6] It then empirically assesses the effectiveness of these preventive measures by country and region.

6.3.1. *Lessons from the past*

Crises are not news. They occurred often in the past three decades, includ-ing Latin America (1980s), Asia (1997), Russia (1998), Argentina (2000), ERM (1992), and Nordic countries (early 1990s), and all diversely influ-enced crisis prevention and management thinking prior to 2008. Capital flight linked with debt, banking, and currency problems played a major role in emerging market crises. In the ERM and Nordic crisis, overvalued

---

[6]Becker *et al.* (2007) discuss how shocks affect countries at different stages of develop-ment and policies to protect against such shocks.

currencies and competitiveness were proximate causes, stemming more fundamentally from excess credit growth, real estate bubbles, and an impaired banking sector.

The overarching lesson taught by these crises was that a stable macro-economic environment and a sound prevention regime were essential for forestalling domestic bubbles and effectively coping with external shocks. The key to achieving both objectives boiled down to identifying key variables capable of providing timely signals of impending crisis and acquiring the pertinent data on a standardized basis for the entire world economy. IMF and other international bodies, rising to the challenge, mounted a major effort to devise a battery of reliable early warning indicators and facilitate the effective monitoring of global economic conditions.[7]

The IMF's work on early warning systems started in earnest after the Mexican crisis in 1994 and was expanded in the aftermath of the Asian crisis in 1997, culminating in a comprehensive early warning model. Its *Global Financial Stability Report* (GFSR) (IMF, 2008) contains a table presenting four vulnerability variables for 27 emerging market countries. They are: current account balances, private sector credit growth, changes in the ratio of private credit to GDP, and the external position of BIS reporting banks. Commodity price sensitivity, gross reserves to short term external debt, inflation and the real policy rate variables were added in October 2008,[8] and the country set expanded to 38.[9] Further modifications were made in April 2009, during the 2008–2009 crisis. External debt refinancing needs, loan to deposit ratios and the share of foreign currency deposits were added to the mix. Although specific indicators varied from

---

[7]The early warning model developed by Kaminsky, Reinhart, and Lizondo (1998) and further developed by Berg and Pattillio (1999) has led to a long line of early warning papers. Abiad (2003) provides an extensive survey and extension. Frankel and Saravelos (2010) extends the survey and also look at performance in the current crisis. Berg, Borensztein, and Pattillo (2005) look at how early warnings have worked in practice compared to various benchmarks, including some basic market indicators. Ghosh, Ostry, and Tamarisa (2009) provide a short, policy-focused discussion of early warning systems.

[8]The real policy rate in the table is defined as the interest rate set by the monetary authority deflated by the past year-on-year inflation rate, so it is not based on ex-ante expected inflation.

[9]The change in private credit to GDP variable was dropped.

set to set, all functioned as proxies for (excess) borrowing, especially in foreign currency or from foreign sources, and domestic macroeconomic imbalances.

The variables chosen by the IMF contain both flows and stocks. For example, the current account balance is a flow variable related to the stock variables foreign debt and international reserves. It is unclear if early warning variables should focus on stocks or flows. For example, a sudden capital flow stoppage that causes a sharp current account deficit contraction can be harmful at relatively modest foreign debt levels, but the likelihood of the stoppage itself may depend on the magnitude of foreign debt relative to foreign reserves.

The 2008 crisis also revealed another deficiency in the IMF's early warning regime. The indicators did not adequately capture the complexity of the international financial system. They took no account of the sophisticated instruments employed by contemporary banking institutions, or cross border financial linkages. These omissions were remedied to some extent in the 2010 GFSR (IMF, 2010b) with a fresh table better attuned to the needs of advanced countries that contain new variables including market spreads, fiscal indicators, external debt and the potential impact of the banking system on national fiscal accounts.[10]

The FSB and BIS recently began collaborating with the IMF in perfecting its crisis prevention regime (IMF, 2010c) and related work on macroprudential frameworks complements this effort (see for example IMF 2011a; 2011b).

6.3.2. *How did early warnings and crisis prevention measures correlate with economic performance in the crisis?*

The 2008 crisis promoted renewed calls for the creation of an effective crisis prevention regime. In this section, we will survey the effectiveness of prior crisis prevention regimes in terms of numerous variables grouped into three main categories: early warnings, policy choice instruments and

---

[10] The IMF provided real figures and identified areas of potential vulnerabilities as shaded boxes in its April 2008 table. This changed in October 2008 when statistics were replaced by a color coded "heat map".

insurance measures. Table 6.1 lists these variables and reports their average values for the full sample of countries, clustered into four aggregates: advanced economies, CEE, developing Asia and the rest of the world (which includes LAC, MENA, SSA, and CIS).

From the regional account of GDP performance presented earlier, we know that advanced countries and the CEE group were hardest hit by the crisis, and that developing Asia did relatively well. Did any or some of the variables listed in Table 6.1 reliably predict these outcomes? The answer is clearly yes. For example, CEE current account deficits were five times greater than those in developing Asia and other emerging markets before 2008. CEE credit growth was extreme. CEE housing prices rose faster than anywhere else; and CEE external debt to GDP ratios were twice the advanced country norm, and far greater than those of other groupings. All these indicators accurately sounded early warnings of impending crisis for the CEE.[11]

Are any or some of the variables listed in Table 6.1 equally effective at the national level? Again, the answer is yes, but there are not sufficient numbers of independent observations to reliably settle the matter with regressions.[12] Simple scatter plots and correlations therefore must be employed instead to assess predictive power, even if causal connections are opaque.[13] Two measures of output will be used for this purpose. The first is the cumulative output gain or loss in 2008–2009 available for 153 countries. The measure is applicable for all countries regardless of whether crisis period output contracts or expands. Sample selection is not an issue, but the cumulative GDP change metric for the years 2008–2009 does not capture the full loss for countries that remained depressed beyond 2009. Therefore the cumulative output discussed above

---

[11]The deficit indicator, however, gave a faulty reading for advanced countries, where fiscal deficit on average were more or less balanced.

[12]In addition, the overlap of countries for some of these variables is imperfect, which means that a regression with all the variables leaves a small number of observations to estimate quite a few coefficients.

[13]Our indicators are subject to the usual ambiguities of endogeneity and causation. Pre-crisis macro, policy, and insurance variables are used to minimize the endogeneity problem, but it does not eliminate it. Given the nature of the crisis, where both its magnitude and timing were largely unanticipated, this is probably not a major concern.

Table 6.1.   Averages of pre-crisis variables for country groups.

	All countries	Advanced	CEE	Dev Asia	Other EM
Pre-crisis variables					
Early warnings					
Current account balance	−2.7	0.1	−10.4	−2.0	−2.6
Credit growth	23.2	12.9	34.9	20.4	24.3
Share prices	215.6	172.1	231.6	180.3	277.1
House prices	55.6	38.9	106.3	50.0	87.0
External debt	70.7	218.1	44.4	25.7	32.2
Inflation rate	6.2	2.4	5.8	6.7	7.5
Past GDP growth	5.4	3.8	6.5	6.5	5.6
Real exchange rate	7.1	2.7	13.9	7.6	9.1
Policy choices					
Fiscal balance	−0.6	0.1	−1.1	−2.2	−0.3
Real interest rate	1.4	1.5	1.3	1.8	1.2
Insurance measures					
International reserves	19.0	12.5	23.1	26.2	19.1
Export concentration	0.4	0.4	0.3	0.4	0.4
Domestic bond market	84.3	99.2	74.9	44.5	87.0
Domestic equity market	82.4	118.4	61.5	91.8	71.2
Foreign banks	40.4	31.8	79.3	27.6	40.9

Note: Variables are: average current account balance 2004–2007 as percent of GDP, average credit growth 2004–2007, change in share prices 2004–2007, change in real house prices 2000–2006, external debt in 2007 as percent of GDP, average inflation rate 2004–2007, average real GDP growth rate 2004–2007, average change in real exchange rate 2004–2007, average fiscal balance for general government 2004–2007, average real interest rate 2004–2007, international reserves 2007 as percent of GDP, export concentration in 2007, total bond market capitalization in 2007 as percent of GDP, equity market capitalization in 2007 as percent of GDP, share of foreign banks in total assets 2007.

is computed for the 77 countries suffering protracted declines. As might be expected, predictive merit is sensitive to the output metric chosen, raising a variety of knotty practical issues.

6.3.2.1. *Early warning indicators — macro outcomes*

Our investigation of the predictive power of the indicators listed in Table 6.1 starts with macro-outcomes that have been used as early warning indicators and then continues sequentially to policy choices and insurance measures. Averages of pre-crisis values for all indicators and country groups are reported in Table 6.1. In Figs. 6.5, 6.7 and 6.8, the same set of variables are plotted against the two output measures defined above; first, the cumulative output change 2008–2009 (computed for all 153 countries) and, second, the cumulative projected output loss (computed for the 77 countries that lost output). Figure 6.5 displays the eight early warning indicators listed in Table 6.1, Fig. 6.7 the two policy choice variables, and Fig. 6.8 the five insurance measures. In all the charts, the left panels show the correlation with the first output measure (for 153 countries) while the right panels display the correlation with the loss measure (for 77 countries).

The first early warning indicator in Fig. 6.5 is the average current account balance during 2004–2007. It shows a modestly positively correlation with cumulated output changes in 2008–2009 (left panel), and a much stronger correlation with the subset of countries suffering output losses in the crisis (right panel). The disparity between the performance of CEE and developing Asian countries (DA) is conspicuous, but of secondary importance for appraising predictive power.[14]

The credit growth indicator shows a very weak positive correlation with output performance for the full sample (Fig. 6.5, left panel). This makes it a poor early warning indicator of cumulative GDP change in 2008–2009. The right panel of Fig. 6.5, however, reveals that it is an excellent early warning indicator for countries that experienced output losses during the crisis. The correlation here is strongly negative; that is,

---

[14]We will later investigate whether other economic variables explain this regional pattern.

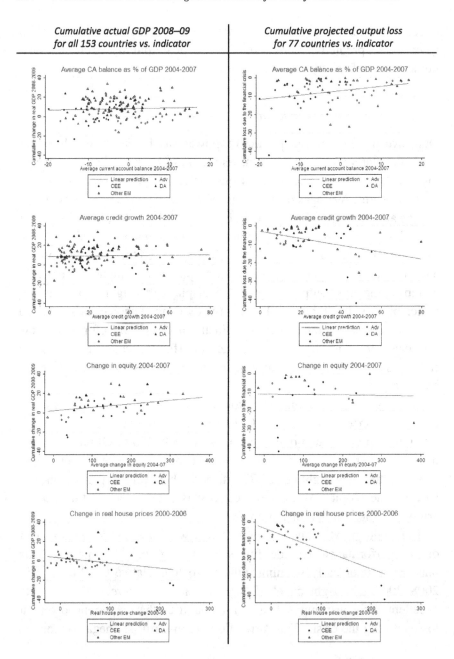

Figure 6.5.   Early warning indicators versus output in the crisis.

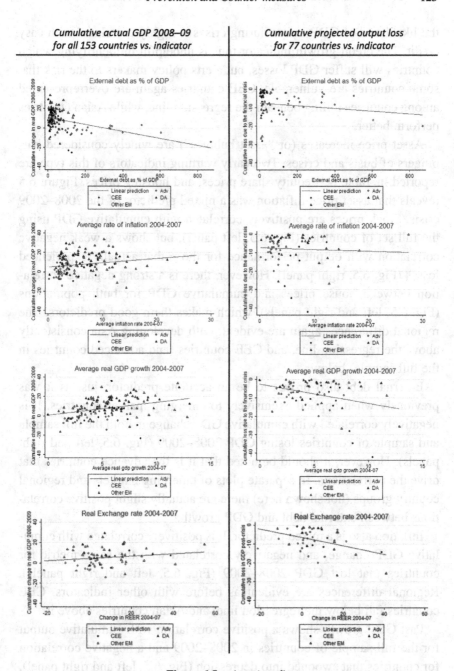

Figure 6.5. (*continued*)

the likelihood of GDP losses during crises is highly correlated with easy credit. The credit growth indicator thus is unhelpful in identifying which countries will suffer GDP losses, but alerts policy makers to the risk that some countries are vulnerable. CEE countries again are overrepresented among countries falling beneath the regression line, while Asian countries perform better.

Asset price increases (or "asset bubbles") are widely considered harbingers of busts and crises. Two early warning indicators of this type are reported in Table 6.1: equity share prices, and housing prices. Figure 6.5 reveals that asset price inflation was a mixed predictor of the 2008–2009 crisis. Stock prices are positively correlated with cumulative GDP using the full set of countries (Fig. 6.5, left panel), but shows a weak negative correlation with output performance for those that actually experienced losses (Fig. 6.5, right panel). However, there is a strong negative correlation between house prices and cumulative GDP for both populations (Fig. 6.5, left and right panels), which makes them good predictors. The regional differences again are evident, with developing Asia consistently above the regression line, and CEE countries (and advanced countries in the full sample) below.

External debt also proves to be an accurate predictor, just as it was previously when applied exclusively to emerging market countries. It is negatively correlated with cumulative GDP change in both the full sample and sample of countries losing GDP 2008–2009 (Fig. 6.5, left and right panels). However, it should be noted that it is the advance countries that drive the correlations. In separate plots of emerging markets and regional country groups (not shown here) there are actually slight positive correlations between external debt and GDP growth.

Inflation also is a mixed predictor. It is positively correlated with cumulative GDP change, and negatively correlated with the same metric for countries that lost GDP 2008–2009 (Fig. 6.5, left and right panels). Regional differences are evident as before with other indicators. CEE countries fall below the regression line, and Asian countries above it.

Past GDP growth shows a positive correlation with cumulative output for the full sample of countries in 2008–2009 and a negative correlation for countries that swooned into depression (Fig. 6.5, left and right panel). As before, this mixed result tells us that the past GDP growth early warning indicator can serve only as a cautionary signal, not as a dependable predictor.

The final early warning indicator plotted is the change in the real exchange rate prior to the crisis. Again we have a mixed predictor that shows a positive correlation with output in 2008–2009 for all countries (Fig. 6.5, left panel), meaning that countries with appreciating real exchange rates prior to the crisis did relatively well during 2008–2009. However, for countries that lost output in the crisis, the correlation is negative (Fig. 6.5, right panel), implying that reduced competitiveness prior to the crisis led to greater output losses for crisis struck countries.

6.3.2.2. *Policy choices*

Policy choice variables provide insight into macro-regulatory intentions of national governments. The two predictors listed in Table 6.1 are fiscal balances and real interest rates, and the corresponding plots with output performance are shown in Fig. 6.7. Fiscal deficits in Keynesian theory are thought to be stimulatory; surpluses either stabilizing or contractive. High real interest rates *ceteris paribus* are believed to be GDP growth retarding; low real interest rates expansionary. However, policy makers (in most cases) only seek to set a nominal policy interest rate, and the real interest rate is then a result of this rate and the realized inflation rate. Realized inflation is in turn a complex equilibrium macro-outcome that depends not only on the nominal policy rate but also on external and domestic balances that are linked to exchange rates and fiscal policy. Policy makers' intentions, therefore, can be deduced from the handling of fiscal balances and real interest rates, providing clues about the likelihood of ensuing crises. This is best done, however, in conjunction with information about nations' foreign exchange rate regimes.[15] The correlations reported later must be interpreted in this broad context.

Here the focus is not on contemporaneous correlations between policy variables and economic outcomes but on how past policies affected crisis outcomes. Past fiscal policy can then be viewed as an indicator of policy

---

[15]For a recent discussion of the choice of exchange rate regimes and associated costs and benefits, see Ghosh, Ostry, and Tsangarides (2011).

makers ability to control fiscal spending in good times (since 2004–2007 where generally boom years), or as possibly contributing to domestic instability by building up balance sheet vulnerabilities in the public sector. In short, the question is: did past fiscal prudence pay off in terms of better economic performance in the crisis? Similar with past real interest rates; did cheap credit in the pre-crisis boom fuel unsustainable asset price increases or balance sheet vulnerabilities in the private sector that later had a negative effect on output in the crisis?

The exchange rate regimes in force in the countries included in the full data set, and the set of countries that succumbed to depression in 2008–2009 are illustrated in Fig. 6.6, with bar graphs indicating how much fixers and floaters gained or lost GDP in the crisis. The two bars on the left report the cumulative GDP performance in the full sample of countries, and the two bars on the right represent the GDP losses experienced in the crisis countries.

The frequency of output loss countries is roughly the same in nations with fixed and floating rate foreign exchange regimes.

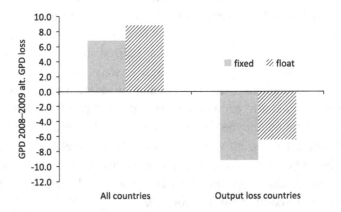

Figure 6.6.   Exchange rate regimes.

Note: The two bars to the left show cumulative growth in 2008 and 2009 for the full sample of countries distinguishing between countries with fixed and floating exchange rates while the two bars to the right show cumulative GDP for countries that lost GDP in the crisis, again distinguishing between countries with fixed versus floating exchange rates. Unweighted averages are shown in all bars. The classification of exchange rate regimes is based on de facto exchange rate regime in 2007 from Ghosh, Ostry and Tsangarides (2010).

Countries with fixed exchange rates, however, fared worse during the 2008–2009 crisis both in terms of cumulative GDP change and the loss of GDP. For the full sample, countries with fixed exchange rates had two percentage points (or 25%) lower output gains on average over 2008–2009, and for the output loss countries, those with fixed exchange rates suffered losses close to three percentage points (or 30%) greater than floaters.

It is interesting to note, however, that while floaters clearly outperformed exchange rate fixers, past fiscal policy was more or less neutral in its effect on cumulative GDP change (Fig. 6.7, left panel). However, in the sample of countries that lost GDP in the crisis, pre-crisis fiscally conservative economies outperformed liberal spenders (right panel). Again, some of the glaring negative outliers are in the CEE region (and the private sector borrowing in the Baltic countries was particularly extreme).

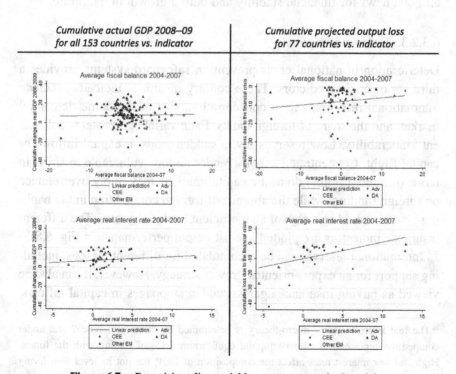

Figure 6.7. Pre-crisis policy variables versus output in the crisis.

Macro-theorists consider the real interest rate a key barometer of domestic imbalances.[16] Very high rates can signal significant risk premia, and very low or even negative rates can be signs of slack investment demand. Cheap money has been a driving force in many financial crises and speculative asset price increases. The correlations between cumulative GDP change and the past real interest rate for both data pools are positive (Fig. 6.7). Low real interest rates go hand in hand with poor GDP performance in both cases, consistent with the hypothesis that cheap credit creates vulnerabilities that lead to poor economic performance down the road.

Again, the interpretation regarding the real interest rate as a policy variable or macro outcome is far from clear, but still it seems that on average, very low real interest rates have been correlated with poor performance in this crisis. If today's low nominal policy rates also translate into low real interest rates (which is not always and everywhere true), this may not be all good news for financial stability and output growth in the future.

6.3.2.3. *Country insurance*

Deterioration in national crisis prevention safeguard systems provides a third set of crisis predictors. These country insurance indicators include international reserves, export concentration, size of the domestic capital market, and the share of foreign banks. Each variable represents a different vulnerability. Low reserves invite sudden stops in capital inflows or capital flight. Concentrated exports render nations vulnerable to shifts in terms of trade. Limited domestic capital markets may imply overreliance on foreign funding, while the absence of foreign competition in the banking systems could be a sign of an inefficient banking system. The different insurance indicators are plotted against output performance in Fig. 6.8.

International reserves can be accumulated for different reasons, including support for an export-oriented growth strategy. However, it can also be viewed as buying insurance against sudden stoppages in capital inflows,

---

[16] The real interest rate in micro-theory is determined by "time preference" and under competition represents the inter-temporal equilibrium price of trading with the future. High and low interest rates affect the composition of GDP, but not its level. See Irving Fisher, *The Theory of Interest*, 1930.

which clearly has been a motive in some countries, not least in Asia where countries witnessed the effects of sharp capital flow reversals in the 1997 crisis. In the 2008–2009 crisis, holding larger international reserves has been positively correlated with better economic performance, both in the full sample and among the output loss countries (Fig. 6.8, left and right panels). The real side of the foreign reserves phenomenon is changes in current account balances, and separate plots (not shown here) indicated

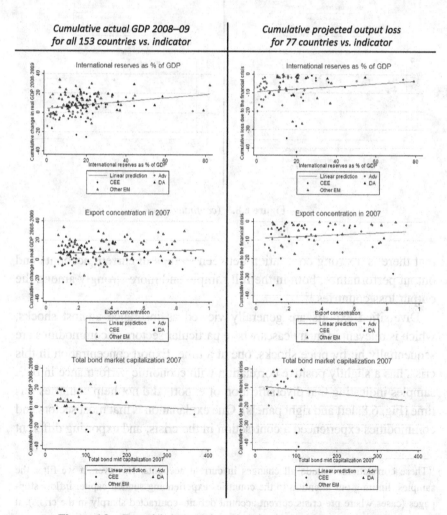

Figure 6.8. Pre-crisis insurance measures versus output in the crisis.

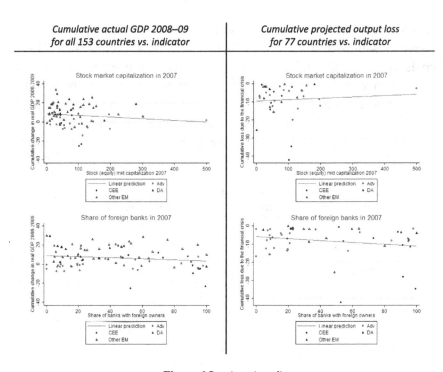

Figure 6.8.   (*continued*)

that there is a strong correlation between swings in current accounts and output performance, both in the full sample and more strongly among the output loss countries.[17]

Diversified exports are generally viewed as insurance against shocks, which is relevant in many cases where particular sectors or commodities are sequentially hit by price shocks, one at a time. Export concentration in this crisis has a slightly positive correlation with economic performance in both samples indicating that diversification of exports did not help countries this time (Fig. 6.8, left and right panels). One explanation is that most sectors and commodities experienced a contraction in the crisis, and exporting different

---

[17]These correlations include all changes in current accounts. However, if we filter the samples, limiting our attention to the countries experiencing sudden capital inflow stoppages (cases where pre-crisis current account deficits contracted sharply in the crisis), it turns out somewhat surprisingly the few countries experience sudden stoppages.

goods only help when shocks hit one sector at the time. This does not mean that countries should ignore the potential value of having diversified exports because this crisis is unusual compared to past episodes (and most likely in the future) when terms-of-trade shocks were more narrowly concentrated.

Diversification has been promoted not only on the real side of the economy but also in finance. Local bond and equity markets have been developed to reduce dependence on international financial flows and are construed here in this sense.[18] However, the indicator may be blurred to the extent that foreign investors account for a large share of a domestic market, or domestic investors behave like foreign investors in countries with relatively open capital accounts. If investors in local markets hedge currency risks and move capital in and out of a country's domestic markets, a country with a large domestic market is also subject to risks of large capital flow reversals that affect exchange rates and funding opportunities in crisis times. In this crisis, the correlations between the size of domestic bond and equity markets and economic performance were slightly negative or non-existent, excluding some outliers (Fig. 6.8, left and right panels).

This should not deter efforts to develop domestic capital markets in countries that are lacking them because such development may have positive effects on various institutional factors important for long-run growth. However, in this crisis, domestic capital markets did not seem to improve economic performance. Given the negative role the financial sector has played in many countries in the 2008 crisis, this may not be too surprising. The lesson for a country that wants to develop its capital markets to enhance future growth prospects is that it is a good idea to think hard about regulation and supervision of these markets from the outset.

Banks are another important part of the financial system and in many developing countries and emerging markets, the participation of foreign banks has been seen as a way to modernize and enhance domestic banking efficiency and stability. There is probably little doubt that foreign banks bring new skills and technologies to domestic banking markets, but the

---

[18]This characterization assumes that domestic capital markets provide services that international markets do not, such as, allowing domestic entities to fund themselves with local currency instruments or by pulling in domestic savings into the financial systems that otherwise are used inefficiently.

question here is whether this contributed to better output performance in the 2008–2009 crisis. The correlation between the share of foreign banks in the domestic banking system and output performance is slightly negative in the full sample (Fig. 6.8, left panel), and more strongly so among output loss countries (Fig. 6.8, right panel).

The share of foreign banks also is strongly correlated with current account balances. A larger share of foreign banks is associated with larger pre-crisis current account deficits. Current account deficits in turn have been shown above to be associated with inferior economic performance in this crisis, especially among output loss countries. If foreign banks provide easy access to foreign credit that allows unsustainable current account deficits, this may create a vulnerability that outweighs the benefits of a more efficient domestic banking system.

6.3.2.4. *Summary of indicators and output performance*

The visual patterns in Figs. 6.5, 6.7 and 6.8 are complemented with Table 6.2, which summarizes the numerical correlation estimates and their statistical significance. The data in Table 6.2 reveal that although correlations are informative, only a handful are statistically significant and there are potential discrepancies in magnitudes and even the signs between the full sample and the output loss countries. There is only one variable, house prices, that displays a statistically significant correlation with the same (negative) sign in both samples. For two of the most discussed variables in the aftermath of the crisis, current account balances and credit growth, there is a very small and insignificant correlation in the full sample, but a statistically significant correlation with the expected sign in the output loss sample.

Several of the variables in Table 6.2 are correlated with each other as well as with economic performance. The distortion could be addressed by including them all in a regression with economic performance as the dependent variable, but as mentioned in Sec. 6.1, this has not been done due to data limitation. There are too few degrees of freedom. Nevertheless, some cross-correlations among the variables are worth mentioning to give a fuller picture of their covariances prior to the crisis. First, credit growth as expected was positively correlated with several variables; asset prices, GDP growth, inflation and the real foreign exchange rate.

Table 6.2. Summary of correlations between variables and output performance.

	Correlations	
	GDP 2008–2009	Output loss
Pre-crisis variables		
Macro outcomes		
Current account balance	0.0494	0.2574*
Credit growth	0.031	−0.3682*
Share prices	0.2757	−0.0281
House prices	−0.3207*	−0.6411*
External debt	−0.3958*	−0.1416
Inflation rate	0.1854*	−0.0554
Past GDP growth	0.3275*	−0.3318*
Real exchange rate	0.1592	−0.4045*
Policy choices		
Real interest rate	0.1365	0.4800*
Fiscal balance	0.0309	0.1208
Insurance measures		
International reserves	0.2599*	0.1352
Export concentration	0.1015	0.122
Domestic bond market	−0.1313	−0.1431
Domestic equity market	−0.1193	0.0688
Foreign banks	−0.1633	−0.2084

Note: The first column corresponds to the scatter plots of all countries in the left hand panels of Figs 6.5, 6.7 and 6.8 above and the second column to right hand panels that show the output loss countries.

More surprisingly, it was only significantly correlated with current account balances in advanced countries and not in emerging market countries. This is unexpected, given the strong correlation between the variables in previous emerging market crises and the pre-crisis development in the CEE region, but it was not something observable in other emerging markets this time. Current account balances showed a significant negative correlation with house price increases in emerging market economies partly because the sample for which we have house prices is incomplete, and overrepresents the CEE region. Current account balances also have been positively correlated with fiscal balances and with the share of foreign banks in the domestic banking system both in emerging markets and advanced countries.

6.4. Crisis Management Strategies

When crisis prevention fails, crisis management has to step in to minimize the damage. Given that many crisis countries have not fully recovered, and the full experience is not observable, it is premature to make a conclusive assessment about the comparative merit of various crisis predictors, and intervention strategies. This section therefore is descriptive. Before turning to the quantitative matters, we provide a brief discussion of the lessons discernible from past crises.

6.4.1. *Lessons from the past*

The key lesson from the past, used at the onset of the 2008–2009 crisis, came from the widely held view that the severity of the great depression was attributable to governments' failure to employ its full kit of policy tools. This lesson pertained exclusively to serious crisis situations; not "business as usual" monetary and fiscal policy which, over the years, had increasingly become rules based and intervention averse.

Accordingly, when Lehman Brothers' bankruptcy threatened to devastate the global financial system in September 2008, contemporary macroeconomic theorists counseled energetic counter-crisis fiscal and monetary intervention, including bailouts for banks and other large financial institutions. This posture was mirrored by the IMF's advice and the design of the economic rescue packages organized by the international community. Suddenly, Keynesian policy was rehabilitated after having fallen from grace in the late 1990s.[19]

---

[19]See Chapter 2 of this volume. The insurgent "Ricardian Equivalence," "Great Moderation," and "Divine Coincidence" doctrines persuaded most macro-theorists that fiscal policy was ineffectual.

Many of these Keynesian prescriptions departed sharply from prior IMF policies recommended during and after the emerging market crises of the 1980s and 1990s. These crisis management strategies stressed adjusting exchange rates to restore competitiveness and confidence, backed up with stringent fiscal and monetary policies aimed at preventing sovereign defaults, hyper inflation and free falling exchange rates. Unlike the "Washington consensus" applied during the Asian crisis in the late 1990s, it focused almost exclusively on macroeconomic factors, disregarding structural reforms presumably because market liberalization, subsidy reduction and privatization were regarded as subsidiary issues for advanced western economies.

6.4.2. *Domestic responses*

Endogeneity clouds the cause and effects of the new crisis intervention strategy and compels us to describe more than explain its effects in different parts of the world. As was discussed earlier, it is too early to tell what policy responses will be able to generate not only short-run relief, but also longer-term sustainable growth in incomes and welfare.

The policy variables scrutinized are fiscal balances, monetary policy in the form of policy interest rates, market rates, inflation and real interest rates, and exchange rate changes versus both the dollar and the euro (see Table 6.3). Four outcome variables are included, current account balances, credit growth and average GDP growth in 2008–2009 and projected for 2010–2012. To facilitate the comparison with pre-crisis policies, we also report changes in the key variables from the pre-crisis benchmark.

The first thing to note is that fiscal deficits, driven mostly by Keynesian policy considerations, have widened across the globe. Advanced countries and the CEE region have seen the largest deterioration in their fiscal balances, 2½ and over 3 percentage points, respectively. Countries in developing Asia entered the crisis with larger deficits and have only added half a percentage point to them in the crisis.[20] In a number of CEE countries, the fiscal position deteriorated significantly despite substantial spending cuts.

---

[20]The deficits reported in Table 6.3 are real outcome rather than targets or estimates, and therefore serve only as oblique indicators of policy makers' choice. No attempt is made here to devise more sophisticated measures of fiscal policy because the assumptions required are too heroic with regard to future growth rates and potential GDP, etc.

Table 6.3. Key domestic policy variables and macro-outcomes.

	All countries	Advanced	CEE	Dev Asia	Other EM	No-loss EM	Loss EM
Fiscal balance	-2.6	-3.2	-4.0	-2.6	-2.3	-2.2	-3.0
change	-1.5	-2.5	-3.2	-0.6	-1.0	-0.5	-2.8
Policy interest rate	6.6	1.6	6.1	6.3	8.8	7.7	8.5
Market interest rate	3.5	0.8	5.9	5.1	5.0	4.3	7.6
change	-1.4	-3.5	0.9	-0.7	-0.2	-0.8	2.4
Inflation	5.0	1.7	4.4	8.2	6.6	6.7	5.7
change	0.0	-0.6	-1.3	2.0	0.0	0.5	-1.5
Real interest rate	0.5	0.5	0.9	-0.4	0.8	0.8	0.3
change	-0.6	-0.7	-0.3	-1.1	-0.3	-0.4	-0.2
Exchange rate change vs. USD	2.6	6.4	-1.4	4.1	1.4	2.1	2.6
Exchange rate change vs. euro	4.1	8.0	0.0	5.6	2.9	3.6	4.1
Current account	-4.3	-1.3	-7.7	-3.2	-5.5	-5.2	-5.6
change	-1.4	-1.9	2.5	-1.9	-2.6	-3.0	-0.4
Credit growth	17.2	7.0	22.9	18.2	17.9	19.0	15.8
change	-2.4	-3.9	-14.8	-1.4	-3.1	-0.6	-7.6
Avg. GDP growth 2008–09	1.9	-1.0	0.3	4.5	3.3	4.7	0.3
Avg. proj. GDP growth 2010–12	4.1	2.1	2.8	5.6	4.6	5.3	3.3

Note: Medians for the group of countries for 2008–2009, changes compared to the period 2004–2007.

Keynesian monetary policy likewise has been expansionary. Advanced countries have been cutting policy interest rates very aggressively, and market interest rates have fallen by 3½ percentage points, without seriously affecting wage and price levels. Inflation as measured by official statistics has declined and is on average less than 2%. In some countries, it is close to zero.[21] Policy interest rates and inflation in emerging markets prior to the crisis were substantially higher than in advanced countries. Inflation remained higher, and actually increased in developing Asia during the 2008–2009 crisis, but this was atypical. The crisis triggered a sharp drop in prices in the CEE region. CEE market interest rates, however, moved in the opposite direction as lenders demanded premia to compensate for increased credit risk.

Exchange rate policy responses to the 2008–2009 crisis differed widely despite a Keynesian inclination toward devaluation because many nations have fixed foreign exchange rate regimes. Nonetheless, many countries with floating or flexible peg exchange rate regimes fostered the depreciation of their currencies, including U.S. and the EU. Others sought to stimulate their economies even more by depreciating their currencies against the "safe" dollar and euro. The only exception is the CEE region, where many countries had fixed their currencies to the euro. When other countries around the world let their currencies fall, this put additional pressure on the CEE region. Part of the region's poor economic performance surely is due to this rigidity.

Finally, policy makers tried to shore up their beleaguered economies with massive support to financial sectors, ranging from direct balance sheet assistance, to large-scale guarantees. Liquidity problems in banks and financial institutions during the 2008–2009 crisis made government financial assistance essential in 16 advanced countries, 3 in the CEE region and 4 in CIS countries. The direct fiscal costs, according to Laeven and Valencia (2010) are around 5% of GDP, while the impact on public debt averages almost 25% of GDP.

---

[21] Some are critical of the official measures of inflation but a full discussion of the extent to which official statistics provide a measure of prices that are relevant to a majority of consumers is beyond the scope of this chapter.

6.4.3. *International community's response*

The years before the 2008–2009 crisis were relatively stable, especially in major emerging market countries receiving large international funding packages from the IMF and other IFIs. As a result, IMF lending declined substantially (Fig. 6.9), and policy makers around the globe convinced themselves that the planet had entered a new, crisis-free age, dubbed the "Great Moderation."

The signs of this new confidence were visible in many places, not least in the board of the IMF where shareholder governments made two decisions that in retrospect look particularly unwise. First, staff at the IMF was cut significantly barely a year prior to the crisis; and, second, it was decided not to push forward with a new crisis-prevention facility designed to deter capital flight in international capital markets.[22] The decision to cut IMF staff was clearly linked to the funding model of the IMF, which predicted lower revenues due to reduced crisis borrowing by large emerging market countries.[23]

Seldom have policy makers been more wrong. The pre-crisis thinking could best be described as lessons unlearned and a widespread "This time is different" mentality. Many economists have used the phrase in the aftermath of the crisis to describe the build-up to the crisis. It is also the title of the 2009 book by Reinhart and Rogoff, which has the subtitle "*Eight Centuries of Financial Folly.*"

Once the crisis hit, it became apparent that the "Great Moderation" had been wishful thinking; that there was an enduring need for an effective crisis prevention regime, and that many countries could not cope with external shocks without international assistance.

A coordinated international policy response was needed and the IMF was the only viable institution for providing it. The G-20 was of course the international political gathering that was setting the course for this work, but it was the IMF that had the infrastructure and competence to

---

[22]The target countries were those pre-qualifying for IMF credit in normal times.

[23]The reason it was hard to convince shareholder governments to increase IMF funding that did not rely on its lending operations was that many questioned the mandate of the IMF altogether in the years prior to the crisis. With capital markets so large and efficient and countries having learnt the lessons from previous crises, an emerging consensus of important shareholders came to believe that the IMF would not be needed.

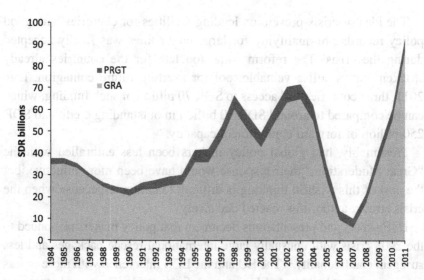

Figure 6.9. IMF credit outstanding.

Note: PRGT lending by the IMF is directed to poorer countries as part of a poverty reduction and growth strategy while GRA lending is the IMF's main lending to countries in need of balance of payments support. SDR is the IMF's unit of account and SDR100 was equivalent to around USD150 late 2011.

deal with large-scale and timely lending programs to countries with balance of payments problem. Even the EU and the eurozone eventually realized that IMF involvement was essential in euro countries.

IMF resources accordingly have been increased. The Fund's lending capacity grew in several steps from around $250 billion to $750 billion after negotiations in various G-20 meetings. It was also agreed that international liquidity should be increased by providing central banks with extra foreign exchange reserves. SDR allocations were increased by $250 billion for this purpose. Part of the international bargain has been to increase the voice of emerging markets on the IMF board. Suddenly, countries that had been viewed as potential IMF borrowers have become funders of the international bailouts, changing the power balance.[24]

---

[24]Discussions on reforming IMF governance began long before the crisis, but the crisis transformed talk into action. The process is incomplete. Quotas and voting power still need further adjustment to accurately reflect the economic importance and strength of member countries.

The idea of crisis-prevention lending facilities for countries with good policy records pre-qualifying for large credit lines was finally accepted during the crisis. The reform came too late for the countries already stricken, but is still a valuable tool for averting future contagion. Late 2011, three countries had access to SDR 70 billion of such funding, which can be compared to around SDR 90 billion in outstanding credit and SDR 250 billion of forward commitment capacity.

Presumably, had global policy makers been less enthralled with the "Great Moderation," their response would have been more effective, but the cost of this wishful thinking is difficult to calibrate because when the crisis struck, authorities reacted decisively.

IMF papers and presentations document that policy makers responded to the 2008 crisis with unusually large international rescue packages and less stringent conditionality.[25] The EU and the ECB intervened with more or less (non)transparent bailouts to EU countries, first outside (Hungary, Latvia, and Romania), and then inside (Greece and Ireland) the eurozone. The European Stabilisation Mechanism was set up in May 2010 with several pillars, including ECB and IMF funding of up to €750 billion. Already the packages to the countries listed above amount to around €100 billion. At the same time, the ECB provided €500 billion in loans to commercial banks in Austria, Finland, Germany, Greece, Ireland, Italy, Portugal, and Spain in early 2011.

In sum, the financial response of the international community to crisis-stricken countries has been substantial. Nevertheless, the constant political battles over how much, when and to whom, and taking a piecemeal approach to arranging various bailout mechanisms, particularly in Europe, has created a significant amount of uncertainty that has impeded the restoration of confidence.

6.5. Conclusions and Lessons for the Future

The 2008 crisis has (re)kindled a heated debate on how to avoid and manage crises as well as rethinking macroeconomic policies more generally.[26]

---

[25] See for example IMF (2010a) and Giorgianni (2009).

[26] A paper that received ample attention both among academics and policy makers is Blanchard, Dell'Arriccia, and Mauro (2010).

Many see the 2008 crisis as a wakeup call that will help the world community implement much needed reform in areas ranging from regulation of the international financial system to reforming the voting shares in the IFIs, to setting-up robust early warning systems, and pushing through structural reforms in advanced countries to stimulate growth and assure sustainable fiscal dynamics. As the world economy is recovering, many of the more ambitious goals are taking a backseat and the attention is shifting to more immediate rescue efforts in countries with the direst needs. Many argue that this is a missed opportunity that will contribute to a new crisis in a not too distant future, and it is not hard to see why this may happen, given the one-way street rescues provided to financial firms "too-big-to-fail."

Despite the global label that is used for the crisis, there are large differences in the crisis's impact among the country groups discussed above. Most notably, the central figures in this crisis are advanced countries, and CEE countries with strong financial and trade ties to the advanced economies. By contrast, developing Asia fared relatively well in the crisis, and in many instances suffered few ill effects. Of course, the global label is appropriate from the standpoint of worldwide aggregate economic activity. Planetary GDP did fall due to the high weight of crisis-stricken advanced countries. Of the 32 advanced countries, 29 suffered output losses, in stark contrast to the MENA region, where only one country experienced an output decline in 2008–2009. Likewise, growth in developing Asia and Sub-Saharan Africa was mostly positive during the 2008 crisis.

Early warning indicators did signal problems in CEE, but when we plot all countries together, most of these indicators were weakly or moderately correlated with economic performance, and served as poor crisis predictors. Some were better when the focus is narrowed to the subset of crisis-afflicted countries, and may serve as effective indicators of future vulnerability. This suggests that a principal virtue of compiling crisis predictors is the impetus they provide for closer case-by-case investigation to resolve ambiguities.

"False positives" add another wrinkle. In some cases, a signal will be truly false in the sense that no crisis is coming, but in others the signal may merely be premature. For example, in Latvia, the IMF raised warning flags several years before the crisis, but they were ignored because the economy kept flourishing for another three years. The signals were correct, but timing was not. This problem is especially perplexing for crises involving speculative bubbles. Many observers did not believe the dot com hype, and claimed it was a bubble well before it burst, but investors who listened to that advice too early lost significant amounts of money in the interim. Timing is also a bothersome empirical issue. It is difficult to include all relevant leads and lags when constructing an empirical model, especially when they are country specific.

At the end of the day, cheap money that fuels rapid credit and funds speculative debt-financed asset investments turns out to be a primary cause of most "bubbles." Once confidence falters, too many debtors simultaneously run into trouble, and the financially overexposed cannot save themselves without government support. Some governments are able to provide the needed assistance, but in many cases, the international community has to come to the rescue.

Most people concur with this diagnosis. However, it does not save the day because interested parties tend to disagree about whether economies are overstimulated. Economists cannot infallibly foretell that money is too cheap, credit is growing too fast and assets are overvalued before crises, leaving the door open to procrastination that assures "this time" really won't be "different."

However, persistent crises cannot be ascribed solely to stochastic ambiguity. It also is the result of a fundamental mismatch between speculators' expected returns (including anticipated bailouts), and social costs. If the well-paid financial players had to pick up the bill after each financial meltdown, they would be much more risk-averse, and welfare losses would be correspondingly lower. Policy makers are in a position to redress this asymmetry, but have been noticeably loath to do so, suggesting that when push comes to shove, they do not place enough importance on crisis prevention.

The 2008 crisis has also made it clear that the link between fiscal deficits and national debt must be confronted. Deficit spending one's way out of recession without accumulating countercyclical surpluses is a temporary palliative setting the stage for even greater crises tomorrow. Several countries have seen their public debt explode in the 2008–2009 crisis, both because of the direct bailout costs borne by the public sector, and the crisis's impact on the tax base and government transfers. Economists at the IMF and elsewhere have rightly called for creating fiscal space in good times to finance counter-crisis deficit spending later.

Becker (1999) has suggested that public debt management strategies should include the risks of bailouts, which would affect both desired debt levels and the composition of public debt. In the model, the public debt manager should basically undo (part) of the private sectors financial decisions by taking the opposite position in the public debt portfolio. This is Ricardian equivalence in reverse. The standard Ricardian argument as in Barro (1974) is that households undo the government deficit by adjusting its savings, which leads to the neutrality of government debt.

In the final analysis, the lesson from our investigation is simply that crises will always be too frequent and severe because of human folly, and governments should be prepared to deal with them in a manner that reduces the negative income and welfare effects for the whole population. This requires major changes to financial sector regulation, reducing moral hazard in lending and borrowing, limiting bailouts, and making significant changes to fiscal policy and public debt management. It also necessitates the creation of crisis prevention regimes, despite their limitations, that press policy makers to take better account of catastrophic risk, and encourage them to prioritize stability over wishful thinking. Our scatterplots have shown that early warning indicators can provide useful signals of mounting risk for the global community, even though they do not always apply to the entire population of countries. Very little of this will of course happen because this time is indeed unlikely to be different.

Acknowledgments

The author is grateful to the editor Steven Rosefielde for valuable comments, suggestions, edits and great patience. Many thanks also to seminar participants at SITE and to Evelina Bonnier for expert research assistance. Remaining shortcomings are of course the author's sole responsibility.

References

Abiad, Abdul (2003) "Early Warning Systems: A Survey and a Regime-Switching Approach", IMF Working Paper WP/03/32.

Barrell, Ray, E. Philip Davis, Dilruba Karim and Iana Liadze (2010) "Bank Regulation, Property Prices and Early Warning Systems for Banking Crises in OECD Countries," *Journal of Banking & Finance*, Elsevier, September, Vol. 34, No. 9, pp. 2255–2264.

Barro, Robert (1974) "Are Government Bonds Net Wealth?" *Journal of Political Economy*, Vol. 81, pp. 1095–1117.

Becker, Torbjörn (1999) "Public Debt Management and Bailouts" IMF Working Paper WP/99/103.

Becker, Torbjörn, Daniel Daianu, Zsolt Darvas, Vladimir Gligorov, Michael A. Landesmann, Pavle Petrovic, Jean Pisani-Ferry, Dariusz K. Rosati, André Sapir and Beatrice Weder Di Mauro (2010) "Whither Growth in Central and Eastern Europe? Policy lessons for an integrated Europe," Bruegel Blueprints Number 453, 12, Bruegel and The Vienna Institute for International Economic Studies (WIIW).

Becker, Torbjörn, Olivier Jeanne, Paolo Mauro, Jonathan D. Ostry and Roman Ranciere (2007) "Country Insurance: The Role of Domestic Policies", IMF Occasional Paper No. 254.

Berg, Andrew and Catherine Pattillo (1999) "Are Currency Crises Predictable? A Test," *IMF Staff Papers*, June, Vol. 46, No. 2, pp. 107–138.

Berg, Andrew, Eduardo Borensztein and Catherine A. Pattillo (2005) "Assessing Early Warning Systems: How Have They Worked in Practice?" *IMF Staff Papers*, Vol. 52, No. 3, pp. 462–502.

Berkmen, Pelin, Gelos, Gaston, Rennhack, Robert and James Walsh (2009) "The Global Financial Crisis: Explaining Cross-Country Differences in the Output Impact," IMF Working Paper, WP/09/280.

Blanchard, Olivier J., Giovanni Dell'Ariccia and Paolo Mauro (2010) "Rethinking Macroeconomic Policy," IMF Staff Position Note No. 2010/03.

Frankel, Jeffrey A and G. Saravelos (2010) "Are Leading Indicators of Financial Crises Useful for Assessing Country Vulnerability?" NBER Working Paper 16047.

Ghosh, Atish R., Jonathan D. Ostry and Charalambos G. Tsangarides (2011) "Exchange Rate Regimes and the Stability of the International Monetary System," IMF Occasional Paper No. 270.

Ghosh, Atish, Jonathan D. Ostry and Natalia Tamirisa (2009) "Anticipating the Next Crisis," *Finance and Development*, Vol. 46, No. 3, pp. 35–37.

Giorgianni, Lorenzo (2009) "IMF-supported Programs in the Crisis: What Have We Learned So Far?" Presentation in Instanbul, October 2. Available at: http://www.imf.org/external/np/pp/eng/2009/100209ppt.pdf.

IMF (2008) Global Financial Stability Report, April.

IMF (2010a) "How Did Emerging Markets Cope in the Crisis?" IMF Policy Paper, June 15.

IMF (2010b) Global Financial Stability Report, April.

IMF (2010c) "The IMF-FSB Early Warning Exercise: Design and Methodological Toolkit."

IMF (2011a) "Macroprudential Policy: An Organizing Framework," IMF Policy Paper.

IMF (2011b) Global Financial Stability Report, September, Chapter 3.

Kaminsky, Gabriela, Saul Lizondo and Carmen M. Reinhart (1998) "Leading Indicators of Currency Crises," *IMF Staff Papers*, March, Vol. 45, No. 1, pp. 1–48.

Kaminsky, Graciela and Carmen Reinhart (1999) "The Twin Crises: The Causes of Banking and Balance-of-Payments Problems," *American Economic Review*, Vol. 89, No. 3, pp. 473–500.

Laeven, Luc and Fabian Valencia (2010) "Resolution of Banking Crises: The Good, The Bad, and The Ugly," IMF Working Paper, WP/10/146.

Lane, Philip R. and Gian Maria Milesi-Ferretti (2010) "The Cross–Country Incidence of the Global Crisis," IMF Working Paper WP/10/171.

Maddison, Angus (2003) *The World Economy — Historical Statistics*, OECD Paris. Available at: http://dx.doi.org/10.1787/456125276116.

Manasse, Paolo and Nouriel Roubini (2005) "Rules of Thumb for Sovereign Debt Crises," IMF Working Paper WP/05/42.

Reinhart, Carmen and Kenneth Rogoff (2009) *This Time is Different: Eight Centuries of Financial Folly*, Princeton University Press.

Appendix

Table A.1.   Countries economic performance in the crisis.

Countries	Crisis loss	duration	GDP0809	Countries	Crisis loss	duration	GDP0809	Countries	Crisis loss	duration	GDP0809
Advanced economies				**Developing Asia**				**MENA**			
Ireland	−20.0	8	−14.4	Samoa	−11.2	5	4.8	UAE	−4.8	3	7.7
Iceland	−16.9	6	−4.9	Fiji	−4.1	4	−2.5	Sudan			18.5
Greece	−16.6	12	2.0	Kiribati	−3.3	4	−2.9	Jordan			17.7
Finland	−13.9	6	−6.2	Thailand	−2.2	2	2.6	Egypt			19.4
Slovenia	−13.6	5	−1.1	Solomon Islands	−2.2	2	12.2	Tunisia			12.3
Japan	−12.4	6	−7.6	Cambodia	−2.0	2	11.3	Oman			29.7
Italy	−12.2	8	−7.6	Malaysia	−1.7	2	7.6	Lebanon			28.4
Sweden	−9.7	4	−5.9	Tonga	−0.5	2	1.1	I.R. Iran			3.1
Denmark	−9.6	5	−6.4	Pakistan			6.7	Syrian Arab Rep.			14.5
Slovak Republic	−8.6	3	7.4	Philippines			8.5	Rep. of Yemen			11.3
United Kingdom	−8.5	5	−5.0	Myanmar			12.3	Bahrain			15.9
Czech Republic	−8.2	4	0.7	Sri Lanka			15.7	Morocco			16.4
Germany	−7.9	3	−2.8	Vanuatu			16.5	Djibouti			17.0
Netherlands	−7.3	4	−0.2	Bhutan			16.6				
Austria	−7.0	4	0.4	Indonesia			16.8				

(Continued)

Table A.1. (*Continued*)

Countries	Crisis loss	duration	GDP0809	Countries	Crisis loss	duration	GDP0809	Countries	Crisis loss	duration	GDP0809
Advanced economies				**Developing Asia**				**SSA**			
Luxembourg	-7.0	3	-4.0	Nepal			17.4	Eritrea	-17.4	5	-16.3
Spain	-6.5	5	-2.0	Bangladesh			17.9	Madagascar	-8.2	4	10.3
United States	-5.2	3	-2.6	Papua New Guinea			18.1	Botswana	-3.7	2	2.5
Portugal	-4.9	7	-2.7	Vietnam			18.3	Seychelles	-1.9	3	-1.8
Belgium	-4.2	3	-1.1	India			18.8	South Africa	-1.8	2	5.5
France	-4.1	3	-2.4	Lao P.D.R.			23.8	Gabon	-1.4	2	3.9
Malta	-3.7	3	3.0	China			29.2	Niger	-1.2	2	16.1
Hong Kong SAR	-2.8	2	1.5	**LAC**				Namibia	-0.8	2	7.7
Canada	-2.5	2	-1.4	Mexico	-11.2	3	-3.7	Guinea	-0.3	2	9.6
Cyprus	-2.1	3	5.4	The Bahamas	-10.2	6	-7.6	Benin			12.7
Norway	-2.0	3	0.1	Venezuela	-9.0	8	6.1	Rep. of Congo			19.0
Switzerland	-1.9	2	1.8	Jamaica	-7.7	6	-4.8	Togo			7.6
Taiwan P.o.C.	-1.9	2	-0.5	El Salvador	-6.9	4	1.2	Burundi			12.7
New Zealand	-1.7	3	-1.9	Paraguay	-3.8	2	7.6	Comoros			3.8
Korea			4.8	Honduras	-1.9	2	6.0	Tanzania			21.3
Australia			5.8	Chile	-1.5	2	5.9	Cameroon			7.8
Israel			9.3	Nicaragua	-1.5	2	4.0	Kenya			5.1
								Mali			14.6

(*Continued*)

Table A.1.   (*Continued*)

Countries	Crisis loss	duration	GDP0809	Countries	Crisis loss	duration	GDP0809	Countries	Crisis loss	duration	GDP0809
Central and Eastern Europe				**LAC**				**SSA**			
Latvia	-42.1	11	-25.7	Costa Rica	-1.1	2	4.5	Malawi			25.8
Estonia	-34.8	9	-23.3	Barbados	-0.5	6	-5.8	Lesotho			9.8
Lithuania	-28.1	8	-9.7	Brazil	-0.2	2	10.1	Cote d'Ivoire			8.5
Romania	-14.4	5	7.0	Suriname			14.7	Zambia			18.0
Hungary	-11.7	5	-5.1	Ecuador			13.4	Senegal			8.8
Montenegro	-11.6	4	7.7	Panama			23.5	D.R. Congo			15.3
Croatia	-10.7	6	-1.2	Uruguay			20.2	Ghana			18.9
Bulgaria	-6.9	4	6.7	Belize			7.5	Cape Verde			14.4
Turkey	-4.7	2	-3.4	Dominican Rep.			14.1	Uganda			25.2
Serbia	-4.5	3	7.9	Bolivia			15.9	Burkina Faso			13.8
Bos. and Herz.	-3.6	3	8.1	Colombia			6.3	Rwanda			27.0
F.Y.R. Macedonia	-0.8	3	9.2	Guatemala			7.1	C. African Rep.			5.7
Poland			11.8	Guyana			7.0	Swaziland			6.0
Albania			18.9	Haiti			4.6	Mozambique			20.2
				Argentina			14.4	Ethiopia			33.4
				Peru			20.6	The Gambia			18.5

(*Continued*)

Table A.1. (*Continued*)

Countries	Crisis loss	duration	GDP0809	Countries	Crisis loss	duration	GDP0809	Countries	Crisis loss	duration	GDP0809
CIS								**SSA**			
Ukraine	−26.7	5	−11.2					Mauritius			12.7
Armenia	−25.7	5	−1.2					Guinea–Bissau			10.3
Russia	−15.7	4	2.2								
Moldova	−12.9	4	8.6								
Georgia	−3.9	2	0.6								
Mongolia	−1.6	2	16.1								
Uzbekistan			26.8								
Tajikistan			19.5								
Kyrgyz Republic			19.3								
Belarus			20.8								
Kazakhstan			7.6								

Note: The three columns are crisis loss, computed as in Becker and Mauro for output loss periods starting in either 2008 or 2009, duration is the time in years to get back to pre-crisis GDP levels, and the GDP0809 column is the cumulative gain or loss in GDP during 2008–2009 compared to the GDP level in 2007.

Table A.2.   Advanced countries by economic performance and exchange rate regime.

	Top 50%	Bottom 50%	Fixed exrate	Flex exrate
Pre-crisis variables				
Early warnings				
Current account balance	1.3	−1.1	0.4	−0.2
Credit growth	12.6	13.2	13.1	12.8
Share prices	142.2	27.5	216.2	82.5
House prices	26.3	50.6	35.4	42.1
External debt	191.8	246.3	266.4	166.4
Inflation rate	2.5	2.4	2.4	2.5
Past GDP growth	4.5	3.2	3.5	4.2
Real exchange rate	3.7	2.0	1.3	4.1
Policy choices				
Fiscal balance	0.1	0.1	-0.4	0.7
Real interest rate	0.9	2.3	1.5	1.5
Insurance measures				
International reserves	19.4	6.0	10.9	14.2
Export concentration	0.5	0.2	0.3	0.5
Domestic bond market	50.1	120.2	103.3	89.5
Domestic equity market	194.2	80.5	128.6	90.4
Foreign banks	34.8	29.0	28.1	35.2

Note: Top 50% refers to the best performing countries in terms of cumulative GDP change 2008–2009 compared with 2007.

Table A.3. Emerging market countries by economic performance and exchange rate regime.

	Top 50%	Bottom 50%	No-loss	Loss	Fixed exrate	Flex exrate
Pre-crisis variables						
Early warnings						
Current account balance	−2.9	−3.9	−2.8	−4.3	−3.7	−3.1
Credit growth	24.9	24.7	22.3	28.7	24.1	25.5
Share prices	155.5	127.9	154.5	123.3	122.3	152.7
House prices	76.8	87.1	63.6	95.2	124.0	56.0
External debt	34.3	30.6	34.3	29.5	39.0	26.9
Inflation rate	7.1	7.2	6.9	7.6	6.2	8.1
Past GDP growth	6.5	5.1	5.9	5.8	5.7	5.9
Real exchange rate	8.8	9.9	8.6	10.6	3.1	13.4
Policy choices						
Fiscal balance	−1.0	−0.5	−1.1	−0.2	−0.5	−1.0
Real interest rate	1.9	0.7	1.3	1.3	0.0	2.5
Insurance measures						
International reserves	21.7	19.8	20.3	21.4	19.9	21.7
Export concentration	0.3	0.4	0.4	0.3	0.4	0.4
Domestic bond market	82.2	74.7	84.4	70.5	69.4	89.6
Domestic equity market	71.2	74.8	75.8	68.9	82.7	62.7
Foreign banks	35.3	51.7	36.2	55.3	46.5	42.1

Note: "Top 50%" refers to the best performing countries in terms of cumulative GDP change 2008–2009 compared with 2007, "No-Loss" refers to the countries that did not experience negative growth in neither 2008 nor 2009.

PART III

THREATS AND DETERRENTS

CHAPTER 7

GLOBAL IMBALANCES

HUAN ZHOU AND STEVEN ROSEFIELDE

It is widely believed that global imbalances (high concentration of planetary debt in some countries like the U.S., matched by reciprocal savings in others like China) contributed to the 2008 financial crisis and exacerbated unemployment in the West.[1] Bubble prevention and efficient recovery therefore require a clear understanding of the linkages and a commitment to protect. However, this imperative is obscured by a pre-occupation with other aspects of the issue, including trade efficiency, exchange rate disequilibria, optimal global payments systems, and reserve currencies. These concerns are worthy, but tangential to prevention and only will be addressed to the extent that they bear on bubbles and macroeconomic disequilibrium.

Global imbalances may cause bubbles by facilitating excess credit creation in the debtor and creditor nations and can aggravate unemployment when excess savings are created through protectionism. The prelude to the 2008 financial crisis provides a clear case in point. In the aftermath of the September 11, 2001, World Trade Center terror attack, U.S. deficit spending rose rapidly for both security and consumption purposes, creating a financial burden funded in large part by correspondingly brisk increases in Beijing's holdings of U.S. treasury debt. China held relatively modest dollar reserves prior to its admission to the World Trade Organization (WTO) on December 11, 2001, but its ability to finance a large portion of U.S. debt subsequently mushroomed (see Tables 7.1 and 7.2 and Figs. 7.1 and 7.2). Its treasury debt purchases, together with those of other trade surplus nations, allowed the Federal Reserve to keep interest and

---

[1] Obstfeld and Rogoff (2009).

Table 7.1. Dollar Reserve Accumulations (1985–2010) in China, Japan, Germany, and Singapore.

Country	1985	1986	1987	1988	1989	1990
Japan	26,718,700	42,256,600	80,972,900	96,728,200	83,957,400	78,500,600
China	1,272,8100	11,453,000	16,304,900	18,541,300	17,959,900	29,586,200
Germany	44,379,900	51,734,000	78,756,300	58,527,600	60,708,700	67,902,200
Singapore	12,846,600	12,939,000	15,227,000	17,072,500	20,371,000	27,790,000

Country	1991	1992	1993	1994	1995	1996	1997
Japan	72,058,800	71,622,700	98,524,300	1.26E+08	1.83E+08	2.17E+08	2.2E+08
China	43,674,300	20,620,400	22,386,900	52,914,100	75,376,700	1.07E+08	1.43E+08
Germany	63,000,800	90,967,100	77,639,900	77,363,200	85,005,200	83,177,900	7,758,6700
Singapore	34,186,600	39,941,400	48,416,200	58,295,800	68,816,100	76,964,000	71,390,100

Country	1998	1999	2000	2001	2002	2003
Japan	2.15E+08	2.87E+08	3.55E+08	3.95E+08	4.61E+08	6.63E+08
China	1.49E+08	1.58E+08	1.68E+08	2.16E+08	2.91E+08	4.08E+08
Germany	74,024,200	61,038,800	56,890,500	51,403,900	51,170,600	50694000
Singapore	75,077,200	77,047,100	80,170,300	75,677,000	82,221,200	96245500

Country	2004	2005	2006	2007	2008	2009	2010
Japan	8.34E+08	8.34E+08	8.8E+08	9.53E+08	1.01E+09	1.02E+09	1.06E+09
China	6.15E+08	8.22E+08	1.07E+09	1.53E+09	1.95E+09	2.42E+09	2.87E+09
Germany	48822700	45139700	41686500	44326500	43137200	59925300	62294900
Singapore	1.13E+08	1.16E+08	1.36E+08	1.63E+08	1.74E+08	1.88E+08	2.26E+08

Source: International Financial Statistics (IFS online).

Table 7.2. Dollar Reserve Accumulations (1985–2010) in Philippines, Malaysia, South Korea, and Indonesia.

	1985	1986	1987	1988	1989	1990
Philippines	614,895	172,8180	968,271	1,003,390	1,416,960	924,352
Malaysia	4,911,840	6,027,380	7,435,330	6,526,500	7,782,960	9,754,080
South Korea	2,869,320	3,319,580	3,583,680	12,346,700	15,213,600	14,793,000
Indonesia	4,974,240	4,051,270	5,592,320	5,048,320	5,453,530	7,459,060

	1991	1992	1993	1994	1995	1996	1997
Philippines	3,245,950	4,403,260	4,675,690	6,038,010	6,396,310	10,058,200	7,297,480
Malaysia	10,885,600	17,227,500	27,249,200	25,422,900	23,774,400	2,7009,400	20,788,200
South Korea	13,701,100	17,120,600	20,228,200	25,639,300	32,677,700	34,037,100	20,367,900
Indonesia	9,257,940	10,448,600	11,262,700	12,132,700	13,708,200	18,251,100	16,586,900

	1998	1999	2000	2001	2002	2003
Philippines	9,274,150	132,69700	130,90200	134,76300	133,29300	136,54,900
Malaysia	25,559,400	30,588,200	28,329,800	29,522,300	3,3360,700	4,3821,700
South Korea	51,974,500	73,987,300	96,130,500	1.03E+08	1.21E+08	1.55E+08
Indonesia	22,713,400	26,445,000	28,501,900	27,246,200	30,970,700	34,962,300

	2004	2005	2006	2007	2008	2009	2010
Philippines	131,16300	159,26000	200,25400	302,10600	331,92900	387,82900	553,62800
Malaysia	65,881,100	69,858,000	82,132,300	1.01E+08	91,148,800	95,431,700	1.05E+08
South Korea	1.99E+08	2.1E+08	2.39E+08	2.62E+08	2.01E+08	2.7E+08	2.91E+08
Indonesia	34,952,500	33,140,500	41,103,100	54,976,400	49,596,700	63,563,300	92,908,000

Source: International Financial Statistics (IFS online).

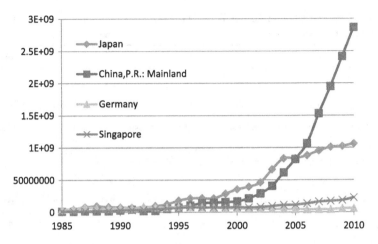

Figure 7.1.   Dollar reserve accumulations (1985–2010) in China, Japan, Germany, and Singapore.

Source: International Financial Statistics (IFS online).

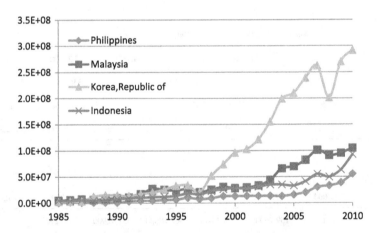

Figure 7.2.   Dollar reserve accumulations (1985–2010) in Philippines, Malaysia, South Korea, and Indonesia.

Source: International Financial Statistics (IFS online).

core inflation rates relatively low (CPI and PCE) at the same time the government binged on deficit spending and prices skyrocketed in hard asset markets (housing, natural resources and collectibles).[2] The segmentation was reminiscent of Japan's bubble economy during the late 1980s, where inflation was concentrated in real estate, collectibles and stocks.

China's excess dollar accumulations and those of other nations did not compel the U.S. to deficit spend, issue subprime mortgage debt, and fuel natural resource demand with its wars in Iraq and Afghanistan, but it facilitated the process by encouraging faith in "divine coincidence."

A tidal shift in macroeconomic thinking during the 1990s and 2000s based on concepts like "Ricardian equivalence"[3] and "rational expectations",[4] together with a "Great Moderation" in business cycle volatility,[5] led economists like Robert Lucas to conclude that governments could achieve all their policy objectives with a single instrument, the short-term interest rate.[6] China's excess dollar accumulations from this perspective were a macroeconomic blessing (together with cheap Chinese imports that tamed inflation), not a bane. The new consensus maintained that full

---

[2]The term "core inflation" was coined by Robert Gordian (1975) in his paper "Alternative Responses to Policy of External Supply Shocks." The concept excludes food and energy prices, which are both volatile and said by macro-theorists to be only weakly connected with the behavior of the rest of the real economy. The Federal Reserve uses the personal consumption expenditures chain price index (PCE) to gauge core economic activity and guide policy. The U.S. consumer price index (CPI) is employed to set social security payments. It is a general price index of the cost of living of urbanites, not a GDP deflator. There is a debate over whether the CPI under or overstates inflation.

[3]The Ricardian equivalence, also called the Barro–Ricardo theorem, postulates that consumers internalized the government's budget constraint, and thus the timing of tax changes does not affect their spending. If true, then traditional Keynesian fiscal policy is ineffectual. See Buchanan (1976), Ricardo (1888), and Barro (1979, 1989).

[4]Rational expectations in economics is the hypothesis that agents' expectations about future values are not systematically wrong. Errors are random. The concept suggests that government fiscal policies are anticipated, and therefore do not have powerful effects.

[5]The Great Moderation refers to the reduction in the volatility of business cycle fluctuations that began in the 1980s and was widely attributed to institutional and structural changes in developed countries. See Stock and Watson (2002). Ben Bernanke stressed the importance of the phenomenon in 2004. This led to the adoption of rules-based, as opposed to discretionary–based, macroeconomic policymaking. See Taylor (2011).

[6]Rosefielde and Razin (2011).

employment and steady growth were more important than peripheral effects on financial speculation, failing to appreciate how easily money and mammoth dollar accumulations could affect hard asset capital appreciation prospects, credit creation, leveraging and an explosion in derivatives that ultimately precipitated a nearly catastrophic run on the bank by financial institutions.[7] Ben Bernanke, Simon Gilchrist, and Masashi Saito had written about financial accelerators,[8] but this theoretical work had no visible impact on policy.

The ballooning effect of China's dollar accumulations on western capital gains and speculative hard asset expectations (analogous to the impact of terms of trade effects on "command income")[9] boomeranged back on Beijing in the form of foreign direct investment-induced real estate inflation.[10] Chinese money lent to the Fed stayed there, but the expectations it created stimulated reverse financial flows from other sources, contributing to a hyper bubble that is still in the making.

Many economists like Evgeny Gavrilenkov (chief economist, Troika Dialog) grasped long ago that global imbalances were inundating the world with bubble-inducing liquidity.[11] The insight provided a sound rule of thumb for speculating in oil and other minerals while the Great Moderation lasted, and still provides useful guidance qualified by anemic GDP recovery of the U.S, intractable high unemployment, and the parlous sovereign indebtedness of Portugal, Italy, Ireland, Greece, and Spain (PIIGs). High speculative demand for cash (Keynesian style liquidity trap) has temporarily severed the link between global imbalances and acute bubble behavior in the west as Reinhart and Rogoff forecasted,[12] allowing policymakers to ignore the danger of a second wave bubble resurgence. Western authorities are acting as if they still believe in divine coincidence

---

[7] Rosefielde and Razin, "The 2008 Global Financial Crisis," Chapter 2 of this volume.

[8] There is a literature on the impact of asset inflation on expectations and monetary policy, but not on the global imbalance linkage. See Gilchrist and Saito (2006) and Bernanke, Gertler and Gilchrist (1999).

[9] Command income is GDP plus additional purchasing power attributable to improvements in a country's terms of trade.

[10] See Akio Kawato, "China's Real Estate Bubble," Chapter 8 in this volume.

[11] Personal interview in Moscow, March 2009.

[12] Reinhart and Rogoff (2009).

over the long run, where the government can run deficits at any level it chooses,[13] in a lax financial regulatory environment because full employment can be assured solely by targeting short term interest rates, ad-libbing in the interim with colossal budgetary deficits and "monetary easing"(QE-infinity) to forestall the Keynesian deflationary bugaboo.[14]

Deflation has been averted and deficits financed with foreign dollar savings. However, macroeconomists have yet to integrate global imbalances and other financial disequilibria into their policies. Ben Bernanke insists that when the tide turns and the public ceases hoarding excess idle cash balances, QE-infinity can be reversed precluding both general inflation and another financial debacle. Perhaps he can, but it would be imprudent to bet on it because while theoreticians fiddle, global imbalances continue to briskly mount affecting speculative expectations beyond the Federal Reserve's control both in the west and China. *Ceteris paribus*, tomorrow's conflagration should be fiercer than 2008.

There is no need to guess whether the next financial crisis will generate mass involuntary unemployment. Reinhart and Rogoff have shown that the real effects of financial crises always are devastating and long lasting. However, inadequate attention has been paid to the possibility that global imbalances exacerbate mass involuntary unemployment through a back channel, when excess savings accrue due to the combined effects of the surplus country's over-exporting and under-importing; that is, the global system is in protectionist disequilibrium.[15]

The term overexporting means that a nation sells more goods abroad than it should under general competition because its currency is undervalued in

---

[13]Larry Summers, "Turning Japanese: The United States Will Suffer a 'Lost Decade,' If We Don't Change Course," OpEd, *Financial Times*, June 14, 2011.

[14]Monetary easing is action taken by the central bank to reduce interest rates and expand the money supply. Quantitative easing is an unconventional monetary policy where the central bank purchases assets (sometimes toxic) with new money. This increases banks excess reserves and lowers interest rates. It is a form of printing money intended to keep inflation above some target (forestalling deflation), while allowing real interest rates to become negative (providing a subsidy for spending). Beranke announced that be would continue a policy of quantitative easing forever of needed to alleviate unemployment. This new policy as of September 2012 has been widely dubbed QE-infinity

[15]See Eric Fisher, "Optimal Asian Dollar Surplus," Chapter 9 of this volume.

the foreign exchange market, or exports are subsidized (protectionism). Underimporting is the opposite. Countries buy less from abroad than they should from their excess, disequilibrium export revenues because import control authorities refuse to spend dollars in order to protect home industries or other unworthy reasons (dollar imports seem expensive at the state fixed exchange rate).

The accumulation of macroeconomically destabilizing imbalances frequently involves both overexporting and underimporting. For example, China's renminbi foreign exchange rate is widely alleged to be undervalued, allowing Beijing to overexport. But China's leaders at their discretion could use the extra dollars acquired by its currency control authorities to purchase just enough dollar imports to keep the current account balanced (forced substitution). This was China's policy before 2001 (see Fig. 7.3). The U.S. under these circumstances (assuming general competition everywhere else) would overimport and overexport (relative to China's disequilibrum optimal import level), maintaining full employment by transferring lost jobs in the import competing to its export sector.

The fact that China perpetually runs a current account surplus (assuming disequilibrium contrary to the Eric Fisher hypothesis),[16] means that

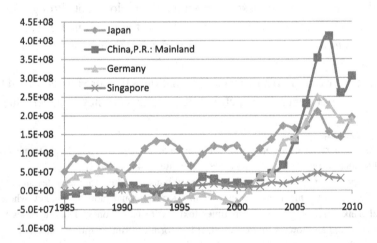

Figure 7.3. Current account surpluses 1985–2010 in China, Japan, Germany, and Singapore.

Source: International Financial Statistics (IFS online).

---

[16]Eric Fisher, "Optimal Asian Dollar Surplus," Chapter 10 of this volume.

some of its surplus is excessive, and consequently imposes an adjustment shock on U.S. As Keynes understood, this shock need not cause involuntary unemployment.[17] Wages could downward adjust and jobs could increase in the non trade competing sector. Keynes claimed however, that this disregarded the multiplier effects of exogenous shocks (in this case China's under-importing) on aggregate effective demand, imposing the adjustment burden manufactured in China on workers abroad. The argument starting from imbalances and proceeding through its beggar-thy-neighbor protectionist effects is general,[18] not specific to China. The same story can be spun for Japan, South Korea, Brazil and a host of other nations running chronic current account surpluses (see Tables 7.3 and 7.4 and Figs. 7.3 and 7.4).

The bottom line here is that the assumption of comprehensive competition, insofar as it is off the mark, masks the adverse employment effects of global imbalances. Whether intended or not, state-trading protectionism has beggar-thy-neighbor consequences that may be camouflaged as they were in U.S. during 2000–2008 by various excess effective demand stimulants, but manifest themselves with a vengeance when bubbles burst. Global imbalances of the non-Eric Fisherian sort therefore are doubly obnoxious. They contribute to bubbles and impose grave hardships on the working population in the aftermath of financial crises. Although, obviously all the blame for bubbles and mass involuntary unemployment cannot be laid at the doorstep of global imbalances, the duty to prevent requires that nations actively defend themselves against the risks raised by chronic overexporting and underimporting.

The U.S. and the EU are loath to confront the issue because doing so might jeopardize what is considered the greater good of liberalizing globalization. Savvy practitioners know full well that the Chinese and many other nations openly engage in sundry protectionist (or mercantilist) practices, but have been content to nudge them toward free trade and urging the appreciation of their foreign exchange rates, as if these policies

---

[17] Keynes (1936).
[18] Beggaring-thy-neighbor is unwarranted in both micro- and macroeconomy theory. Dani Rodrik has argued that China's trade is driven by technology transfers. The issue is important, but separate from the imbalances question. See Rodrik (2006) and Yao (2009).

Table 7.3.   Current account surpluses (1985–2010) of China, Japan, Germany, and Singapore.

	1985	1986	1987	1988	1989	1990
Japan	51,128,900	85,876,600	84,350,600	79,249,300	63,214,900	44,078,200
China	−1.1E+07	−7,034,000	300,000	−3,802,000	−4,317,000	11,997,000
Germany	18,021,200	39,137,800	44,842,500	54,725,000	58,032,100	47,659,400
Singapore	−3,636.12	318,726	−108,643	1,936,920	2,963,660	3,121,870

	1991	1992	1993	1994	1995	1996	1997
Japan	68,203,500	1.13E+08	1.32E+08	1.3E+08	1.11E+08	65,792,200	96,813,900
China	13,272,000	6,401,000	−1.2E+07	6,908,000	1,618,390	7,243,000	36,963,000
Germany	−2.3E+07	−2.2E+07	−1.8E+07	−3E+07	−2.8E+07	−1.2E+07	−7,817,180
Singapore	4,880,320	5,914,850	4,211,060	11,399,800	14,230,300	13,984,200	15,313,600

	1998	1999	2000	2001	2002	2003	2004
Japan	1.19E+08	1.15E+08	1.2E+08	87,797,700	1.12E+08	1.36E+08	1.72E+08
China	31,472,000	21,115,000	20,518,400	17,401,000	35,422,000	45,874,800	68659200
Germany	−1.4E+07	−2.7E+07	−3.2E+07	400,895	41,105,400	46,930,400	1.28E+08
Singapore	18,449,200	14,440,700	10,178,300	11,202,700	11,756,500	21,880,600	19,293,600

	2005	2006	2007	2008	2009	2010
Japan	1.66E+08	1.71E+08	2.1E+08	1.57E+08	1.42E+08	1.96E+08
China	1.34E+08	2.33E+08	3.54E+08	4.12E+08	2.61E+08	3.05E+08
Germany	1.41E+08	1.83E+08	2.49E+08	2.28E+08	1.89E+08	1.88E+08
Singapore	26,665,900	35,125,700	47,084,100	36,010,900	32,628,100	

Source: International Financial Statistics (IFS online).

Table 7.4. Current account surpluses (1985–2010) in Philippines, Malaysia, South Korea and Indonesia.

	1985	1986	1987	1988	1989	1990
Philippines	−36,000	952,000	−444,000	−390,000	−1,456,000	−2,695,000
Malaysia	−600,070	−101,494	2,575,370	1,867,280	314,526	−869,911
South Korea	−795,100	4,709,400	10,058,400	14,505,400	5,344,200	−2,014,400
Indonesia	−1,923,000	−3,911,000	−2,098,000	−1,397,000	−1,108,000	−2,988,000

	1991	1992	1993	1994	1995	1996	1997
Philippines	−1,034,000	−1,000,000	−3,016,000	−2,950,000	−1,980,000	−3,953,000	−4,351,000
Malaysia	−4,182,810	−2,167,320	−2,990,950	−4,520,140	−8,643,570	−4,461,950	−5,935,250
South Korea	−8,417,400	−4,095,200	821,100	−4,024,200	−8,665,100	−2.3E+07	−8,383,700
Indonesia	−4,260,000	−2,780,000	−2,106,000	−2,792,000	−6,431,000	−7,663,000	−4,889,000

	1998	1999	2000	2001	2002	2003
Philippines	1,546,000	−2,875,000	−2,228,000	−1,750,000	−282,000	285,000
Malaysia	9,528,650	1,2603,700	8,487,890	7,286,840	7,189,740	13,381,200
South Korea	40,371,200	24,521,900	12,250,800	8,032,600	5,393,900	11,949,500
Indonesia	4,096,970	5,782,900	7,992,090	6,900,920	7,823,520	8,106,790

	2004	2005	2006	2007	2008	2009	2010
Philippines	1,625,000	1,980,000	5,341,000	7,112,000	3,627,000	9,358,000	8,465,000
Malaysia	15,079,400	19,979,900	26,199,500	29,770,100	38,914,400	31,801,000	
South Korea	28,173,500	14,980,900	5,385,340	5,876,000	3,196,600	32,790,500	28,213,500
Indonesia	1,563,020	277,554	1,0859,500	1,0492,600	125,885	10,191,900	6,294,350

Source: International Financial Statistics (IFS online)

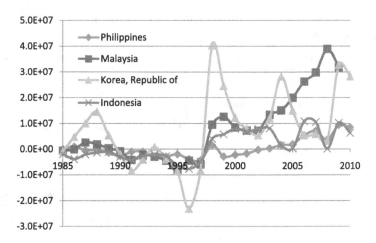

Figure 7.4. Current account surpluses (1985–2010) in Philippines, Malaysia, South Korea, and Indonesia.

Source: International Financial Statistics (IFS online).

alone will solve the problem. They only need look at Japan, which runs chronic current account surpluses with an overvalued yen to appreciate that exchange rate adjustment is insufficient to eliminate anticompetitive disequilibria for protracted periods.

In a world suffused with divine coincidences, anticompetitive disequilibria would not matter in the big picture. Nations could enjoy full employment, steady growth, improved living standards and welfare while safely ignoring global imbalances. However, as the 2008 crisis made plain, this is not a universe that we should expect to inhabit. Policymaking therefore should be modified so that prime goals like globalization and liberalization are adjusted to accommodate a duty to prevent global crises.

This can be accomplished by acknowledging the duty, accepting the constraint, and debating appropriate countermeasures. There are institutions already in place like the WTO that can be assigned to grapple with aspects of the task. An intelligence unit should be formed to investigate the protectionist dimension of chronic surpluses both on the import and export sides of the ledger. WTO politics preclude full revelation, but official compilations can be used as a benchmark for deeper probes by independent national bubble prevention agencies, as circumstances dictate.

When evidence of protectionism is compelling, victimized states should take countervailing antiprotectionist action regardless of employment conditions. Eliminating anticompetitive current account surpluses in times of full employment will dampen bubble creating speculative expectations. Countering these excesses in hard times will alleviate victim pain and simultaneously clear a path for responsible monetary policy. Given the magnitudes of U.S. budget deficit and national debt, the burden of fighting unemployment has fallen by default on the Federal Reserve. Absent the anticompetitive component of global imbalances, unemployment most likely would be substantially lower than it is today. The Fed would not have had to resort to QE-infinity. It could have focused its activities properly on combating inflation.

The disequilibria caused by anticompetitive global imbalances cannot be quarantined, and should they continue growing this decade as they did in the last decade, then the planet is apt to experience another great bubble and bust. Policymakers will probably just grin and bear it, but they should not. The fire next time is entirely preventable.

References

Barro, Robert (1989) "The Ricardian Approach to Budget Deficits," *The Journal of Economic Perspectives*, Vol. 3, No. 2.

Bernanke Ben, Mark Gertler and Simon Gilchrist (1999) "Financial Accelerator in a Quantitative Business Cycle Framework," In John Taylor and M. Woodward (eds.), *Handbook of Macroeconomics*, Vol. 1C, Amsterdam: Elsevier Science, North Holland.

Buchanan, James (1976) "Perceived Wealth in Bonds and Social Security: A Comment," *Journal of Political Economy*, Vol. 84, No. 2, pp. 337–342.

Gilchrist, Simon and Masashi Saito (2006) "Expectations, Asset Prices, and Monetary Policy: The Role of Learning," IMES Discussion Paper Series 2006-E-18, August.

Gordian, Robert (1975) "Alternative Responses to Policy of External Supply Shocks," *Brookings Papers on Economic Activity*, Vol. 6, No. 3, pp. 183–206.

Keynes, John Maynard (1936) *The General Theory of Employment, Money and Interest*, London: Palgrave Macmillan.

Obstfeld, Maurice and Kenneth Rogoff (2009) "Global Imbalances and the Financial Crisis: Products of Common Cause," Paper Presented at the Federal Reserve Bank of San Francisco Asia Economic Policy Conference, Santa Barbara, CA, October 18–20.

Reinhart, Carmen and Kenneth Rogoff (2009) *This Time is Different: Four Centuries of Financial Folly*, Princeton NJ: Princeton University Press.

Ricardo, David (1888) "Essay on the Funding System," in *The Works of David Ricardo*, London: John Murray.

Robert, Barro (1979) "On the Determination of the Public Debt," *Journal of Political Economy*, Vol. 87, No. 5, pp. 940–971.

Rodrik, Dani (2006) "What's so Special About China's Exports?" *China and World Economy*, Vol. 14, No. 5, pp. 1–19.

Rosefielde, Steven and Assaf Razin (2011) "Global Financial Crisis," In Steven Rosefielde, Masaaki Kuboniwa and Satoshi Mizobata (eds), *Two Asias: The Emerging Postcrisis Divide*, Singapore: World Scientific.

Stock, James and Mark Watson (2002) "Has the Business Cycle Changed and Why?" *NBER Macroeconomic Annual*.

Taylor, John and M Woodward (1999) *Handbook of Macroeconomics*, Vol. 1C, Amsterdam: Elsevier Science, North Holland.

Taylor, John (2011) "The Cycle of Rules and Discretion in Economic Policy," *National Affairs*, Vol. 7.

Yao, Shunli (2009) "Why are Chinese Exports not so Special?" *China and World Economy*, Vol. 17, pp. 47–65.

CHAPTER 8

CHINESE PROTECTIONISM

JONATHAN LEIGHTNER

8.1. Introduction

Crises can originate internally or externally to a country. When the U.S. went into crisis in 2008, it produced problems for China because Chinese exports to the U.S. fell as a result. This chapter focuses on how to prevent crises that originate externally and will use China as an example. Clearly, China faces the prospect of crises generated both internally (especially from excessive speculation in real estate) and externally. Furthermore, it is sometimes difficult to classify the origin of a crisis as either external or internal. For example, the 1997 financial crisis of Thailand started with Thailand opening an international banking center into which flowed large volumes of foreign money, funding a speculative bubble in real estate (Leightner, 1999; 2007). Reasonable people could disagree on whether Thailand's 1997 crisis originated externally or internally. Having admitted this difficulty, I will proceed to discuss preventing crises which clearly contain an important element of external orientation.

Section 2 of this paper discusses how China's 1986–2008 growth model made China vulnerable to the West's 2008 crisis. Section 3 describes what China is currently doing and what China still needs to do in order to reduce its vulnerability to similar crises in the future. Section 5 explains that the U.S. in 2011 continues to use policies that keep U.S. interest rates near 0%, while China has started to increase interest rates in order to combat inflation. As Chinese interest rates rise, foreigners will want to move their assets into China (Wei, 2011). This could add fuel (funds) to the speculative bubble that appears to be raging in China's real estate market. Section 5 discusses how China can reduce its vulnerability to these problems. Section 6 explains how China's accumulation of foreign reserves could be used against the U.S. causing a crisis in the U.S. that originated in China. Such a crisis would generate a secondary wave of crises throughout Asia. The only way to stop such a crisis is if there was an international agency that would monitor currency flows and that would prevent massive sellings of currency reserves. Section 7 concludes.

8.2. China's Export Driven Growth Model of the Recent Past[1]

Between 1986 and 2007, China used several strategies to promote exports. Its exchange rate is fixed at a level less than market clearing, which generates a shortage of China's currency, the yuan. In order to eliminate this shortage, China prints more yuan and exchanges it for U.S. dollars or U.S. treasury bonds (or for other foreign assets). China attempts to "sterilize" (neutralize) the resulting increase in the supply of yuan by imposing strong capital controls and by forcing Chinese banks to purchase government bonds. When Chinese banks purchase government bonds, excess yuan is removed from the market. However, sterilization interferes with bank profit maximization and its effectiveness is subject to debate. Irrefutable evidence that China has kept its exchange rate below market clearing levels is China's foreign reserves increasing from US$1.9 trillion in January 2009 to US$2.85 trillion dollars in December 2010, *ceteris paribus*.[2] No other country in all of known history has held such a large amount of foreign reserves.

China also promotes labor-intensive exports by suppressing labor unions and the wage rate. The dual strategy of suppressing both the wage rate and the exchange rate causes the domestic market to develop very slowly, or not at all. This dual strategy also makes it possible for the rich owners of export industries to keep most of the returns as profits (thus enriching themselves) while most laborers remain in severe poverty.

---

[1]Sections 8.2 and 8.3 of this paper are similar, but not identical, to Secs. 1 and 3 of Leightner (2009, 2011).

[2]People's Bank of China. Available at: http://www.pbc.gov.cn/publish/html/2010s09.htm and /2009s09.htm. Accessed June 17, 2011. Most of these reserves were accumulated after July 1997. Wei (2011) says that China's foreign reserves are 3.2 trillion dollars as of July 2011. Here "*ceteris paribus*" would include any existing import restrictions.

The resulting rise in Chinese income inequality is dramatically illustrated by the Gini coefficient.

The Gini coefficient is zero if a society is completely equal (everyone has an equal share of income) and this coefficient is one if a society is completely unequal (one person has all the income). China's Gini coefficient was only 0.28 in 1983, making China one of the most equal countries on the earth. This is especially significant because it is easier to improve and sustain equality in small countries, like Japan and Sweden, and harder in large countries like China. However, the degree of inequality skyrocketed in China after 1983. By 2001, China's Gini was 0.447, making China less equal than Thailand (Gini = 0.43), Korea (Gini = 0.32), Indonesia (Gini = 0.34), India (Gini = 0.325), and the U.S. (Gini in 2000 = 0.408). Although China is not yet as unequal as Mexico (Gini = 0.55) or Brazil (Gini = 0.59) there is probably "no other case where a society's income distribution has deteriorated so much, so fast" (Naughton, 2007: pp. 217–218). Furthermore, China's Gini has continued to rise; as of 2006 it was 0.47 (Xin, 2008) and this author has heard unofficial estimates that in 2009 China's Gini was 0.50.

With a highly unequal income distribution, Chinese producers do not have a domestic market for what they produce; thus China must export. For trade to occur there must be both a buyer and a seller — if China exports, then other countries have to import. China entices other countries to buy Chinese goods and services by keeping the prices of its exports extremely low. Prices are kept low by keeping the cost of Chinese production low via wage repression and by fixing the exchange rate below its market clearing level (and thus accumulating foreign reserves). China's net "exports" (exports minus imports or "trade surplus") equals the amount that China produces in excess of what it consumes domestically and, thus, it equals China's "excess savings." Excess savings (trade surpluses) can be maintained only if other countries have off-setting excess consumption (trade deficits). Thus China's 1986–2007 "Export Promotion" strategy could have been named China's "Excess Savings Strategy" and this strategy necessarily implies that there must be countries with offsetting excess consumption (Leightner, 2009; 2010b; 2011).

Modigliani and Cao (2004, pp. 165–166) state,

By the early 90s, the Chinese personal saving rate had reached a remarkable level of nearly 30%.... This occurred despite the fact that, even with the high growth rate, the per-capita income remained one of the lowest in the world. The saving rates are stunningly high in comparison with those of the U.S., one of the world's richest nations. During those same years, the personal saving rate in the U.S. was 7.6%: and even the "private" saving rate, which is the sum of personal saving and corporate saving (profit retention), rises to only 10%.... Since then the saving rate has slipped further with the personal down to 3% and the private down to 5%.

If corporate savings is added to household savings, then China is saving approximately 50% of the income it generates.

"An 'Excess Savings' strategy can be maintained if and only if, year after year (forever more), a country accumulates more and more savings" (i.e., if they never use the U.S. dollars they continue to accumulate). If a country was to spend the foreign reserves they had previously accumulated, then that country would run a trade deficit. When the rest of the world produces goods and services and exports them to the U.S. but never uses what it was paid for those goods and services, it is equivalent to the world giving the U.S. a huge gift. It is equivalent to your employer giving you a pay check, which you never cash. The U.S. gains tremendously. The big losers are the Chinese consumer and worker. The winners in China are the rich who own the companies that export — they get to keep the profits which are artificially high due to the suppression of labor and wages" (Leightner, 2011).

The U.S. has gained tremendously from the world's increased appetite for U.S. dollar reserves between 1997 and 2007.[3] Not only does the U.S. receive goods and services in exchange for countries taking printed paper

---

[3] Total reserves (minus gold) for all countries in the world grew 3.23 fold from 1,265 billion SDRs in 1997 to 4,080 billion in 2007. For just developing countries, total reserves grew 4.55 fold from 683 billion SDRs in 1997 to 3,107 billion in 2007. For just Asian countries, total reserves grew 4.92 fold from 384 billion SDRs in 1997 to 1,891 billion in 2007. For just China, total reserves grew 9.13 fold from 106 billion SDRs in 1997 to 968 billion SDRs in 2007 (IMF, 2008). Much, but not all, of these increases in foreign reserves were held in U.S. dollars or U.S. treasury bills.

(U.S. dollars and treasury bonds), the U.S. also gains in other ways. Lindsey (2006), focusing on China's fixed exchange rate, explains:

> The Chinese clearly undervalue their exchange rate. This means American consumers are able to buy goods at an artificially low price, making them winners. In order to maintain this arrangement, the People's Bank of China must buy excess dollars, and has accumulated nearly $1 trillion of reserves (this is now over $2.8 trillion). Since it has no domestic use for them, it turns around and lends them back to America in our Treasury, corporate and housing loan markets. This means that both Treasury borrowing costs and mortgage interest rates are lower than they otherwise would be. American homeowners and taxpayers are winners as a result.

Lindsey admits that U.S. producers of goods that compete with Chinese imports lose from China's fixed exchange rate; however, he adamantly insists that the U.S. homeowner, tax payer, and consumer gain more than U.S. producers lose. "What Lindsey (2006) did not consider is that China and the rest of the world accumulating U.S. dollar reserves would fund[4] a speculative bubble in the U.S. that would lead to the worse recession the U.S. has suffered since the great depression. Nor did Lindsey consider the possibility that China might someday cash in their U.S. dollar reserves" (Leightner, 2011).

The deceptive actions of certain U.S. corporate leaders and confusion about the risks associated with financial derivatives resulted in the U.S. speculative bubble. Once that bubble burst, the U.S. reduced its imports, creating problems for China's Export Driven Growth Model. Recall that an export promotion strategy requires an importer.

China could return to its pre-crisis export promotion strategy if and only if two unlikely conditions occurred after the crisis. First, the U.S. would have to return to its excess consumption. However, this is unlikely in the near future since many Americans have been scared by the crisis

---

[4]It is important to realize that I am NOT blaming China for the current world financial crisis. China (in conjunction with many other countries) did "finance" the bubble that caused the crisis, but the core of the problem (and thus where blame should be placed) is with the deceptive actions of American business leaders.

into saving more. Second, China would have to return to its perpetual accumulation of U.S. dollar reserves. Although China has continued to accumulate **foreign reserves** after the crisis, China's top leadership — Hu Jintao, Wen Jiabao, and Zhou Xiaochuan — have made it very clear that they will not continue to accumulate **U.S. dollars** for very long (see Leightner, 2011 for details). China's holdings of U.S. Treasuries have not been steadily increasing since 2009. They were 939.9 billion in July 2009, only 843.7 billion in June 2010 (for a more than 10% reduction), climbed to 1175.3 billion by October 2010, and then fell to 1144.9 billion in March 2011, and then climbed to 1159.8 in May 2011 (http://www.ustreas.gov/tic/mfh.txt, accessed July 2011, June 2011 and August 2010). Furthermore, China continues to diversify its foreign reserves — adding more Euro, Japanese and South Korean assets.

8.3. Reforms Needed for a Chinese Consumption Growth Model

The international financial crisis that began in 2008 convinced China that it cannot rely upon U.S. and European demand for its exports. China wants a new and more reliable buyer for its goods. The currently underdeveloped massive domestic market in China is the greatest source of potential buyers for Chinese goods on this earth. Realizing that, Hu Jintao actively is advocating a domestic consumption driven growth model for China's future.[5] However, for the full potential of this market to be realized, major reforms will need to be made in China.

Buyers need income in order to be able to buy. Thus, China must re-distribute income from the wealthy (who tend to save more of their income) to the poor (who spend a larger percent of their income). In 2010, China's top legislature (the National People's Congress) proposed a major reform in income distribution to "be launched as soon as possible," which

---

[5]When the author of this paper went to a conference on "Can emerging economies return to the same growth model after the crisis" in Hainan, China October 31–November 1, 2009, every single scholar from China talked about how a domestic consumption growth model was the best plan for China's future. However, one Chinese provincial leader proudly declared that income had risen in his province by 10% last year and savings by 16%. He claimed that these statistics prove that his province was following Hu Jintao's consumption driven growth model.

aims to increase incomes, reduce the wealth gap, and make the middle class the largest sector of society ("Legislature," 2010). These proposals are to be included in the 12th Five-Year Plan (2011–2015).

Until recently, the Chinese communist party always suppressed labor strikes. Thus it surprised many when, in response to a 2010 labor dispute at a Japanese-owned factory in China, Wen Jiabao told a Japanese delegation that "Labor disputes are occurring at some foreign companies (located in China), where there is a problem of relatively low wages. We would like (Japan) to address this issue" (Chang, 2010). Apparently, China is now allowing labor strikes and slow-downs in foreign-owned factories located in China in an effort to get higher wages for Chinese workers.

China began making policy shifts to help workers, at the expense of the factory owners, even before the 2008 financial crisis. For example, China's new labor law officially took effect in January 2008.[6] This law requires that all employers give their employees written contracts and that an employee can be given a maximum of two contracts with fixed ending dates. At the end of the second fixed ending date contract, the employee must be fired or given a permanent labor contract. Under a permanent labor contract, the worker can only be fired if the worker breaks his obligations as outlined in the written contract.

The policy shifts discussed above should increase disposable income for China's relatively poorer masses. However, China needs to do more than just increase disposable income. China needs to eliminate the fear that is the primary driving force behind China's excess savings rate. The Chinese people are afraid of getting sick, and of not having enough money to pay the doctor. Many Chinese medical doctors enthusiastically embraced Deng Xiaoping's sayings, "to get rich is glorious," "some will get rich before others," and "whatever makes profits is good for China," A doctor maximizes his profits by giving his patients expensive treatments that keep the patients alive but still sick. If a patient gets well, they stop going to the doctor and the doctor loses them as a source of income. Furthermore health insurance only covers a small percent of China's population and the limited health insurance that does exist requires

---

[6]This author does not know to what extent this new labor law is actually being enforced.

payment by the insured up front. The Chinese people are afraid that they will get sick and not have enough money to pay their medical expenses.

The Chinese people also are afraid that corrupt government officials or corporate leaders will misuse and lose their pension funds. People can either save or consume their disposable income. Chinese households save almost 30% of their disposable income out of fear of major health care problems and/or pension funds failing (Prasad, 2009 and Leightner, 2010b). Until China's health care system and pension system problems are fixed, the Chinese people will continue to save, limiting (or preventing) the success of any consumption promoting strategies of the government.

If China could also prevent the exploitation of rural migrants in urban areas and the taking of farm land by local governments (Leightner, 2010a), then a consumption driven model would get a boost from rural spending. Most importantly, if the Chinese could trust each other because any form of corruption or illegal activity was vigorously prosecuted in a fair, transparent and efficient legal system that was accessible to all, regardless of wealth, then the Chinese would fear less and consume more. Finally it is essential that China ensures that the products it produces are safe. Repeated cases of lead paint on toys, melamine in milk and lime in flour reduce the consumption of domestically produced goods.

If the above problems were significantly reduced, then increased consumption could lead to several waves of domestic investment and, thus, growth. Both Japan and the U.S. have enjoyed periods of consumption driven growth. During the 1960s, a substantial increase in the real income for Japan's working class led to several waves of domestic demand driven investment and growth (Ozawa, 1985). During the first wave, Japan's working class purchased automatic rice cookers, washing machines, air conditioners, TVs and automobiles. In response, Japanese companies expanded old factories and built new factories to increase their production of these consumer products. These products also increased the leisure time for Japanese housewives. By 1969, the average Japanese housewife spent less than 8 hours per day on household chores, in contrast to before the war spending 11 hours. Increased leisure time produced increased purchases of, and investment in, the production of domestically made leisure goods and services (Leightner, 2011).

In the 1920s, the U.S. enjoyed several waves of demand driven growth. Rosenberg (2003: p. 4) explains:

> Though invented earlier, the full impact of the automobile on the U.S. economy was not felt until the 1920s. Car production increased three-fold during this decade. This generated strong demand for investment in the automobile industry as well as in other industries dependent on car production such as tires, auto parts, plate glass and steel. Roads and traffic lights needed to be built and gas stations soon followed. The automobile fostered the growth of the suburb. With suburbanization came increased spending on new housing. Many of the new homes would be electrified and have telephones and radios. Thus, investment spending in the electric power, telephone and communications industries took off.

The U.S. and Japan enjoyed periods of consumption driven growth and so could China, if China would implement the key reforms discussed above.

Finally notice that a consumption-driven growth model is not anti-trade. Instead, redistributing money to labor and the poor will cause an increase in the domestic demand for goods, which will cause production for goods sold domestically to increase, *ceteris paribus*. As this happens the percentage of the economy dependent on trade will naturally decline without any anti-trade policies imposed. As a country becomes less dependent on trade, the probability falls that it will face a crisis due to declining foreign demand.

8.4. A Potential Crisis from International Capital Flows

Zheng Xinli (a member of the National Committee of the Chinese People's Political Consultative Conference and deputy director of the Subcommittee of Economy of the advisory body) wrote in July 2011,

> As part of world's ongoing economic adjustments, global inflation triggered by the depreciation of the dollar will continue into the future, which will increase imported inflationary pressures on China, threaten the country's foreign reserve security and constitute an immediate, and indeed, the biggest challenge to its development over the next five years. The

quantitative easing policy adopted by the U.S. Federal Reserve, aimed at shifting the U.S.' economic losses to other countries, has fuelled sharp devaluations of the dollar and global inflation. Given that 70% of China's foreign reserves are dollar-denominated assets, every 1% depreciation of the dollar will lead to more than $10 billion of its foreign reserves evaporating. Also, the dramatic price rises of bulk commodities such as oil, iron ore, beans and cotton in recent years, as a result of the US' adoption of the weak dollar policy, have brought huge pressures to China's manufacturers that are heavily dependent on imports of these commodities. China has achieved success in fending off the first impacts of the global financial crisis, but it has yet to come up with effective measures to better resist the new wave of global inflation in a bid to maintain the safety of its financial assets.

China, like most countries, attempts to fight inflation by decreasing its money supply which causes domestic interest rates to rise. In contrast, interest rates in the U.S. are stuck at approximately 0% due to the U.S. Federal Reserves' continuing policy of quantitative easing. People like to put their assets into countries that have the highest interest rates because they earn the greatest possible return there. Thus as China's interest rate rises, there will be increasing demand for the Chinese yuan and increasing pressure for the Chinese yuan to appreciate. In response, China will either have to purchase even more foreign reserves in order to keep the yuan fixed or it will have to allow the yuan to appreciate.

In this situation, China has several conflicting goals. First, China would like to shift to a consumption driven growth model, without damaging their exports. However, purchasing additional foreign reserves would continue the past policies that aided the producer and exporter at the expense of the consumer. Allowing the yuan to appreciate would hurt exporters, but help consumers. Wei (2011) writes,

The [yuan internationalization] move had important unintended side effects, including giving companies and investors a way to profit from the difference in interest rates between China and other countries, and opening a path for "hot money" to flood the country.... China's stumble in trying to get its currency more widely accepted outside its borders underlie a fundamental contradiction at the heart of Beijing's plans: the Chinese authorities want to keep a tight grip on the value of the yuan to keep exports booming, while at the same time encourage more foreign companies and investors to use it.... There is a "tension in the short run between managing yuan appreciation and increasing the yuan's prominence in global trade and finance transactions," says Brooking Institute China scholar Eswar Prasad.

Furthermore, China has advocated the world shifting away from using the U.S. dollar as the dominant world reserve currency (Leightner, 2011). China has also made it clear that they would like for the yuan to be included in a basket of currencies that would replace the U.S. dollar. Some Chinese scholars have openly advocated the world switching from primarily using the U.S. dollar to the world using the Chinese yuan as the reserve currency. For the Chinese yuan to be considered a reserve currency, it must be more freely floating. China's progressive and steady stream of currency reforms of the last three years indicate that China's dominating goal is to make China's yuan a reserve currency (Blumenstein *et al.*, 2010; LeVine, 2009).

The stronger China's capital controls, the smaller foreign capital flows into China, and, thus, the lower the risk of foreign capital funding a speculative bubble, *ceteris paribus*. The more China dismantles those capital controls in an effort to move the Chinese yuan closer to a free float and, thus, closer to being a world reserve currency, the greater the risk of foreign capital flows funding a speculative bubble (Wei, 2011). Therefore, if China wants to reduce its risk of an externally originating crisis from foreign capital flows, then it must stop (and possibly reverse) its steady and progressive liberalization of its capital account.

The Thai 1997 crisis illustrates the danger that China faces as it eliminates its capital controls while its interest rate rises relative to world interest rates. Thailand opened an international banking sector in 1996 which (for all practical considerations) eliminated Thailand's capital controls. Because interest rates in Thailand, at that time, were 5% higher than world interest rates, foreign capital came flooding into Thailand. Those foreign funds financed the speculative bubble in the Thai real estate market which lead to the Bangkok Bank of Commerce case, the soiling of the reputation of the Central Bank of Thailand, Songprasong Land company defaulting on a one million dollar interest payment for some European debentures and a temporary stopping of the Thai stock market so that Thai regulators could increase the reserve requirements for Thai financial institutions. These events gave George Soros the ammunition he needed to lead a successful speculative attack against the Thai baht (Leightner, 1999 and 2007).

8.5. What China Could do to the U.S. with Its Foreign Currency Reserves

In recent years, China has projected two very different images to the world community. On one hand, China looks like a successful world power when it hosts the Summer Olympics and the World Fair and puts men in outer space. On the other hand, China claims that it is just a developing country, and not a world leader, when challenged to take a leadership role on global moral issues like genocide in the Sudan.

The branch of political economy called "Realism" would argue that China is out to increase its power as much as possible and would dominate the world if it could. China is now the second largest economy on the earth. Indeed China sees the U.S. as its only major remaining rival. If China could cause the U.S. to fall, then China could assume the top, most powerful, position.

China's holdings of U.S. dollar assets, which China accumulated while under its export promotion strategy, is the bullet that China could use to shoot the U.S. If China successfully switches to a domestic consumption driven growth model, then China would no longer need the U.S. as a buyer of its goods and could then cause a fall of the U.S. dollar (by dumping their U.S. dollar assets) without significantly hurting itself.

Some scholars believe that China will not sell its U.S. dollar assets because it would drive down the value of their remaining U.S. dollar assets (Wines *et al.*, 2009). Leightner (2010c: p. 35) finds that the value of the U.S. dollar would fall by 4.42 % in Europe and Asia if China sold 10% of its foreign reserves.

[Thus] if 1.27 trillion of China's reserves are in U.S. dollar assets (or 65% of the total reserves as estimated by Molinski, 2007), then China selling

10% of its reserves (for 195.4 billion dollars) could cause the value of China's remaining reserves to fall by 50.5 billion dollars ($1.27 \times 0.90 \times 0.0442$), greatly diminishing China's return. Given this large effect, China has the incentive to either sell none of its U.S. dollar reserves or to sell all of its U.S. dollar reserves. If China was convinced that the value of the U.S. dollar would fall by a significant amount, no matter what China did, then it would be rational for China to sell as many of its U.S. dollar assets as possible and as quickly as possible. If China sold all of its U.S. dollar reserves then the value of the U.S. dollar would plummet by at least 44% which would cause the value of U.S. exports to fall by 44% (as measured in other currencies) and the dollar price the U.S. pays for imports to increase by 44%. Such changes in exports and imports would drive the U.S. economy much further into recession.

This author has heard several Chinese scholars say that China's currency, the yuan, should move "from the periphery to the center where it belongs." China is now steadily implementing currency reforms (Blumenstein *et al.*, 2010) which could be viewed as a preparation for the yuan to make a bid to replace the dollar as the world's reserve currency (LeVine, 2009). If China wants the yuan to replace the dollar as the world's reserve currency, then China might want to orchestrate a massive fall in the value of the dollar (by selling all of its holdings of U.S. dollar assets at one time), once the yuan is ready.

China would minimize its own losses from a massive selling of its U.S. dollar reserves if it set up people to sell parts of those reserves at the same time in different locations. If timed well, then most of China's reserves could be sold at the exchange rate that prevailed immediately before China began its selling. For this to work, China must not divulge its plans to anyone. For the rest of Asia, such a move would destroy the value of their U.S. dollar reserves, causing a fall in international confidence in the rest of Asia. Such a move could throw Asia, and indeed the entire international financial system, into crisis.

What can the world and the U.S. do to prevent such a scenario? China has legitimately accumulated 2.85 trillion dollars of foreign reserves by December 2010, of which 2 trillion is U.S. dollar denominated assets (based on Zheng's 2011 claim that 70% of China's reserves are U.S. dollar denominated). It is as if China has loaned the U.S. 2 trillion dollars and there is no ethical way for the U.S. to avoid its responsibility for that debt. Zheng (2011) expressing Chinese concern over the safety of its U.S. denominated financial assets is legitimate.

However, the world and the U.S. can legitimately argue that there should be restrictions on how that debt is used. All around the world, people purchase knives; however, the legal systems of the world tell those people that they cannot use those knives to stab other people. Furthermore, to purchase guns, there is often a required waiting period. The world community should tell China that it cannot use its massive foreign reserves to destroy the U.S. by selling all (or a major part) of its reserves at one time. Furthermore, requiring even an hour waiting period when massive blocks of currency are sold would make it possible for the world to recognize any synchronized selling of currency blocks at different locations. Finally, if there was an international agency that prohibited the use of foreign reserves in economic warfare, then that agency could nullify massive sells of a currency. China would be allowed to slowly divest its U.S. dollar reserves, it would just be prohibited against dumping its reserves in such a way that would destroy the U.S. and destabilize the international financial system.

Such an agency could also be justified based on the public good nature of trust. When a few Thai banks went into crisis in 1996–1997, they destroyed confidence in the entire Thai banking system which caused all Thai banks (the good and the bad) to be hurt (Leightner and Alam, 2002). Likewise when Thailand went into crisis in 1997, it caused international confidence in all of Asia to fall, generating crises in Indonesia and South Korea. Problems in Asia led to a fall in confidence for all developing countries, leading to crises in Brazil and Russia. Because trust is a public good, it is appropriate to set up agencies that will protect that trust for the good of the entire world. China must not be allowed to use its massive foreign reserves in economic warfare.

8.6. Conclusion

In 2008–2009 China faced an externally originating crisis due to its exports to the U.S. falling. In order to reduce the possibility of being hurt in a similar way in the future, China's government is advocating a switch from an export driven growth model to a domestic consumption driven growth model. Whether or not China will be able to successfully make this switch is not yet obvious. China will have to fix some major problems (like its broken health care and pension systems) before such a switch could occur.

Meanwhile, interest rates are rising in China (as China combats inflation by lowering its money supply) while interest rates in the U.S. remain at practically zero (due to the continuing commitment of the U.S. to quantitative easing). This situation opens China up for another type of externally originating crisis if China continues to liberate its foreign capital controls. If China wants the Chinese yuan to become a world reserve currency, then it needs to liberate its capital controls. However, liberating its capital controls while Chinese interest rates are much higher than world interest rates could lead to a flood of foreign capital entering China, which then might fund a speculative bubble in China's real estate market.

Finally, China's current holding of 2 trillion dollars of dollar denominated assets makes it possible for China to orchestrate a massive fall in the value of the dollar. Such a fall in the value of the U.S. dollar might make it possible for China to replace the U.S. as the world's dominant country. If China can successfully switch to a domestic consumption driven growth model, then China would no longer need the U.S. as a buyer of its goods. In that case, causing the U.S. to fall so that China can rise might be viewed as worth any associated risk by Beijing. The only way to prevent this scenario is to set up an international agency that would prohibit the use of foreign currency reserves in economic warfare. Such an agency would not prohibit China from slowly and steadily divesting its U.S. dollar denominated assets; however, it would prevent any massive selling that could destroy the U.S., destabilize the international financial system and throw all of Asia (including China itself) into another crisis.

References

Batson, Andrew (2009) "China Takes Aim at Dollar," *Wall Street Journal*, March 24. Available at: http://online.wsj.com/article/SB123780272456212885.html. Accessed on 9th October 2009.

Blumenstein, Rebecca, Andrew Browne and Dinny McMahon (2010) "China Deflects Pressure for Yuan Rise," *Wall Street Journal*, September 1, Vol. 1–6, p. A9.

Chang, Anita (2010) "China Premier Wen Jiabao Says Japanese Companies Wages Too Low," *Huffington Post*, August 29. Available at: http://www.huffingtonpost.com/2010/08/29/wen-jiabao-china-wages-japanese-companies_n_698297.html. Accessed on 1st September.

IMF (2008) *International Financial Statistics Yearbook: 2008*.

"Legislature Proposes Narrowing the Gap in Wealth," *China Daily On Line*, August 24, 2010.

Leightner, Jonathan E. (2011) "Chinese Overtrading," In Steven Rosefielde, Masaaki Kuboniwa and Satoshi Mizobata (eds.), *Two Asias: The Emerging Postcrisis Divide*, Singapore: World Scientific Publishers.

Leightner, Jonathan E. (2010a) "Alternative Property Systems for China," *China: An International Journal*, Vol. 8, No. 2, pp. 346–359.

Leightner, Jonathan E. (2010b) "Are the Forces that Cause China's Trade Surplus with the USA Good?" *Journal of Chinese Economic and Foreign Trade Studies*, Vol. 3, No. 1, pp. 43–53.

Leightner, Jonathan E. (2010c) "How China's Holdings of Foreign Reserves Affect the Value of the U.S. Dollar in Europe and Asia," *China and World Economy*, Vol. 18, No. 3, pp. 24–39.

Leightner, Jonathan E. (2009) "How the Crisis is Killing One Asian Development Model, While Birthing Another One," (in Chinese), In Chi Fulin and Yin Zhongyi (eds.), *Transformation of Development Models and Reforms in the Post-Crisis Period*, Beijing: Huawen Publishing Corporation, pp. 134–144.

Leightner, Jonathan E. (2007) "Thailand's Financial Crisis: Its Causes, Consequences, and Implications," *Journal of Economic Issues*, Vol. 41, No. 1, pp. 61–76.

Leightner, Jonathan E. (2005) "Utility Maximization, Morality, and Religion," *Journal of Economic Issues*, Vol. 39, No. 2, pp. 375–381.

Leightner, Jonathan E. (1999) "Globalization and Thailand's Financial Crisis," *Journal of Economic Issues*, Vol. 33, No. 2, pp. 367–373.

Leightner, Jonathan E. and Ila M. Semenick Alam (2002) "Financial Crisis Hypotheses and the Productivity of Thailand's Financial Institutions," In Tsu-tan Fu, Cliff J. Huang and C.A. Knox Lovell (eds.), *Productivity and Economic Performance in the Asia–Pacific Region*, Northampton, MA: Edward Elgar Publishing, Ltd, pp. 410–432.

Leightner, Jonathan E. and Tomoo Inoue (2007) "Tackling the Omitted Variables Problem without the Strong Assumptions of Proxies," *European Journal of Operational Research*, Vol. 178, No. 3, pp. 819–840.

LeVine, Steve (2009) "China's Yuan: The Next Reserve Currency?" BusinessWeek, May 26. Available at: http://www.businessweek.com/print/globalbiz/content/may2009/gb20090522_665312.htm. Accessed on 14th October 2009.

Lindsey, Lawrence B. (2006) "Yuan Compromise?" *Wall Street Journal*, April 6, p. A14.

Modigliani, Franco and Shi Larry Cao (2004) "The Chinese Saving Puzzle and the Life-Cycle Hypothesis," *Journal of Economic Literature*, Vol. 42, No. 1, pp. 145–170.

Molinski, Dan (2007) "Dollar Pummeled on Report by China over its Reserves," *Wall Street Journal*, November 8, p. C5.

Naughton, Barry (2007) *The Chinese Economy: Transitions and Growth*, Cambridge, Massachusetts: MIT Press.

Ozawa, T. (1985) "Macroeconomic Factors Affecting Japan's Technology Inflows and Outflows: The Postwar Experience," In N. Rosenberg and C. Frischtak (eds.), *International Technology Transfer: Concepts, Measures, and Comparisons*, New York: Praeger, pp. 233–234.

Prasad, Eswar S. (2009) Rebalancing Growth in Asia. Available at: http://www.fullermoney.com/content/2009-07-17/RebalGrowthinAsia.July09.pdf. Accessed on 3rd August 2009. An earlier version of the paper was presented at the NIPFP-DEA conference in New Delhi in March of 2009.

Rosenberg, Samuel (2003) *American Economic Development Since 1945: Growth, Decline, and Rejuvenation*, New York, Palgrave Macmillan.

Wei, Lingling and Rob Davis (2011) "China Stumbles in Yuan Grand Plan," *Wall Street Journal*, July 15.

Wines, Michael, Keith Bradsher and Mark Landler (2009) "China's Leader Says He is Worried Over U.S. Treasuries," *The New York Times On-Line*, March 14. Available at: http://www.nytimes.com/2009/03/14/world/asia/14china.html?_r=1 &pagewanted=print. Assessed on 1st May 2009.

Xin Zhiming (2008) "Transfer Payments Set to Rise," *China Daily*, April 17, p. 13.

Zheng Xinli (2011) "Coping with Global Inflation," *China Daily*, July 14. Available at: http://www.chinadaily.com.cn/opinion/2011-07/14/content_12898687.htm. Accessed on 14th July 2011.

CHAPTER 9

CHINA'S ECONOMIC FUTURE

AKIO KAWATO

Winston Churchill famously said that the Soviet Union "...is a riddle, wrapped in a mystery, inside an enigma, but there is a key. The key is Russian national interest."[1] The same principle applies to China's economy. It is a riddle, wrapped in a mystery, however it can be deciphered through the lens of conflict between capitalistic growth, and the remnants of socialist authoritarianism. On one hand, it seems as if the economy is an unstoppable growth engine,[2] and on the other hand "catch up" theory and the Soviet experience suggest that it will run out of steam, or even implode. Which of these futures is the most likely,[3] and what role will China play in tomorrow's world?

9.1. The Negative Factors in the Chinese Economy

At first the global financial crisis did not seriously impair China's GDP growth, thanks to the government's 50 billion dollar counter crisis

---

[1]"I cannot forecast to you the action of Russia. It is a riddle, wrapped in a mystery, inside an enigma; but perhaps there is a key. That key is Russian national interest." Radio broadcast in October 1939.

[2]IndexMundi says that China's GDP in real purchasing power in 2010 stands at 10.09 trillion dollars (the U.S. GDP in 2010 was 14.5 trillion dollars). Available at: http://www.indexmundi.com/china/gdp(purchasing power parity).html.

[3]The same uncertainty applied to Japan's economic future before it was beset by two "lost decades." See Paul Krugman, "The Myth of Asia's Miracle," *Foreign Affairs*, Vol. 73, No. 6, (November/December 1994), pp. 62–78. *cf.* Zbigniew Brzezinski, *Fragile Blossom: Crisis and Change in Japan*, New York: Harper and Row, 1972.

stimulus package,[4] but loose monetary policy and credit expansion stoked the fires of inflation,[5] overheated the realty market,[6] and created an Everest of potentially bad loans in major state banks.[7] The situation is fluid and regionally diverse. Realty prices started falling in many places in 2011,[8] raising the specter of deflation.

This could hurt the construction sector, the current mainstay of China's economic growth,[9] and aggregate economic growth could be

---

[4]The Chinese State Council declared on November 9, 2008, that 4 trillion Yuan will be allocated toward the end of 2010 to stimulate the economy. One third of it will be financed by the budget of the government.

[5]In June 2011 the CPI rose by 6.4% as compared to June 2010.

[6]An objective picture about the realty market prices is very hard to obtain. Christian Science Monitor for example reports on April 15, 2011, that those prices in Beijing rose 8 times in recent 8 years.

[7]Under the umbrella of the stimulus package published on November 9, 2008, the "Local Financial Platforms" (地方融资平台), disguised financial bodies of local governments, actively borrowed money from state banks, and invested the money on development and construction.

About the sum of their total borrowings a spokesman of the People's Bank of China denied the rumors that the amount is around 14 trillion Yuan (2.22 trillion dollars).

(Available at: http://finance.sina.com.cn/money/future/fmnews/20110713/021910137511. shtml.)

The Japanese journal *"Toa"* (「東亜」) reported that the amount was more than 7 trillion Yuan as of the end of 2009 (p. 4, April 2010). Even this "smaller" sum corresponds to 15% of the entire lending (47 trillion Yuan) by all financial institutions in China (from the same URL as above).

[8]Dow Jones Newswires on June 26 2011 reported that the prices of new homes in Beijing plunged 26.7% month-on-month in March, referring to the Beijing News on June 21.

[9]According to 中国统计年鉴 (*"China Statistical Yearbook"*, National Bureau of Statistics of China) 2007, "Investment on fixed assets" occupied 52% (an exorbitantly high level) of the total GDP of China in 2006. The amount of the investment on fixed assets grew by 23.9%. (Available at: http://www.stats.gov.cn/tjsj/ndsj/.) This means that the growth of the investment on fixed assets counted for as much as 78.5% of the economic growth of China in 2006 (GDP grew by 14.7%). Therefore, if financing of construction and investment be disrupted, it will severely affect the whole economy. On July 5, 2011, Asian stocks fell after Moody's Investors Service announced Chinese mainland lenders may hold more problem loans on their books than had been anticipated (Bloomberg on the same day). The next day, the Singaporean official investment fund "Temasek Holdings" has sold 3.6 billion U.S. dollars of the stocks of the Chinese main state banks.

slowed by reduced bank lending. Prospects for robust foreign direct investment (FDI) growth also are dimming due to other factors. First of all, the myth of the "endless supply of cheap labor forces from provinces" no longer holds; wages in the coastal area are rising steeply.[10] The appreciating yuan is eroding the competitiveness of foreign-owned export companies. Moreover, Chinese authorities are abolishing favorable treatment previously accorded foreign firms, further reducing profitability.[11] These adverse trends are prodding foreign exporters to investment elsewhere, in Vietnam, ASEAN, and Latin America.

The inflow of FDI continued in 2011,[12] but it was targeted at import substitution opportunities, rather than export creation. Japanese and other foreign firms are intent on producing directly for China's home market.[13]The "Use the Chinese cheap labor for export-oriented production" model is losing its allure; a shift that may retard China's economic growth.[14]

---

[10]"Thousands of Workers Protest at Sanyo's China Plant, " *Yahoo!Finance*, January 1, 2012. "Thousands of Chinese workers protesting over compensation and job security at a Sanyo Electric Co Ltd plant clashed with police in southern Shenzhen, media said on Monday, the latest outbreak of labor unrest in China's manufacturing hub."

[11]In January 2008, a new Labor Law came into force. Now even foreign firms are obliged to grant life-time employment to workers employed for more than ten years. From December 1, 2010, all preferential treatments in taxation were to be abolished for the foreign firms in China (*Nikkei* Newspaper, October 23, 2010). Last but not least the gradual appreciation of Yuan coupled with the recent inflation raised the Yuan's rate effectively by more than 10% on annual basis (Treasury Secretary Geithner's White House briefing, January 14, 2011). This will work against the foreign firms which use China as a platform for exports to the U.S.

[12]In the first half of 2011 the overall amount of FDI increased by 18.4% as compared to the same period in 2010. (*JETRO*, Vol. 15, 2011.Available at: http://www.jetro.go.jp/jfile/report/07000722/cn_2011_1_invest.pdf.)

[13]Japanese firms directed 50.9% of their total investment in China to non-manufacturing sector in the first half of 2011 (*ibid.*)

[14]For an analysis of this complex matter see Chapter 8 in this volume. China's growth is likely to slow due to diminishing returns to FDI as it catches up to the west's high per capita income frontier. See Rosefielde, Steven, Masaaki Kuboniwa and Satoshi Mizobata, eds., *Two Asias: The Emerging Postcrisis Divide*, World Scientific Publishers, Singapore, 2011.

9.2. Does China Possess Conditions for Sustained Growth in the Light of the British Experience of Industrialization?

Can China continue its rapid ascent under these new conditions? It would not be the first time that its growth faltered. Is it destined to repeat past failures? The British experience illuminates the matter.

Before the Industrial Revolution, global wealth grew slowly. The whole world was a zero-sum economy, and only military conquest and plunder (for example, Spain's "discovery" of Peruvian gold) increased the wealth of nations. When the supply of gold and silver dwindled, and slavery was prohibited in the 18th century, British merchants and the gentry sought prosperity in mass-producing cheap cotton textiles for the European, American and Indian markets. India wanted to protect its domestic cotton manufacturing industry, but the British prevailed and profited. Wealth grew thanks to industrialization with a flow from Asia to Europe,[15] allowing Britain to thrive for 150 years, but eventually its forward progress slowed to a crawl.

Today, the situation is just the reverse. China has become the world's workshop, and the de-industrialized West has become the principal buyer of Beijing's manufactures. Enormous wealth is being transferred from the "advanced countries" to China through foreign direct investment and current account surplus to the west that have allowed the Middle Kingdom to accumulate 3.2 trillion dollars worth of foreign currency reserves. This exchange is mutually beneficial, but China is reaping the lion's share,[16] just the reverse of the earlier pattern.

This is not the first time China has been the world's workshop. It was the dominant worldwide supplier of porcelain, silk goods and other luxury items for long periods during the Middle Ages in the West. China's economy reached its apogee in the 11th century. It produced iron with coke and invented paper, the compass and gunpowder. During the Ming Dynasty, the Middle Kingdom became a great maritime commercial power,[17] and small textile workshops flourished near large cities.

---

[15]There is a controversy on who, Britain or India, benefitted more from the British rule.

[16]Ironically, Europe and the U.S. are being adversely affected by large narcotics inflows from China, just as China was previously harmed by British opium in the 19th century.

[17]Zheng He's great voyages made in 1405–1433. According to "Míngshi", the length of the largest ship was about 140 m.

These advances were real, but they did not constitute an authentic industrial revolution — mass, machine-based, production. There were many constraints. First, the domestic market was saturated with cheap manufactures, and the population was overwhelmingly composed of poor farmers and peasants. China did not have markets abroad, and even if competitive large-scale industrial enterprises had developed, the Imperial government would have suppressed them to buttress its monopoly powers. The Chinese elite preferred to safeguard its high social status and privileges, defend monopolies and sinecures, serve the government, and suppress new entrants. Although small scale private business was bustling in medieval China, big businesses like salt production and foreign trade were under strict government control. Indeed, China had many prerequisites for industrialization: capital, labor, iron, coal, and technology, but lacked sufficient domestic demand, colonies, and competitive scope.

9.3. Bloated Government — China's Imperial and Socialist Legacies

China attempted to modernize twice after the Ming Dynasty. Toward the end of the Qing Dynasty, it built European-type factories in the coastal area, but these state-led initiatives, concentrated in the munitions sector, were inefficient. It tried again during the Republican period,[18] but the civil war and the Second Sino-Japanese War thwarted the effort.

Today China is once again a global player and its domestic economy is gradually becoming more vibrant. But Party-state prerogatives as before could easily become paralytic.[19] Chinese state enterprises have started to grow more powerful again,[20] partly due to the global financial crisis's adverse affect on small private firms, and partly to government reconsoli-

---

[18] In order to make up for the decrease of imports from Europe Chinese investors built more than 600 factories in China during 1912–1919 (Matsumaru, Michio *et al. History of China*, Vol. 5, Yamakawa Publishing House, Tokyo, 2002, p. 142).

[19] The "party-state" is a concept which Sun Yat-sen imported from the new-born Soviet Union. Sun Yat-sen considered that the one-party dictatorship, in which government, army and economy are directly subjected to one party, would serve best for unification of the country and a quick economic development.

[20] In China it is called 国进民退 (state firms go forward as private business goes back).

dation. In November 2009, almost all private firms were obliged to host Communists Party's sub-organization. And some politicians started to play the old communist ideology card[21] in anticipation of the next Communist Party Congress (in 2012), which would choose Hu Jintao's successor.

Authoritarian rule may hothouse rapid economic growth at low stages of economic development,[22] but in an advanced economy it is likely to be counterproductive.[23] The absence of free elections, moreover, makes it difficult for China to eradicate debilitating and destabilizing problems like corruption and income inequality. On the other hand a haphazard democratization may destabilize the society because politicians and political parties would rush for control of state revenues and assets, instead of responsibly governing the country. Achieving socially beneficial governance is likely to be China's greatest challenge.[24]

9.4. How Long Will Deng Xiaoping's Magic — Beijing Consensus Helped by Foreign Capital — Hold?

Shortly after Mao Zedong's death, Deng Xiaoping began a market-oriented industrialization campaign. He partially liberalized the economy by deregulating agriculture and light industry in 1979, and after the Tiananmen incident in 1989, opened China to direct foreign investment. Firms in Taiwan, Hong Kong and then Japan, suffering from rapid

---

[21] This pertains most of all to Bo Xi-Lai, in Chong-Qing Party Secretary, who got dismissed in March 2012, He promoted collective performance of old revolutionary songs.

[22] Alexander Gerschenkron, *Economic Backwardness in Historical Perspective*, Cambridge MA: Belknap Press, 1962.

[23] One may counterargue that if Japan were able to develop its economy thanks to its strong "authoritarian" government, China would be able to emulate this. But besides the presence of free election in Japan there are stark differences between Japan and China; Japanese government (in principle) does not directly meddle in business (especially in manufacturing industry), the pools of personnel for the government and private firms are strictly separate, and private ownership of property is very well protected in Japan under rule of law.

[24] Incidentally, the party-state is very similar to the Chinese imperial rule with strong bureaucracy — their tradition for more than 1,000 years. This system is more congenial for the Chinese than the Western-type democracis.

appreciation of their currencies after the Plaza Accord in 1985, rushed to invest their money in China as an outsourcing platform for their exports to the U.S. and the EU.

The West (including Japan) built factories in China, exported machinery and high-tech components to them for final assembly with "cheap Chinese labor" for re-export abroad. The dollars earned from these exports were held by the government and invested for the most part in U.S. treasury bonds, financing American economic growth and boosting consumer imports from China. This economic symbiosis was mutually agreeable. All participants were willing to maintain the political status quo to preserve regional stability, vital for free trade and investment.

The Lehman Brothers crisis disrupted this cozy relationship. China's exports plunged from 337.8 billion dollars in 2008 to 296.4 billion dollars in 2009.[25] To compensate for the loss, the Chinese Government introduced a huge 4 trillion Yuan stimulus package.[26] It brought a respite for the economy[27] and bolstered rapid growth encouraging Beijing to become more assertive with its neighbors and the U.S. However, the massive spending and loan program stoked inflation and a real estate bubble that is beginning to burst. Deng Xiaoping's model for economic development with its heavy dependence on foreign investment and exports appears to be sputtering. As long as China's growth depends on wealth transfers from abroad, its growth will hinge on the west's economic health and import absorption possibilities. China has an alternative. Beijing leaders can attempt to switch to domestic-demand-driven growth as leaders now claim they are doing,[28] but this apparently poses severe inflationary risks.

China is trying to build a vibrant modern economy with a Soviet type "party-state" governance system strewn with social injustice. It has been able to manage the growth process successfully thus far thanks to the large inflow of the wealth from abroad and loose bank credits, but how long it can last — that is the critical question.

---

[25]In 2010 the Chinese exports to the U.S. rebounded to the level of 364.9 billion dollars.
[26]See footnote 2.
[27]For examples subsidy was given for purchasing electric appliances and automobiles. Thanks to this measure the sales of both items went up substantially.
[28]See Chapter 8 of this volume.

9.5. Muddling Through Instead of a Catastrophe

China could muddle through. There are pluses that might counterbalance the negatives, even if its real estate bubble bursts. First, major banks may be allowed to write off their loans to the local financial "Platforms" (regional and municipal authorities). Second, a part of Beijing's huge foreign currency reserves may be shifted to major state banks to strengthen their balance sheets.[29] Third, the Chinese government may increase bank deposits by creating money through compulsory purchase of government bonds by People's Bank of China (a Bernanke-style QE2 gambit). The indebtedness of the Chinese government is still very low in comparison to Western populist governments.[30] Lastly, China is entitled to avail itself of IMF credits, even though it seems to have sufficient foreign currency reserves to handle almost any contingency.[31] Its hard currency reserves vastly exceed the IMF's.[32]

Likewise, China's exports to the U.S. started to rebound. They peaked in 2008 at 337.8 billion dollars, plunged to 296.4 billion dollars in 2009, but recovered in 2010 to a record high 364.9 billion dollars (the U.S.'s trade deficit vis-à-vis China reached 273.1 billion dollars — a record, too).[33] And if the U.S. economy starts rolling again (and an EU crisis is averted), the halcyon days may be restored. Beijing, Washington and others will prosper, and China will become more cooperative.

Once an economy accumulates substantial capital, savings and industrial capacity, it can muddle through avoiding a total collapse. I remember

---

[29] In December 2003, 45 billion US dollars were transferred from the foreign currency reserves to Bank of China and Construction Bank of China. (*People's Daily*, http://j. people.com.cn/2004/01/07/jp20040107_35652.html). Now, the total sum of the loans to the local real estate "Platforms" is estimated at 7–14 trillion Yuan (1–2 trillion dollars). Even if 50% of these loans become insolvent, it is well below the amount of China's foreign currency reserves.

[30] The Chinese government foresees less than 10% of financial deficit for 2011. (Japanese "*Economist*", April 5, 2011, Hidetoshi Tashiro).

[31] At the end of March 2011 it exceeded 3 trillion U.S. dollars. This amount dwarfs the capacity of the IMF.

[32] The capital of the IMF is to be doubled to about 800 billion dollars pending ratification by some member countries.

[33] Calculated by the U.S.-China Business Council (Available at: http://www.uschina.org/statistics/tradetable.html).

my Russian friends' astonishment after visiting Japan in the nineties, saying, "If an economic depression is like that in Japan, we Russians would be eager to have one!" China, too, may have passed the threshold where its deficiencies are no longer life threatening. Its civilian-based economy is far more robust than the Soviet Union's structurally militarized regime.[34] It may well surpass the U.S. as the world's largest economy soon (but not per capita income), and play an increasingly large role on the world political stage. But even then America will be able to retain a military and soft power edge (values, media and etc.).

China, thus, is unlikely to become a unipolar hegemon, or sink into the abyss. Likewise, Asia need not divide into two camps — decrepit Japan and prosperous China, or vice versa. As David Ricardo demonstrated two centuries ago, China's continued growth should benefit Japan's economy, not harm it.[35]

The economies of the East Asian countries are becoming more and more intertwined. Firms of Japan, the U.S., the EU, China, India, South Korea, Taiwan, ASEAN countries have built a vast integrated economic network based on the division of labor. Rivalries will persist, but their fates are co-dependent. The U.S. is a vital element of this system: guarantor of the values of freedom and democracy, mainstay for maintaining the status quo and provider of capital and innovation. It may even reinvigorate its own industrial production as the wage level in China rises to the American norm. The U.S. dollar will remain as the most important instrument for international commerce.

This emerging global system is intricate, but if major powers behave rationally, Asia with Japan, the U.S. and China in it will successfully muddle through.[36]

---

[34]Rosefielde, Steven, *Russian Economy from Lenin to Putin*, New York: Wiley, 2007. The term "structural militarization" was coined by Vitaly Shlykov, Deputy Chairman of Yeltsin Defense Council.

[35]Ricardo, David, *On the Principle of Political Economy and Taxation*, 1817. Japan has been enjoying large trade surplus vis-à-vis China.

[36] After writing this chapter there arose three major changes; firstly the slowing down of China's economic growth secondly mounting grievances with attack on foreign properties and thirdly defying foreign policy which antagonizes surrounding countries. It things further develop in this manner, it may trigger a new Cold War with China in the role of the USSR.

CHAPTER 10

OPTIMAL ASIAN DOLLAR SURPLUS

ERIC FISHER

10.1. Introduction

This chapter explores a two-country model where money serves as a store of value. It shows that imbalanced trade is the norm. It emphasizes that a surplus country absorbs its trading partner's fiscal expansion because every country experiences gains from trade. But the deficit country is in a stronger bargaining position since it has a greater role for money as a store of value under autarky. In dividing the gains from trade equally, the surplus country is willing to tax its own residents as a part of the cost of gaining access to the world trading system.

This presents a novel way of thinking about the large bilateral trade imbalances that have given rise to the Asian dollar surplus in the last decade. A trade surplus is just the counterpart of a pattern of asset accumulation. I will argue that China has accumulated a historically unprecedented level of dollar-denominated assets as the counterpart of the gains from becoming more deeply integrated into the world trading system. No country benefits from running perpetual trade surpluses, but every country benefits from the gains from trade. I will show that a natural way of dividing the gains from trade might well give rise to a pattern of asset accumulation in which one country agrees to accommodate the deficit of another because the latter gives up some local seigniorage. Both countries gain from trade, but when they split the surplus equally, one country runs a deficit and the other runs a surplus willingly.

I use the model of overlapping generations to flesh out these ideas. The paradigm emphasizes that money serves as a store of value; it builds on

Samuelson's (1958) notion of the social contrivance of money. I have shown elsewhere (Fisher, 1990) that countries can run *any* pattern of trade in this model. The intuition is that one has to think of the overall pattern of asset creation in the world economy, and one government's surplus can be offset by another's deficit. There is an ineluctable element of cooperation in the creation of international liquidity. This idea echoes the old notion that in a system of fixed exchange rates $n-1$ countries are free to choose independent debt policies but the $n-th$ country must adjust so that the world's needs for liquidity are met. In a world with only two countries, the surplus country accommodates its trading partner's deficit, while providing sufficient liquidity to insure the dynamic efficiency of the world economy.

The model of overlapping generations allows for a simple and cogent description of seignorage, the resources that accrue to a monetary authority by virtue of its ability to create money. Seigniorage is the transfer of purchasing power to the residents of a country that creates money balances. An important equilibrium condition is that every currency bear the same rate of return; the intuition is that all moneys are perfect substitutes as stores of value. In a model with several countries, there are several monetary authorities. Indeed, in a world with complete capital mobility and free trade in goods, the simplest *definition* of a country is that it has a monetary authority whose currency is valued. One country can create all the liquidity for the world economy, or all countries can agree, implicitly or explicitly, on a division of seignorage when the need for international liquidity arises.

Monetary theorists who emphasize that the model of overlapping generation is a model of money *per se* are disingenuous. I prefer to stress that it is a model of national debt, since paper assets bear a rate of return equal to that on capital in economies with an explicit structure for production across time. Hence the strict interpretation, in this chapter, of seigniorage is the pattern of creation and then absorption of national debts in a model with several countries. If one country creates debt in excess of the savings needs of its own residents, it will run a trade deficit. This trade imbalance follows immediately from the accounting identity that emphasizes the equality between a trade deficit and the acquisition of claims on local capital by foreigners. Hence my theoretical explanation for the Asian dollar surplus is that the Chinese willingly accommodate a large fraction of the national debt of the U.S.

It is easy to see the advantage in this arrangement for the deficit country: it gets imports in return for otherwise worthless fiat money. But what is in it for the surplus country? Both countries gain from trade, and the right way of framing this question is to ask: Are the surplus country's gains from trade sufficient to offset the burden imposed by absorbing the trading partner's fiscal expansion? This way of posing the question highlights the insight that the two countries are involved in an implicit bargain over how to divide the gains from trade. I model the outcome of the bargaining process as the Nash solution to a cooperative game. Rubinstein (1982) shows how this division might arise as the Nash equilibrium in a repeated (noncooperative) game with discounting. For me, the Nash bargaining solution just picks one point in the core of a cooperative game that characterizes the world economy aptly.

This solution has attractive efficiency properties. The equilibrium allocations are Pareto optimal; intuitively, real interest rates are not less than the growth rate of the world economy. The country under autarky that has a role for the social contrivance of money is in a stronger bargaining position. It needs to be bribed a bit more to enter into the world trading system. The price of this bribe is that its trading partner accommodate a modest deficit.[1]

There are two kinds of gains from trade in any dynamic general equilibrium model: (1) the usual static ones in which trade across space cannot make any country worse off; and (2) the dynamic ones in which the social contrivance of money facilitates trade across time. This kind of gain may permit a Pareto improvement from a situation of *inter-temporal autarky*. Members of each generation can borrow and lend across international borders; the monetary theorist thinks of this kind of inter-temporal trade

---

[1]Of course, no country in the world — most especially China or the U.S. — is under autarky. Here I am using the international economist's pleasant theoretical fiction of describing an equilibrium for a country if it were forced to separate itself from the world trading system. In fact, the country whose autarkic allocations are not Pareto optimal is the one that has the greater need for the social contrivance of money. In essence, creating an interest-bearing national debt raises current welfare with no deleterious effect on future generations.

as inside money, since these asset trades clear in each generation. But there is another kind of asset trade inherent in the creation of outside money in the form of international reserves for the world economy. In the right circumstances, the creation of world debt makes everyone in the world economy — now and in the future — better off.

My analysis abstracts from important considerations of default risk. I use the concept of a perfect foresight equilibrium. No country ever defaults on its sovereign debt, and no interest rate includes any risk premium. This is an obvious limitation of the model, and China bears the risk of implicit default to the extent that the U.S. will monetize its national debt in the future. Indeed, China is currently paying a substantial inflation tax on the stock of dollar-denominated debt that it already owns. This tax will be exacerbated to the extent that the dollar continues to depreciate against a broad basket of international currencies. Extending my theoretical observations to a stochastic environment is an open and likely fruitful avenue of future research.

My contribution is to show that two governments, both rational actors, will agree on a large imbalance of asset flows because one needs access to international markets and the other has a role under autarky for a positive level of national debt. Song, Storesletten and Zilliboti (2011) develop another model grounded in neoclassical economics. Theirs concentrates on asset market imperfections. Local entrepreneurial firms finance investments through internal savings. State-owned firms have low productivity but survive because of better (political) access to credit markets. Productive firms grow more quickly than politically connected ones if local entrepreneurs have sufficiently high savings. The downsizing of financially integrated politically connected firms forces domestic savings to be invested abroad, generating a foreign surplus. Their work plays on tensions within China, whereas mine highlight those between China and the U.S.

The rest of this chapter is structured as follows. In the Section 2, I review some salient facts about China's pattern of accumulation of dollar-denominated assets; the point here is to emphasize that understanding trade imbalances is perhaps best accomplished by analyzing a model of long-run asset accumulation. Section 3 presents the model and derives its equilibrium. Section 4 discusses the division of seigniorage from the

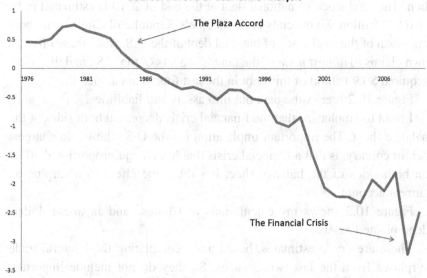

Figure 10.1. Net international investment position of the U.S.

creation of international reserves, and Section 5 gives some concluding remarks and suggestions for the direction of future research.

10.2. China's Dollar Surplus

Figure 10.1 shows the net international investment position of the U.S.

At the end of 2009, it was −$2.7 trillion. Chinese ownership of the official assets of the U.S. in the middle of 2010 was roughly $2.25 trillion.[2] Let me put these numbers in perspective. The U.S. GDP was approximately

---

[2]The Bureau of Economic Analysis shows assets owned by foreigners in the U.S. The total assets owned by corporations based in Hong Kong at the end of 2007 were $10.1 billion. Assets owned by corporations based in China were not reported because they were so few. So I calculated that all assets owned by China are held in the form of official assets, and the USITC reports bilateral trade balances with China from 1986 through the middle of 2010. I have reported their sum.

$14 trillion. Since the capital-output ratio of the U.S. is roughly 2.5, a good estimate for the value of all *tangible* assets in the U.S. is around $35 trillion. The total stock of national debt at the end of 2010 is estimated to be also $14 trillion. So officials in the People's Republic of China own about one-sixth of the total stock of national debt of the U.S. Also, these officials own claims to *almost none* of the tangible assets of the U.S., and they have acquired $0.9 trillion of this debt in the last four years alone.

Figure 10.2 breaks the data out into assets and liabilities.

I want to emphasize that the financial crisis decreased both sides of the balance sheet. The important implication for the U.S., the world's largest debtor country, is that a financial crisis that has an equiproportional effect on both sides of the balance sheet has the same effect as a surplus on current account.

Figure 10.3 shows my calculations of Chinese and Japanese dollar-denominated assets.

These are crude estimates, based upon cumulating the bilateral trade surpluses from the last two decades. So they do not include important

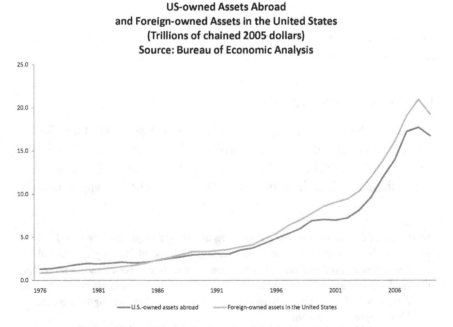

**US-owned Assets Abroad
and Foreign-owned Assets in the United States
(Trillions of chained 2005 dollars)
Source: Bureau of Economic Analysis**

──── U.S.-owned assets abroad   ──── Foreign-owned assets in the United States

Figure 10.2.   U.S. assets abroad and foreign assets in the U.S.

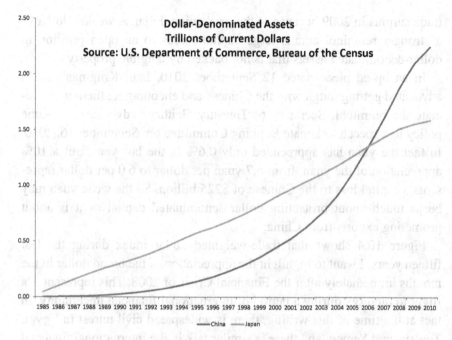

Figure 10.3. Chinese and Japanese dollar-denominated assets.

valuation effects. Figure 10.3 shows the salient aspect of the bilateral international economic relations between China and the U.S.: exponentially increasing dollar asset accumulation by the Chinese that began well before the recession of 2001 and during a time of fiscal surplus during the Clinton administration. This pattern of asset ownership has important implications for the inflation tax.

Inflation as measured by the GDP deflator has averaged 2.3% per annum in the last 20 years. Even though official assets bear interest, they are denominated in nominal dollars. A conservative estimate of the inflation tax that the Chinese Communist Party is paying on its dollar assets is $50 billion. China's bilateral trade surplus with the U.S. in 2009 was $225 billion, so this inflation tax is a substantial portion of the real economic activity that China exports on net to this country.

The Federal Reserve Board's broad trade-weighted dollar index has depreciated by around 10% in the last year. The Chinese have an asset position that is obviously subject to substantial exchange rate risk, and a conservative estimate is that they lost the entire value of their bilateral trade surplus in 2009 because of the weakening dollar. A weaker dollar or a stronger renminbi entails large capital losses to an open position in dollar-denominated assets that is not backed by tangible property.

In an op-ed piece dated 12 September 2010, Paul Krugman (2010) advocated getting tough with the Chinese and encouraging them to appreciate the renminbi. Secretary of Treasury Geithner advocated the same policy in a speech to Senate Banking Committee on September 16, 2010. In fact the yuan has appreciated only 0.6% in the last year. But a 10% appreciation of the yuan, from 6.7 yuan per dollar to 6.0 per dollar represents a capital loss to the Chinese of $225 billion. So the weak yuan may be as much about protecting dollar-denominated capital as it is about promoting exports from China.

Figure 10.4 shows that trade-weighted dollar index during the last fifteen years. I want to highlight the appreciation of the broad dollar in the months immediately after the Financial Crisis of 2008. This represents "a flight to quality" during a period of international financial uncertainty. In fact at the time of this writing, there is widespread civil unrest in Egypt, Tunisia, and Yemen, and there is similar talk in the international financial press about the current appreciation of the dollar.

Figure 10.4.   Trade weighted dollar.

I want to emphasize that the dollar has been and will likely remain the leading store of value in the the world economy. Also, this dollar surplus, flowing into Asia, is substantial. In what sense does it benefit the U.S.? The federal deficit is $1.5 trillion in 2010. In 2009, it was $1.4 trillion, and the bilateral trade surplus with China was $0.23 trillion. *The Chinese Communist Party is financing about one-sixth of the current federal deficit.* Without this inflow of financial capital, is likely that long-term interest rates in the U.S. would be higher, perhaps substantially so.

Figure 10.5 shows the nominal exchange for the yuan during the last 15 years. During most of the period of China's accumulation of dollar-denominated assets, the yuan was fixed at near eight per dollar. Thus any variation in the real exchange rate had to do with differences in inflation rates. Inflation in the U.S. is measured fairly accurately, although not perfectly. Inflation in China is a problematic measure of the change of producer prices at best. Hence, it is not too much of a stretch to consider the real exchange between China and the U.S. to be much more constant that the multilateral real exchange rate shown below in Fig. 10.5.

These observations are the launching pad for an analysis of asset accumulation within the model of overlapping generations. For simplicity, the

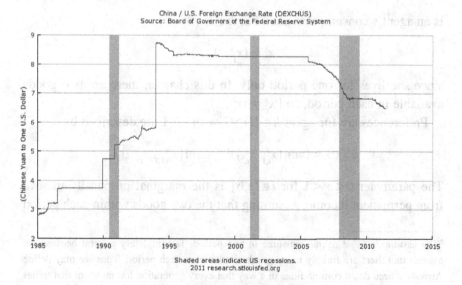

Figure 10.5. Yuan per dollar.

model abstracts from uncertainty, and there is no rule for real exchange rate fluctuations. But it does emphasize that the long-run real exchange rate might best be thought of as a way of dividing seigniorage in the creation of international reserves for the world economy.

10.3. The Model and its Equilibrium

10.3.1. *Agents, preferences, and endowments*

The model of overlapping generations with several goods and two countries can be notationally cumbersome. There is also a subtle element of confusion because agents are born at time t and consume at times t and $t + 1$.[3]

I will index an agent by the superscript h. The set of agents born in generation is G_t for $t \geq 0$. A generation consists of one agent from country a and one from country b. The set of all agents is $H = \cup_{t=0}^{\infty} G_t$, I partition this set into $H = H^a \cup H^b$, and agent $h \in G_t \cap H^i$ is a resident of country $i \in \{a,b\}$ born at time t

The co-finite sequence

$$x^h = (0,\ldots, x_t^h, x_{t+1}^h, 0,\ldots)$$

is an agent's consumption plan. For $h \in G_0$,

$$x^h = (x_1{}^h, 0,\ldots)$$

since she lives for one period only. In this chapter, there are two goods available in each period, and $x_t^h = (x_{t,1}^h, x_{t,2}^h)$

Preferences are for agent $h \in H^i \cap G_t$ with $t \geq 1$ are described by

$$u^h(x^h) = (min\{x_{t,1}^h, x_{t,2}^h\})^{1-\sigma^i} (min\{x_{t+1,1}^h, x_{t+1,2}^h\})^{\sigma^i}$$

The parameter $0 < \sigma^i < 1$ for $i \in \{a,b\}$ is the marginal propensity to save from permanent income. Assuming that the two goods within each period

---

[3]The assumption that agents consume in two periods is completely general because we assume that there are finitely many goods available on each period. Thus we may define Arrow–Debreu dated commodities in a way that every generation has an agent that trades with those who will survive him. See Balasko, Cass and Shell (1980).

are perfect complements allows me to derive a simple expression for the gains from trade. There are potentially large gains from trade across space if endowments are not identical. Preferences for $h \in G_0$ are described by

$$u^h(x^h) = min\{x^h_{1,1}, x^h_{1,2}\}.$$

The initial agent in either country has a marginal propensity to save of zero, since she will live for only one period.

Endowments for an agent $h \in G_t$ with $t \geq 1$ are

$$\omega^h = (0,\ldots, \omega^h_t, \omega^h_{t+1}, 0, \ldots).$$

Endowments for an agent $h \in G_0$ are

$$\omega^h = (\omega^h_1, 0, \ldots)$$

I assume that $\omega^t_h = (1, 1-2\theta)$ if $h \in H^a$ and $\omega^h_t = (0, 2\theta)$ if $h \in H^b$. The parameter $0 < 2\theta \leq 1$ gives the share of the world endowment of the second good that country b owns.

I have chosen endowments such that total resources in the world economy are

$$r = \sum_{h \in H} \omega^h = (2, 2, \ldots)$$

and the parameter θ captures both country b's size and its dependence upon world trade. Endowments are on the edge of a four-dimensional Edgeworth hypercube in each period. Country b has no good 1 at any time, and it has a share 2θ of the world's supply of good 2. If $\theta \approx 0$, then country b is small and also dependent on country a, and if $\theta \approx 1/2$, then the two countries are equally sized and also equally dependent on each other.

10.3.2. *The consumer's problem, government policy, and equilibrium*

Let

$$m^h = (0, \ldots, m^h_t, m^h_{t+1}, 0, \ldots)$$

be agent h's demand for asset balances in each of the periods of her life. Here $m^h_t = (m^h_{t,a}, m^h_{t,b})$ is a portfolio of assets at time t denominated in two different currencies. Those of agents $h \in G_0$ are simply

$$m^h = (m^h_1, 0, \ldots)$$

The government of country $i \in \{a,b\}$ imposes lump-sum taxes or transfers

$$\tau^h = (0,\dots,\tau_t^h,\tau_{t+1}^h,0,\dots)$$

on each of its residents $h \in H_t$ with $t \geq 1$. The analogous expression for $h \in G_0$ is

$$\tau^h = (\tau_1^h,0,\dots)$$

I assume that $\tau_t^h = (\tau_{t,a}^h, 0)$ if $h \in H^a$ and $\tau_t^h = (0,\tau_{t,b}^h)$ if $h \in H^b$. In fact, that is the only cogent definition of nationality in this model; agents are taxed or subsidized in their own currency only.

Write $p_t = (p_{t,1}, p_{t,2})$ and consider goods prices $p = (p_1, p_2,\dots)$. These are present prices, so one can infer both terms of trade and inter-temporal rates of return from them. Asset prices are $q_t = (q_{t,a},q_{t,b})$ and the profile of these prices is $q = (q_1,q_2,\dots)$

Agent $h \in H$ chooses x^h and m^h to maximize

$$u^h(x^h)$$

subject to

$$p \cdot x^h + q \cdot m^h \leq p \cdot \omega^h + q \cdot \tau^h$$

Write

$$M_t = (M_{t,a}, M_{t,b}) = \sum_{s=0}^{t} \sum_{h \in G_s} \tau_t^h$$

as stocks of assets denominated in two currencies that have been injected into the world economy up until time t. Let

$$M = (M_1, M_2,\dots)$$

Then an *equilibrium* is a list goods prices p, asset prices q, allocations $(x^h)_{h \in H}$, and asset demands $(m^h)_h$, $h \in H$ that solve the consumer's problem and also satisfy material balances

$$\sum_{h \in H} x^h \leq \sum_{h \in H} \omega^h$$

and asset balances

$$\sum_{h \in H} m^h \leq M$$

10.3.3. *Properties of equilibrium*

Balasko and Shell (1981) and Fisher (1990) show that the present price of any asset is constant. Hence we may write

$$q_t = (q^a, q^b)$$

for two arbitrary constants and for all $t \geq 1$. The intuition is that the rate of gross return on any store of value is unity. Hence neither asset is denominated in rate of return and also neither the nominal nor the real exchange rate is determined. Bonds denominated in either currency bear the same real rate of return.

This result also implies that only the present value of the tax transfer policies matter for the consumer's decision. Auerbach, Gokhale, and Kotlikoff (1994) call these present values *generational accounts*. Fisher (1995) extends their work to the open economy and explains that the conventional measure of the current account — a cash flow accounting concept — need not be economically meaningful. The timing of the imposition of the lump-sum taxes and subsidies does not matter for the consumer's decision, but the timing of the transfers does matter for the asset market market equilibrium, since the date of the receipts of transfers determines the profile of the stock of world assets.

Since the goods within each period are perfect complements, there is a multiplicity of equilibria. I will concentrate on the simplest equilibrium. In this case,

$$p_t = (p_{t,1}, p_{t,2}) = (z_t, z_t).$$

for some time-dependent scalar z_t. In other words, the terms of trade in each period favor neither good because of the extreme symmetry that I have assumed for the world economy.

We will begin our study of equilibrium with the simple case where there are no lump-sum taxes and transfers:

$$M = (0,0,\ldots).$$

Since the prices of the two goods are identical in each period, we may determine the shares of income in each generation. These shares include no wealth from the creation of seigniorage in either currency. Consider $h \in H^a \cap G_t$. This agent's share of generational wealth is

$$\frac{p \cdot \omega^h}{p \cdot \sum_{h \in G_t} \omega^h} = 1 - \theta$$

Our assumptions about endowments and preferences make for a simple distribution of income within each generation. The analog for an agent in country b is θ.

Since preferences are homothetic (but not necessarily identical) and the distribution of income is also simple, I can aggregate preferences and solve in closed form for the supporting prices. Define

$$\sigma = (1-\theta)\sigma^a + \theta\sigma^b \tag{1}$$

The parameter σ is the world's average propensity to save from permanent income

The materials balances condition in the market for good $i \in 1,2$ and time $t \geq 2$ is:

$$\sigma (z_{t-1} + z_t) + (1-\sigma)(z_t + z_{t+1}) = 2z_t.$$

This equation is derived in three steps. The present value of income of $h \in G_t \cap H^a$ is $2(1-\theta)(z_t + z_{t+1})$ and that of $h \in G_t \cap H^b$ is $2\theta(z_t + z_{t+1})$. Each generation splits its income equally between the two goods in each period. Hence expenditures are summarized by σ defined in (1). Finally, the value of aggregate supply in the world of each good is $2z_t$.

This condition is equivalent to the homogeneous second-order difference equation:

$$(1-\sigma)z_{t+1} - z_t + \sigma z_{t-1} = 0 \tag{2}$$

The roots of its characteristic equation are $\lambda_1 = 1$ and $\lambda_2 = \sigma/(1-\sigma)$ The general solution to this difference equation is:

$$z_t = c_1\lambda_1^t + c_2\lambda_2^t \tag{3}$$

where c_1 and c_2 are constants to be determined.[4]

---

[4]I will not analyze the special case where $\sigma = 1/2$ and the characteristic equation has two roots at unity.

Two comments are in order. First, if $\lambda_2 > 1$, then we are in what Gale (1973) calls the Samuelson case. Otherwise we are in the classical case, where it is traditionally alleged that there is no role for fiat money. Hence if $\sigma > 1/2$, then there is room in the world economy for what Samuelson (1958) called the social contrivance of money. In fact, in this case if there is no creation of international real balances, then the equilibrium allocations are not Pareto optimal. Thus there is a compelling case for one or both of the governments to create world liquidity.

Second, the Pareto optimality of the equilibrium allocations depends upon the preferences of all the agents in the world economy. Consider a large economy in the Samuelson case, where $\theta \approx 0$ and $\sigma^a > 1/2$. It has negative autarkic real interest rates. Let it trade with a small partner with $\sigma^b < 1/2$. Such an economy would have high real interest rates under autarky.[5] In the integrated world economy, an equilibrium without any international seigniorage — real balances used for inter-generational trade — would not support Pareto optimal allocations. The creation of such reserves would make all agents better off in the world economy, including all the agents in country b, which under autarky had no room for domestic money. Since the autarky allocations in country b are still feasible, they are Pareto dominated by those in trade. Even if country a creates all the international reserves in the world economy, every generation in country b is benefited (or not hurt). To the best of my knowledge, this observation has not been made broadly in the literature before.

10.4. Creation of International Reserves

10.4.1. *A complete description of equilibrium*

I will concentrate on the simplest possible policies that create liquidity in the first period only. They do so by imposing lump-sum taxes or subsides on the members of G_0 only. Let agent $h \in H^i \cap G_0$ receive lump-sum transfer $\tau^h = M^i$. These transfers are denominated in units of local currency, and if $\tau^h < 0$, then agent h is taxed by his local government. In most simple

---

[5] Since country b has none of good 1, an autarkic equilibrium would not exist. But think of a modified economy having $\varepsilon > 0$ of that good in each period.

models of overlapping generations, there is a constant stock of fiat money that is given to the initial generation and no agent is ever taxed. But there is a compelling case to allow policies with taxes because this is exactly how one services the national debt in an economy whose real interest rate exceeds its growth rate. Also, it is exactly how a "surplus country" accommodates an overly expansionary policy in its trading partner.

Since there are two types of fiat money, their relative price $e = q^a/q^b$ is the nominal exchange rate. An increase in e is an *appreciation* of currency a. Since all goods are traded freely at all times, the law of one price automatically holds. Since the sub-utility functions describing preferences over consumption choices are identical, each country would have the same ideal price index. Then the absolute and relative versions of purchasing power parity also hold.

For a fixed sequence of prices p, the spot exchange rate e is the real exchange rate for country a, and $1/e$ is that for country b. An increase in e is a real appreciation since the same quantity of fiat money from country a buys more goods in every period. The nominal exchange rate e is constant in a perfect foresight equilibrium. Kareken and Wallace (1981) first emphasized that there was a continuum of equilibrium rates. Fisher (1996) showed that only certain exchange rates might support equilibrium allocations in the world economy that were Pareto optimal.

The total stock of real balances in the world is:

$$M = q^a M^a + q^b M^b.$$

Since we have the total stock of international reserves, we can solve the second-order difference equation (2) exactly. The two initial conditions are the present prices normalization $p_{t,1} = 1$ and materials balances in the first period. Since $p_{t,1} = 1$, $z_1 = 1$. The materials' balances condition for good $i \in 1,2$ in period $t = 1$ is

$$1 + M/2 + (1-\sigma)(1 + z_2) = 2,$$

where I have used the fact that $z_1 = 1$. This equation also imposes the condition that half of all income is spent on each good in period $t = 1$. This equation is equivalent to

$$z_2 = (\sigma - M/2)/(1-\sigma).$$

Recall that $\lambda_1 = 1$. Then some algebra yields:

$$c_1 = \frac{\lambda_2 - z_2}{\lambda_2 - 1}$$

and

$$c_2 = \frac{z_2 - 1}{\lambda_2(\lambda_2 - 1)}.$$

One can already see important elements in the logic of the creation of international reserves. If $M = 0$, then $z_2 = \sigma/(1-\sigma) = \lambda_2$. Thus $c_1 = 0$ and $c_2 = 1/\lambda_2 (1-\sigma)/\sigma$, and the supporting prices are

$$p = (1,1,\ldots, (\sigma/(1-\sigma))^t, (\sigma/(1-\sigma))^t,\ldots)$$

These prices support Pareto optimal allocations for $\sigma<1/2$, which is the classical case for the world economy. Hence if world real interest rates are positive, then there is seemingly no room for additional international reserves. This idea generalizes to the notion that if world real interest rates exceed the long-run growth rate of the world economy, then any government that issues fiat money serving as international reserves will eventually have to raise taxes to pay the interest burden on its national debt.

If $M/2 = 2\sigma-1$, then $z_2 = 1$. It follows that $c_2 = 0$, and the supporting prices are

$$p = (1,1,\ldots,1,1,\ldots)$$

These prices support the golden rule allocations. This observation shows the role of the two monetary authorities in providing for sufficient but not excessive international reserves.

Define

$$\tilde{M} = max\{0,4\sigma-2\}.$$

The quantity $\tilde{M}$ is the unique stationary supply of seigniorage that supports Pareto optimal allocations. Only if

$$\tilde{M} = q^a M^a + q^b M^b \tag{4}$$

will the world have sufficient reserves to satisfy the financial needs of the world economy. There is no guarantee that one country will achieve the right level of international liquidity on its own. Equation (4) shows there is an ineluctable element of cooperation in the creation of international reserves if the national monetary authorities are interested in the dynamic efficiency of the world economy. Hence, if one country is "too expansionary", then its trading partner must "accommodate" by running a tighter fiscal ship.

10.4.2. *Bargaining over the division of seigniorage*

What are the natural limits on the creation of seigniorage $q^a M^a$ and $q^a M^b$? Two forces are at play. First, every generation gains from trade. Second, the original generation in either country may expect a reserve level of utility that reflects its ability to create seigniorage in the autarkic economy. If the world economy is in the classical case, then $\tilde{M} = 0$ supports Pareto optimal allocations, but this does not imply that $M^a = M^b = 0$. If the world economy is in the Samuelson case, then $\tilde{M} > 0$ and either $M^a \neq 0$ or $M^b \neq 0$ or both.

I model the division of seigniorage in the world economy as a cooperative game, and I will highlight the Nash (1950) bargaining solution. This solution maximizes the product of the gains from the creation of international reserves. In the simplest case, the two agents in the original generation bargain over reserves that will implement the Pareto optimal allocations in the world economy.

What are the reservation levels that the two members of generation 0 bring to the bargaining table? Let $\tilde{M}^a = max\{0, 4\sigma^a - 2\}$ be the money stock in Country a that implements Pareto efficient allocations under autarky. The autarkic level of utility for the original agent in Country a is:

$$\bar{u}^a = 1 - 2\theta + \tilde{M}^a / 2$$

where I have used the facts that the first good is in excess supply in autarky and also that the marginal utility of income is unity. The analogous autarkic level of utility for the original agent in Country b is:

$$\bar{u}^b = 0$$

since no agent in that country has any of the second good. There is no role for money in this closed economy since the marginal utility of income in

Country b is zero; this fact is an important implication of the simplifying assumptions that both goods are perfect complements within each period and that country b is entirely dependent upon trade because of its skewed profile of endowments . Since $\bar{u}^a > \bar{u}^b$, Country a has bargaining power in the division of seigniorage in the world economy. Indeed, its outside option is stronger if it has a role for national debt in its own closed economy.

Assume that both economies open for trade, and write p as the sequence of prices that supports the equilibrium allocations when the world stock of money is $\tilde{M}$. Recall that Country a creates $q^a M^a$ of these reserves and Country b creates $qbMb$ of them. Now agent $h \in G_0 \cap H^a$ achieves utility:

$$u^a = 1 - \theta + q^a M^a / 2$$

and $h \in G_0 \cap H^b$ has:

$$u^b = \theta + q^b M^b / 2$$

In both of these equations, the marginal utility of income is $1/2$ since the price of each good is unity.

The Nash bargaining solution maximizes the product of the gains from trade, inclusive of the gains from the creation of international seigniorage. This maximization assumes that the two countries choose the optimal level of seigniorage for the world economy. In this case, the Nash solution chooses $q^a M^a$ and $q^b M^b$ to maximize

$$(u^a - \bar{u}^a)(u^b - u^{-b}) \tag{5}$$

subject to $q^a M^a + q^b M^b = \tilde{M}$. The solution to Eq. (5) has

$$q^a M^a = \frac{\tilde{M} + (\tilde{M}^a - \tilde{M}^b)}{2} \quad \text{and} \quad q^b M^b = \frac{\tilde{M} + (\tilde{M}^a - \tilde{M}^b)}{2} \tag{6}$$

Equation (6) states an elegant rule: *Each country has an equal share in the creation of world seigniorage when the two economies move from autarky to free trade*. It is important to note that this rule respects the levels of national debt that maximize autarkic welfare, and in our simple example $\tilde{M}^b = 0$ since there is no role for national debt in an economy whose GDP is zero.

Consider the interesting and entirely plausible case that the world economy is in the classical case but Country a is in the Samuelson case.

Now $\tilde{M} = 0$ but $\tilde{M}^a > 0$. Inside money created by agents in the world economy coming after Generation 0 now satisfies the needs for savings in Country a. It is sufficient to ensure that the equilibrium allocation are Pareto optimal, but this move from autarky to trade has hurt the agent in Country a in Generation 0. *Now the original agent in Country a will be granted* $q^a M^a > 0$ *as compensation for having lost her rights to local seigniorage.* But then $q^b M^b = -q^a M^a$, since there is no room for outside money in the world economy. Since generational trade among all the other agents in the world economy is balanced, this pattern of money creation corresponds to a deficit in Country a and a surplus in Country b.[6]

During the last 50 years — a period roughly corresponding to the life economic generation in this kind of model — the average debt to GDP ratio in the U.S. has been almost 38%.[7] This is about $6 trillion in current dollars. Hence, it is entirely plausible that the People's Republic of China, which has absorbed less than $3 trillion of this stock of debt might be able easily to double its holdings. This is a massive stock of assets, and the inflation tax on a stock of $6.0 trillion is $180 billion, even at a modest 3% rate of inflation. This flow is almost as large as the entire bilateral trade surplus that China runs with the U.S. This observation is the central point of this chapter.

10.4.3. *How general is this example?*

Not much about this example is special. In the classical case, real interest rates exceed the rate of growth of the world economy, a state of affairs that likely characterizes our own world. The idea that the large country is in the Samuelson case assumes that the social contrivance of money actual improves local welfare under autarky. This assumption seems consistent with the obvious empirical observation that U.S. has had a positive stock of national debt for at least 70 years.

It is somewhat paradoxical that the country with lower autarkic real interest rates runs a trade deficit, since one would normally expect that

---

[6]I have shown (Fisher, 1995) that the current account, a cash flow accounting measure, is not well defined; instead the pattern of generational deficits and surpluses is.

[7]I used Table B-79 from the *Economic Report of the President*, and I am only considering national debt held by the public in the years from 1963 through 2012 inclusive.

capital flows from the country with low interest rates to the one with higher ones. But the mechanism that I have highlighted has to do with the *division of seigniorage* in the world economy. In each generation, agents in Country *b* lend to those in Country *a*, but this lending takes the form of inside money. There is not enough *outside money* on net in the world economy, and a sensible division of this seigniorage would give a larger share to the country that had its own outside money in autarky.

I have discussed the creation of seigniorage as a bargaining problem over the division of of international reserves, but I just as easily could have highlighted negotiations about the "proper" real exchange rate. Fix for a moment the national debts of the two countries $M^a > 0$ and $M^b < 0$. I am again assuming that the world economy is in the classical case. Now, the Nash bargaining problem breaks down into choosing two real values for local assets q^a and q^b such that $q^a = M^a/\tilde{M}^a$ and $q^b = q^a M^a/M^b$. Hence the "right" real exchange rate has a little bit of the flavor of the quantity theory of money, but the actual present prices of assets are both pinned by an argument that depends upon splitting the gains from trade among the members of Generation 0.

If the world economy were in the Samuelson case, then there would be room for the creation of strictly positive stocks of international reserves. However, the division of seigniorage would still favor the country where outside money played a role in autarky. If both countries were in the Samuelson case, then the world economy would certainly be so. Country *a* would still be in a position to bargain for a larger share of these reserves because the structure of country *b*'s economy is such that there is no role for money under autarky. In that sense, the gains from commodity trade within each period are logically prior to any gains from inter-temporal trade using the social contrivance of money. This is perhaps the first time in the literature in monetary theory that this point has been made so clearly.

10.5. Conclusion

An unusual aspect of my analysis is that the country with high autarkic real interest rates actually runs a trade surplus. Song, Storesletten and Zilliboti (2011) highlight the paradox that the rate of return on Chinese capital seems to be so high and yet the Chinese current account is in huge surplus. Their model uses firm-specific productivities and differential access to credit markets as a way of reconciling these two facts. My model is simpler. It shows why two rational governments would agree to accommodate an asset imbalance of significant magnitude.

What are the real benefits that accrue to China from unfettered access to world markets? They are surely greater than a simple analysis of the gains from trade might suggest. Export-led growth in manufacturing sectors have eased the transition from a rural to urban society that is the demographic underpinning of China's seemingly rapid economic growth. An increasing concentration of wealth among the politically well connected has surely relieved some of the political pressure on that the Communist party felt in the years leading up to Tiananmen Square. Although I have modeled the gains from trade in a very simple way, there are surely much deeper than can be described in an Edgeworth Box.

Even in my simplified setting, a complete characterization of the results is quite difficult. Indeed, I really only presented an example. But the example has salience, and I am sure it generalizes. I plan to continue this vein of theoretical research because I think it captures an important element of the macroeconomics of international trade. It is certain than models of overlapping generations with only one good per period are much too simple. The open areas for research are to generalize the results and to examine non-stationary debt policies. My example taxes and transfers in the initial generation only, but the same logic dictates that the deficit country can run perpetual deficits, even when world real interest rates are positive.

What have we learned? Using old themes in international finance, I have constructed a robust example where a country that can create money under autarky will run a deficit. The surplus country accommodates this pattern of trade because every system of fixed exchange rates has a very large and ineluctable element of cooperation inherent in it. Even a casual glance at the international financial news in the last three years would lead one to believe that the U.S. and China are indeed negotiating about the "proper level" for the yuan or the "appropriate fiscal" discipline for the U.S. I have highlighted those ideas in a simple macroeconomic model of two countries.

References

A J Auerbach, J Gokhale and L J Kotlikoff (1994) "Generational Accounting: A Meaningful Way to Evaluate Fiscal Policy," *The Journal of Economic Perspectives*, Vol. 8, No. 1, pp. 73–94.

Y Balasko, D Cass and K Shell (1980) "Existence of Competitive Equilibrium in a General Overlapping–Generations Model," *Journal of Economic Theory*, Vol. 23, No. 3, pp. 307–322.

Y Balasko and K Shell (1981) "The Overlapping–Generations Model. II: The Case of Pure Exchange with Money," *Journal of Economic Theory*, Vol. 24, No. 1, pp. 112–142.

Fisher, E O'N (1996) "On Exchange Rates and Efficiency," *Economic Theory*, Vol. 7, pp. 267–281.

Fisher, E O'N (1990) "Sustainable Balance of Trade Deficits," *Journal of Monetary Economics*, Vol. 25, No. 3, pp. 411–430.

Fisher, E O'N (1995) "A New Way of Thinking about the Current Account," *International Economic Review*, Vol. 36, No. 3, pp. 555–568.

Gale, D. (1973) "Pure Exchange Equilibrium of Dynamic Economic Models," *Journal of Economic Theory*, Vol. 6, No. 1, pp. 12–36.

Kareken, J and Wallace (1981) "On the Indeterminacy of Equilibrium Exchange Rates," *The Quarterly Journal of Economics*, Vol. 96, No. 2, pp. 207–222.

Krugman, P. (2010) "China, Japan, America, and the Renminbi," *The New York Times*.

Nash, J F. Jr. (1950) "The Bargaining Problem," *Econometrica*, Vol. 18, No. 2, pp. 155–162.

Rubinstein, A (1982) "Perfect Equilibrium in a Bargaining Model," *Econometrica*, Vol. 50, No. 1, pp. 97–109.

Samuelson, P A. (1958) "An Exact Consumption-Loan Model of Interest with or without the Social Contrivance of Money," *The Journal of Political Economy*, Vol. 66, No. 6, pp. 467–482.

Song, Z, K Storesletten and F Zilibotti (2011) "Growing like China," *American Economic Review*, Vol. 101, pp. 202–241.

CHAPTER 11

TOWARD AN EAST ASIAN ECONOMIC COMMUNITY

YUN CHEN AND KEN MORITA

11.1. Introduction

Regional integration, particularly the subject of East Asian Community (EAC) has become a hot issue in the post-Cold War era. We have shown in a prior contribution that integration is a departure from path dependent individual national development (Morita and Chen, 2008), and explored its security ramifications. This chapter delves more deeply into both matters. We contend that the main purpose of integration is to build collective security systems, patterned on the European Union (EU) precedent renouncing intra-regional warfare.

Polanyi *et al.* (1957) has shown that order and peace are essential for global profit making, but didn't devise a strategy for building a stable regional regime. The European Community (EC) and its successor EU, inspired by Richard Nicolaus Eijiro Coudenhove-Kalergi and Jean Omer Marie Gabriel Monnet, provide one promising paradigm. EU supranationality serves as the touchstone of our analysis, and a platform for investigating the economic benefits of an Asian Economic Community (AEC). We also develop a related defense of the virtue of idealism.

One manifestation of this idealism is our advocacy of a post-nation state global order. Globalization, as we construe it, is about building a "global village" with transnational (supranational) regional components of the EC type (without monetary union), and is a positive force for creating an Asian Economic Union (AEU) with a common currency. The primary obstacle to date for achieving an Asian Community Union with limited trans-governmental coordination and/or an Asian Union of any type (with or without a common currency) with more comprehensive supranational governance has been finding the right catalyst. We contend that the Okinawa issue provides this missing link. It is an important political issue for Japan, Okinawans and neighbors, begging for the kind of solution offered by supranationality. Toward this end, we have devised an original "Okinawa Plan" that addresses both regional and U.S. military basing problems, and argue that it kills six birds with one stone.

We recognize that supranationalism in the EU has hit some bumps along the road. It has been beset by Euro-sclerosis and a colossal sovereign debt crisis. Nonetheless, we do not deem these developments fatal. The cooperative spirit that infuses supranationalism in its varying degrees will enable its leaders to learn and overcome all problems. Accordingly, we anticipate that supranationalism will provide its members with superior prevention and crisis management.

The paper has three parts. In Sec. 1, we investigate the purposes of an East Asian Community. In Sec. 2, we derive lessons from the EU's successful experience, particularly the benefits of a common security system, and North Atlantic Treaty Organization (NATO). In Sec. 3, we present our "Okinawa Plan", examine supranationality's special benefits and delve into the creative potential of idealism.[1]

11.1.1. *East Asian Community: purpose*

Why should East Asian states relinquish their nationhood for supranationality?[2] Figure 11.1 diagrams the justification.

11.1.2. *Nation states: functions and shortcomings*

It identifies positive and negative functions of nation states. The principal positive function is collective security, which involves the renunciation of internecine aggression, and collective deterrence. The nation state also serves as a vehicle for advancing national economic welfare. All these

---

[1] Similar arguments have been devised for the creation of other supranational entities. See Rosecrance (2010).

[2] The concept of "nation state" was first established in Western Europe by the Peace Treaty of Westphalia signed in 1648.

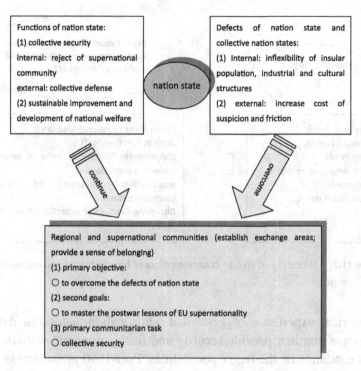

Figure 11.1. Justification for transforming nation states group to post-national communities.

Source: Authors.

elements satisfy the basic human needs elaborated in Maslow's hierarchy (Maslow, 1943), including subsistence, security, respect and self-actualization. These are essential ingredients of sustainable political entities and other organizations,[3] outlined in Fig. 11.2.

---

[3]We would here trace the history of human society. In the primitive society, the authority of tribal elders was established by defending the security against attacks of wild animals and neighboring tribes. Moreover, the existence of an authority contributed stability of the tribe. In ancient times in China, there existed a wise man who did not want to take responsibility of such an authority. (According to Zhuangzi, when Yao Di tried to abdicate in favor of the then wise man, Xu You, his offer was refused.) Undoubtedly, as regards the human society, it was "the more tracing the history, the more wild like a jungle". Therefore, tensions between human beings and between human society and nature were more serious with more tracing the history. Politicians' jobs have never been easy. In either case, it

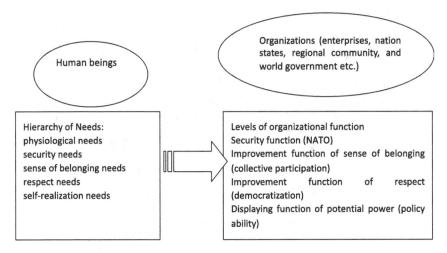

Figure 11.2. Hierarchy of Needs: common points of human beings and organizations.
Source: Authors.

Historical experience suggests that while nation states can dampen internecine conflict, provide security and foster economic welfare, they fail to capitalize on the larger possibilities. Post-1990 globalization testifies to these possibilities and points to the likelihood that supranational organizations will eventually replace nation states.

11.1.3. *The Imperative of regional communities*

The limited ability of Asian nations to solve key internal problems and the potential benefits of supranationality can be illustrated with a few examples. Japan's age structure has become an impediment to growth that cannot be easily remedied at home, but can be mitigated by immigration from other parts of East Asia. China by contrast has an ample population,

---

should be reasonably said that the security function has been most fundamental responsibility of the nation states, based upon which any nation states have their own armies. Needless to say, in addition to the carrying out the self-defense responsibility, the nation state has to meet any other needs (belonging, respect and self-realization) of the people. In order to do, they try to have various institutional designs and to employ any kinds of public policies. As mentioned above, because the nation state has met the peoples' needs, the nation state has been generally supported by them as we recognize at present.

but its industrial structure relies too heavily on cheap factors of production, and could benefit from shared, superior regional technologies that enhance productivity and promote workers' rights and environmental protection. Likewise, while East Asian nations do cooperate, the quality of intra-regional relations is degraded by lingering nationalistic concerns that can be surmounted with supranational organizations.[4]

11.1.4. *Regional community: viability*

This evidence is inconclusive because as organizational size increases, efficiency from multiple perspectives sometimes declines. The solution of some problems could be offset by efficiency loses elsewhere that might undermine supranational viability. The successes of the EU, however, suggest that efficiency losses will not be fatal, or large enough to outweigh the social benefit.[5]

11.1.5. *Regional community: primacy of peace*

Peace is the *sine qua non* of a successful supranational order. The EU experience demonstrates that the ill-founded fears and insecurities which often lead to war can be overcome. In the next section we probe how the European security problem has been solved.

11.2. EU and NATO: Foundations for Peace

NATO is the cornerstone of postwar European peace. It provides essential lessons for building an AEC or AEU. The secrets of NATO's

---

[4]We call pre-communitarian relations among nation states "aggregate because they are infected with distrust and discord". For example, when world financial crisis happened, East Asian countries were highly motivated to cooperate. However, under the recent South Korean patrol boat case, they have become suspicious one another.

[5]We think that the "transaction cost" concept in conjunction with "asymmetry of information" might be important, and believe that government scale economies after World War II broadly explain increases in the organization size of enterprises, countries, UN, and EU. Also, by analogy, the concept of global village can be likened to barrier free international trade that allows participants to exhaustively search opportunities without artificial barriers. Furthermore, we contend that the postwar trend toward supranationality presages the "end of history" for nation states.

success are its unified security system, common armed forces and transparency. The peace it provides has empowered other aspects of the EU, including its integrated economic regime, but is no longer dependent on NATO itself. Now that the EU has matured it can transfer NATO's assets to its own independent security establishment. This process illustrates how collective defense institutions can be built initially to overcome historical animosities, and then perfected under a new collective order.[6]

11.3. The "Okinawa Plan": Toward the East Asian Community

We believe that the NATO/EU experience can be duplicated in East Asia. The first step following the west's example is to devise a framework to get the ball rolling. We propose an Okinawa Plan. It is simple. We suggest that East Asian Community establish a collective armed force headquartered in Okinawa with troops dispersed across the region. Okinawa already has the

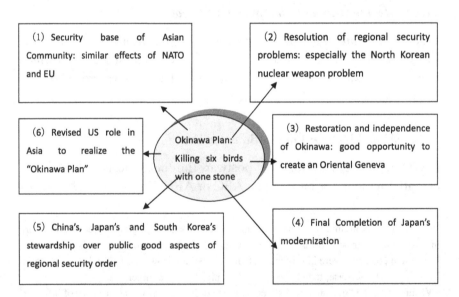

Figure 11.3.   "Okinawa Plan": Killing six birds with one stone.

Source: Authors.

---

[6]Russia has intimated that it would consider joining the EU in October, 2000.

requisite infrastructure.[7] The creation of an East Asian common defense organization in Okinawa holds out the possibility of killing six birds with one stone (see Fig. 11.3).

11.3.1. *Collective security pact: platform for building the East Asian Community*

The consummation of a collective security pact will provide a platform for building the East Asian Community, in accordance the NATO's precedent. It will also diminish lingering animosities.

11.3.2. *Reconciliation*

The adverse legacy of World War II and the cold war lingers in East Asia on the Korean Peninsula and the Taiwan Straits.[8] Other issues like the opacity of China's military spending and the disputes over U.S. military bases similarly roil the waters. New issues like terrorism and piracy also have caused frictions. The "North Korean nuclear weapon problem" appears to be the most explosive, despite six party attempts to defuse the controversy. Nonetheless, there seems room for compromise even here. Some of North Korea's concerns are justified and can be ameliorated with confidence-building measures. We believe that this obstacle can be surmounted if East Asia addresses the problem with goodwill. A collective security pact would be a giant step in this direction. The same principle applies to the resolution of regional national resource disputes.

11.3.3. *Okinawan prosperity*

We expect the Okinawa Plan will make Okinawa prosperous by transforming it into a regional military and government hub. Okinawa might

---

[7]Hainan is another attractive site, but its location is too far south and there could be objections to placing it in China.

[8]The history of the Taiwan problem is as follows. China was half-colonized in the modern era when it lost Taiwan to the Japanese. This remains a source of humiliation. Reunification would redress the grievance. However, this solution would be unfair to the Taiwanese people, unless it was achieved through an amicable agreement.

even become an international Mecca like Geneva, taking into account its natural assets and scenic beauty. The transition also would have the benefit of restoring Okinawans' dignity and facilitating improved relations with the Japanese mainland.[9]

11.3.4. *Completion of Japan's modernization*

Japan's attitude toward Okinawa remains pre-modern to the extent that it refuses to accept Okinawa's autonomy. Headquartering the East Asian collective security force in Okinawa would not only redress Okinawans' "mental and spiritual problem", it would also allow Japan to become a fully modern, enlightened society. Similar benefits should be generated by a resolution of the Taiwan conflict.

11.3.5. *East Asian Community: order and leadership*

11.3.5.1. *From cold war to regional harmony*

The Okinawa plan and derivatively the creation of the East Asian Community will bring China into the regional security network. During the Cold War, and its aftermath an adversarial mentality dominated that now can be transformed into a spirit of regional amity and harmony (Chen, 2009; Chapter 2). Moreover, Japan's misperceptions of the China threat impede a basing solution for Okinawa. Once this issue is resolved, it will be easier to achieve a warming of relations between Beijing and Tokyo.

---

[9]Formerly, Okinawa was the independent "Ryukyu Kingdom" (which was also a member of ancient China-led tributary system). At the beginning of 17th century, the Ryukyu Kingdom was occupied by the Satsuma clan (located at the southern end of Kyushu Island). In 1879, Okinawa became a Japanese prefecture. After World War II, between 1945 and 1972, Okinawa was controlled by the U.S. The island was returned to Japan in 1972, which assumed administrative responsibility over U.S. military bases. These facilities accounted for 75% of all US military bases (in US exclusive use) in Japan, and were expanded during the Vietnamese War. As a consequence of this history Okinawans harbor grievances against the Japanese and Americans, which can be assuaged by granting them a central position in the East Asian Economic Community.

The transformation of relations within East Asia also will facilitate cooperative leadership among key large member, that is, China, Japan and South Korea. Just as in the EU where Germany and France have played pivotal roles, East Asia's leaders will be empowered to fulfill their responsibilities.

11.3.5.2. *The America dimension and new global leadership*

The creation of the East Asian Community does not banish America from the orient. America and the EU have preserved a deep constructive relationship despite Europe's embracing supranationality, and the same should apply in Asia. The new relationship is one among equals that requires the U.S. to curb its leadership role in providing global public governance goods, [10] with the supranational east picking up the slack.[11] Joint leadership sharing is mature and win-win for all concerned (Chen and Morita, 2010).

11.3.6. *American military withdrawal from East Asia*

If the "Okinawa Plan" is implemented step by step, the U.S. will withdraw its military forces from Okinawa, and benefit from the cost savings, assuming as we claim that America is not an hegemonic nation and East Asians step up and fill the leadership gap. A transition process, like the one orchestrated by NATO will be needed to allay residual anxieties.

11.4. Concluding Remarks

11.4.1. *Bumps in the road*

The EU experience reveals that even after supranationality is achieved, new challenges arise. After a good start, the EU today finds itself grappling

---

[10]The U.S. has been a new type of super power country, different from previous hegemonic countries like Portugal, Holland and UK (see Modelski and Thomson, 1987). It seems never to have had territorial ambitions. Instead, The U.S. has pursued its interests through mutually beneficial trade.

[11]China is conflicted about assuming these responsibilities because it has not yet entirely outgrown its hegemonic aspirations. This however will not last forever.

with Euro-sclerosis (growth retardation) and a colossal sovereign debt crisis. Both problems seem daunting, but we believe that its cooperative spirit will allow European leaders to discover and implement requisite remedies. Nation states face similar dilemmas, and we are confident that the supranational approach will prove its mettle. It will both enhance prevention and facilitate crisis management.

11.4.2. *Value of idealism*

Killing six birds with one stone is ambitious.[12] Nonetheless, the EU example is encouraging. The world can be saved by idealists.

We believe that East Asian people should commit themselves to the EAC mission. Imaginary enemies are not required; the Okinawa Plan is sufficient. Also, the process is paramount. There is no need to resolve outstanding issues as a precondition for establishing an East Asian Community. All that is required is a commitment to journey down the road together, just as EU leaders did after the World War II.

Two hundred years ago, the German philosopher, Immanuel Kant, wrote an essay entitled *Zum ewigen Frieden* (Perpetual Peace) and advocated building an united alliance by republics. He exemplifies the peace-spiritedness essential for creating harmonious futures. The peaceful international order which emerged after the World War II has been the result of this idealism, and there is no reason why it cannot succeed in East Asia too.

References

Chen, Yun (2003) "Sino-Japanese Relations from Viewpoints of Characteristics of Japan's Foreign Policy," (in Chinese) In Bao, X. and Z. Zang, *Changes of Japanese Politics and Foreign Policy* (in Chinese), Beijing: Shishi Publishing.

Chen, Yun (2005a) "Sengo nihon no koudo keizai seichou wa shakai shichou wo dou kaetaka? (What had the post-war Japanese high speed economic

---

[12]According to Hamada (2007), assuming that trade volume will become three times more when common currency is introduced [roughly estimated by using the method of Oneal and Russet (1997)], it is possible to say that the probability of occurring "war" becomes around 15% less (p. 99). Such an investigation suggests us there can be a seventh bird with one stone. However, in this chapter, we will not analyze but only refer the possibility of it.

growth changed the social trend of thought in Japan?)" Vol. 22, *Chugoku 21* (*China 21*) Contemporary Chinese Research Association, Aichi University.

Chen, Yun (2005b) "Comparisons of South-East Asian Model with East Asian model: Some suggestions towards Shared Growth (in Chinese),"in Yuan Zhigang, Y., Gu Yunshen and Chen Hao, *Reform of Financial and Management System Towards Internationalization* (in Chinese), Shanghai, Fudan University Press.

Chen, Yun (2005c) "American Factors in Asian Order and Introversion of Asian Countries (in Chinese)," In Dai, X. and D. Guo, *East Asian Development Model and Regional Cooperation* (in Chinese), Shanghai: Fudan University Press.

Chen, Yun (2005d) "Political Economy of East Asian Development Model: Some Incubative Principle in Authoritative Development Model (in Chinese)," *Conference Proceedings of Annual Meeting of Shanghai Political Association*, Shanghai, China.

Chen, Yun (2009) *Transition and Development in China: Towards Shared Growth*, Farnham, Ashgate Publishing.

Chen, Yun and K. Morita (2009) "Chugoku Kaihatsu Model no Seijigaku: Seichou no Kyouyu no Shisa (A Political Analysis of Development Model in China: Towards Shared Growth)," *Keizai Ronsou* (*The Hiroshima Economic Review*), March, Vol. 32, No. 3.

Chen, Yun and K. Morita (2010) *Chugoku no Taiseiikou to Hatten no Seijikeizaigaku: Gendai Kokka he no Chousen* (*Political Economy of Transition and Development in China: Challenge towards Modern Nation*), Tokyo, Taga Shuppan.

Dai, Xu (2009b) *The Fires of War in the Prosperous Society: A Chinese Colonel's Opinion about National Defense* (in Chinese), Beijing, Xinhua Publishing.

Dai, Xu (2009b) *A Totem in the Sea: A Chinese Aircraft Carrier* (in Chinese), Beijing, Huawen Publishing.

Hamada, K. (2007) "Ajia ni Okeru Keizai Tougou to Anzen Hoshou (Economic Integration and Security in Asia)," in Yabushita, S. and K. Shimizu (eds.), *Chiiki Tougou no Seijikeizaigaku* (*Political Economy of Regional Integration*), Tokyo, Toyokeizai Shinpousha.

Modelski, G., and W. R. Thompson (1987) "Testing Cobweb Models of the Long Cycle", in Modelski G. (ed), *Exploring Long Cycle*, Boulder, Lynne Rienner Publishers.

Morita, K. and Yun Chen (2008) "Chiiki Tougou to Keiro Ison: Ajia no Tougou wo Megutte (Regional Integration and Path Dependence: On the Asian Integration)," *Keizai Ronsou* (*The Hiroshima Economic Review*), July, Vol. 32, No. 1.

Morita, K. and Yun Chen (2010) "Regional Integration and Path Dependence: EU and East Asia", *Economic Papers* (Warsaw School of Economics, Institute for International Studies), Vol. 44.

Oneal, J. R. and B. M. Russet (1997) "The Classical Liberals Were Right: Democracy, Interdependence, and Conflict, 1950-1985", *International Studies Quarterly*, Vol. 41, No.2.

Polanyi, K., C. M. Arensberg and H. W. Pearson (eds.) (1957) *Trade and Market in the Early Empires*, New York, The Free Press and The Falcon's Wing Press.

Rosecrance, R. (2010) "Bigger is Better: The Case for a Transatlantic Union," *Foreign Affairs*, Vol. 89, Issue 3.

Song, Qiang, Zhang Zangzang, Qiao Bian and Gu Qingsheng (1996) *China Can Say No* (in Chinese), Beijing, Chinese Business Association Press.

Song, Xiaojun, Wang Xiaodong, Huang Jisu and Song Qiang (1996) *China is Unhappy* (in Chinese), Nanjing, Jiangsu Renmin Publishing.

CHAPTER 12

ASIAN UNION

STEVEN ROSEFIELDE, JONG-RONG CHEN, AND MASUMI HAKOGI

Asian governments are attracted to the possibilities of deepening their cooperation by moving up the supranational institutional ladder to higher levels of multinational regional governance. The Association of Southeast Asian Nations (ASEAN) for example announced its intention to create an ASEAN Community at its Ninth Summit in October 2003 based on three pillars: ASEAN Security Community, ASEAN Economic Community and an ASEAN Socio-Cultural Community. An Action Program was adopted in Vientiane the following year.[1] It plans to create an ASEAN Economic Community (AEC) by 2015, which ultimately could serve as a stepping stone to a Southeast Asian variant of the European Union (EU).

Would this be sage? Could it or some alternative Asian Union prevent regional bubbles and facilitate crisis management if prevention failed? Europeans and others often speak as if EU supranationalism is a panacea that can prevent and cure all ills, while pursuing other lofty purposes. Are they right?

12.1. Empty Promises

The rhetoric of EU architects and practitioners is compelling. They laud the EU's noble purposes: the prevention of intra-European armed conflict,

---

[1]ASEAN was established in 1967 and currently has 10 members: Indonesia, Malaysia, the Philippines, Singapore, Thailand, Brunei, Myanmar, Cambodia, Laos, and Vietnam. It has a population of 600 million (more than the EU). ASEAN often meets with Japan, China, and South Korea. These convocations are called ASEAN PLUS THREE. Taiwan is excluded as a gesture to China. North Korea, often called the hermit kingdom, is treated as a rogue state. Available at: www,asean.org/21083.pdg.

the cultivation of social democracy, and promotion of pan-European prosperity. Although, the EU is sometimes described as an United States of Europe, the Maastricht Treaty (1993) founding the union is an organization rather than an unified multinational state like the former Soviet Union, or a centrally dominated federation like America.[2] The arrangement can be likened to the UN, which serves as a sounding board, a forum for member consensus building, and a vehicle for moral suasion with various programmatic applications, but lacks supranational taxing authority and reliable compliance mechanisms. Heads of state, as in the EU European Council provide guidance, but do not participate in routine transnational governance.

---

[2]The EU has 27 members: Germany, France, Britain, Italy, Denmark, Netherlands, Belgium, Luxembourg, Ireland, Greece, Spain, Portugal, Austria, Sweden, Finland, Estonia, Latvia, Lithuania, Poland, Czech Republic, Hungary, Romania, Bulgaria, Slovakia, Slovenia, Cyprus and Malta. (Croatia, Macedonia, Iceland, Montenegro and Turkey are official candidate members) It is an "organization" supervising more than 500 million people, rather than a supranational sovereign government because it lacks power to adequately tax, transfer and compel member complicance. (The key treaties governing the European common space are: Paris Treaty, 1952, Rome Treaty 1958, Maastricht Treaty 1993, Lisbon Treaty 2009.) The EU's political headquarters are located in Brussels, Luxembourg and Strasbourg. Each EU country controls its own legislation (parliament), fiscal policy and programs, courts, internal security and defense. Some members like Great Britain, Sweden, Denmark and Norway determine their own monetary policy (independent currencies), while other like Germany, France and Italy have delegated this responsibility to the European Central Bank, which governs the euro. The EU government has seven institutions: The European Parliament, the Council of the European Union, the European Commission, the European Central Bank, the Court of Justice of the European Union, and the European Court of Auditors and the European Council, (The European Council made up of the President of the European Council, the President of the European Commission and one representative per member state(either its head of state, or head of government) guides the EU. The European Council is the supreme political authority, negotiating treaty changes and defining union policies and strategies. It convenes at least four times a year. Both the European Parliament and the Council of the European Union have legislative oversight and amendment responsibilities. The European Commission is the EU executive arm, assisted by the European Council. The interpretation and application of EU law and treaties is the responsibility of the Court of Justice of the European Union. The Common Foreign and Security Policy Committee discusses and coordinates external relations.

EU leaders also speak glowingly about practical results.[3] They claim that the region is more peaceful, progressive and prosperous than it otherwise would have been, and that it outshines America. The results of the Maastricht Treaty as they see it serve as a beacon attracting fresh candidates and the EU leaders envision a greater Europe spanning Eurasia from the Atlantic to the Pacific, and continental Europe from the Arctic Ocean to the southern shores of Mediterranean Sea. Nations located beyond this perimeter are excluded from the fold, but are encouraged to emulate the community's recipe for success in their own backyard.

Many Asians are listening, however, the case for an Asian Union is not as cogent as EU rhetoric suggests. There is a conspicuous gap between boasts and performance. The Germans, Austrians, French, British and Italians have refrained from armed combat with each other, but have been notably bellicose elsewhere, including wars with Serbia and Libya. Social democracy has spawned countless abuses, and EU economic growth after 1975 has been lackluster.

Per capita GDP growth decelerated persistently after Europe completed its postwar recovery phase, converging asymptotically toward zero and falling further behind America instead of catching up as supporters often erroneously imply (see Fig. 12.1), despite conspicuous advantages. EU comparative performance should have benefited from its relative economic backwardness (especially among new EU members), the widening of the European common space (the European Common Market), the formation of the EU (1993), and the adoption of the euro in 1999 as a common currency facilitating investment among less developed member states. Unemployment rates similarly

---

[3]The four main practical accomplishments of the EU, beyond cultivating a common identity intended to forestall another intra European and world war are (1) the formation of the European Common Market in 1957 [renamed the European Economic Community (EEC) in 1993] to promote intra-regional trade by eliminating tariff and quota barriers. (2) The European Council's decision to permit unimpeded tourist travel within the common space for EU citizens and foreigners (Schengen Agreement, 1985). However, work permits remain strictly controlled hampering labor mobility. (3) The transunion standardization of product characteristics, labor, business, and human rights regulations promoting liberalization and competitiveness (mostly under the aegis of the European Commission). (4) The creation of the euro to facilitate pan-union business and travel, and earn international seignorage.

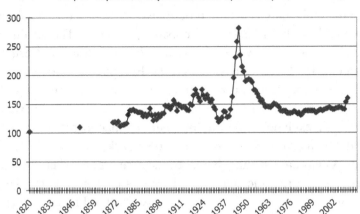

Figure 12.1.   U.S. per capital GDP: EU Benchmark 1990 Geary Khamis dollars (Western Europe = 100).

Source: Angus Maddison, World Economy: Historical Statistics, Paris: OECD, 2003, and website updates.

Note: The West European series above only includes core nations: The UK, Germany, Austria, France, Italy, Belgium, Netherlands, Switzerland, Denmark, Norway, Sweden and Finland.

have been loftier than the U.S. Other things equal, the EU should have converged to America's high per capital income frontier, but instead fell back.

The phenomenon is often described as Eurosclerosis, and has proven resistant to standard remedies. EU leaders sensibly tried to arrest the decline by liberalizing, opening markets, creating a common European "space" (the European Union), adopting a common monetary unit (the euro) and broadening its membership. They promised their peoples that sustainable growth would be increased by a full percent at every milestone, but the prophecy went unfulfilled. They assured everyone that Europe would be bubble free, only to have many union members savaged by the 2008 global financial crisis. Worse still, this failure to prevent continues to fester, enmeshing Portugal, Italy, Ireland, Greece and Spain (PIIGS) in a sovereign debt crisis, some believe, threatens the European Union's survival. Few expected the Soviet Union's demise, and although unlikely, it is not unthinkable that the EU may perish.

Would an Asian Union ultimately be forced to cope with similar perils? The question raises three distinct issues. (1) If Asia cloned the EU, would it likely discover solutions that continue to elude the West? (2) Do the vulnerabilities of supranational organizations place them at high risk for Asia-sclerosis and crises? (3) Are there special factors at play in Asia that favor or disfavor transnational regional arrangements?

12.2. Pitfalls

There is no reason to suppose that Asians would be any cleverer than Europeans if they adopted identical systems. Solutions may exist for the EU's quagmire, but the East needs to be wary of pitfalls.

The broad argument for selective collective governance is that it eliminates wasteful duplication, facilitates standardization and in some instances, allows policymakers to accept improvements that otherwise would be politically unpalatable. The EU experience, however, reveals that practice seldom follows theory. Brussels has persistently added layer upon layer of EU government to national bureaucracies, and seldom eliminated wasteful duplication. Standardization has advanced in Europe, but so too has stifling regulatory enforcement. Likewise, policymakers doubtlessly have used EU authority to foster competition, but obviously not enough to eradicate Eurosclerosis.

The broad argument against selective collective governance starts with these counterfactuals, but extends to destabilizing aspects of political horse trading. EU history illustrates the danger. One of the Maastricht Treaty's founding goals was to kill two birds with one stone, stimulating catch up among low per capita income members and spurring collective EEC growth by implicitly underwriting the creditworthiness of laggards.[4] Foreign direct investors from within the EU, together with outsiders around the globe sensing bonanza began outsourcing and speculatively investing in low factor cost (labor, land, capital) Europe; both newly accessioned states from the east (Poland, the Czech Republic, Hungary, Romania, Bulgaria, Estonia, Latvia, Lithuania, Slovakia and Slovenia) and less developed countries in the west (PIIGS). The adoption of the euro fanned the fire by eliminating foreign currency risk for the PIIGS, but not the eastern members because they retained their own currencies.

---

[4]Steven Rosefielde and Assaf Razin, "PIIGS," Chapter 4 of this volume.

The bubble caused labor and other factor costs to soar, without corresponding productivity gains vis-a-vis other member states, particularly Germany, discouraging further outsourcing, and making it extraordinarily difficult for PIIGS to cope with diminished post-crisis aggregate effective demand. They cannot rely on the ECB (European Central Bank) to work efficiently as a lender of last recourse to floundering commercial banks, or purchase the PIIGS' sovereign debt. Their only residual instrument is fiscal policy, but decades of excess public spending have placed tight constraints on further debt accumulation, forcing them to shoulder the quadruple burdens of high debt service, depression, massive unemployment and vanishing social services. PIIGS cannot depend on yet-to-be-developed EU financial institutions for government facilitated debt restructuring. EU government financial credits could have mitigated the sovereign debt problem. High unemployment likewise could have been ameliorated by stronger EU labor mobility, but none of these options proved to be politically viable.

The ECB too might have aided the PIIGS by excessively printing money and devaluing the euro, but the Germans remembering the 1922–1923 hyperinflation scourge refused to oblige. The PIIGS consequently are compelled to resolve the disequilibrium roundabout restoring competitiveness through a painful process of factor cost reduction and productivity enhancement that is slow and risky. They could choose to default on their debt forcing creditors to share the burden,[5] but might

---

[5]The root cause of the EU's problem is not excessive debt per se, but the ability of less productive members to run EU threatening deficits in a common currency regime, without the option of individual country devaluations. See Bruno Dallago and Chiara Guglielmetti, "Eurozone and Global Imbalances: Two Europes?" in Rosefielde, Steven, Masaaki Kuboniwa and Satoshi Mizobata, eds., *Two Asias: The Emerging Postcrisis Divide*, Singapore: World Scientific, 2011. As we know from the theory of optimum currency areas, there are benefits and costs of currency integration. Benefits are the reduced costs of doing business. If they are large, forming currency areas leads to large increases in trade. This is not what happened in the eurozone after the monetary union was established. The key problem is building a consensus on how best to restore price equilibrium after asymmetric shocks, bubbles and slumps that disparately affect individual member states. Labor mobility (Robert Mundell), fiscal integration (Peter Kenen), a strong central bank serving as lender of last recourse, and a fiscal unit to bail out sovereign debts lubricate equilibration, but don't automatically resolve conflicting member interests. The EU sovereign debt issue is tutoring members about the trade-offs that must be made, if the monetary union is to survive.

well find themselves ensnared in a vicious contractive spiral without a fiscal antidote.

The EU's contemporary sovereign debt crisis, central to any assessment of Europe's malfunctioning governance, is more than a matter of faulty policy, or easily rectified organizational misdesign. EU proponents desired an utopian Saint Simonian federation, and tried to construct it through piecemeal negotiation, but wound up with a dysfunctional mechanism resistant to consensus reform. Once upon a time, when Europeans were mislead into believing that union vouchsafed perpetual prosperity, it was relatively easy for people to invest in the dream, but Eurosclerosis and the sovereign debt crisis have revealed that while there always are free riders, there are no "free lunches." Sacrifices for expected gain are one thing; for expected losses something entirely different. It will take an Herculean effort for the EU to extricate itself from this morass. Social democrats are going to be reluctant to confront the organization's flawed design, eradicate dysfunctional dependences and slenderize government programs and regulation. The Soviet Union's demise proved that planned socialism (where private property, business and entrepreneurship are criminalized) failed the competitive systems test. Now, it seems that the EU is on a path to demonstrate that market socialism is similarly inferior, even judged by the flagging American standard.

An Asian Union would be constructed with different cultural priors,[6] but the risk of dysfunctional supranational systems architecture would be simi-

---

[6] Europe's sociocratic mindset (socio-kratia: rule of "society:) bears substantial blame. First, social democratic leaders disregard majority preferences whenever socialist principle dictates. Second, socialists flout Lockean minority property rights and business protections. As a consequence, European governors not only overprogram, overregulate, misprogram and misregulate, they also curtail economic liberty and overtax. These democratic abuses do not destroy the economy immediately, but they take their cumulative toll in reserved effort, red tape and inefficiency. Worker ardor is dampened by entitlements (including barriers to dismissal that make hiring more like marriage with stiff alimony payments in case of divorce), and investors are daunted by regulatory monkey business and over-taxation. Choices of all kinds are warped, and government administrative layering adds cost, but not value.

These socialist losses apply to each and every social democratic European country regardless of external relationships, just as they did in Eastern and Central Europe during the postwar Soviet era. The extension of socialism across the European space compounds the

lar. Some members inevitably would seek to be free riders imposing mammoth obligations on others, without a unified central authority powerful enough to simultaneously keep the forces of destabilization in check, while preserving the union. Many arguments can be concocted for transnational organizations, but crisis prevention does not seem to be one of them.

12.3. Asian Cultural and Material Disparities

This brings us to the question of whether there are any special Asian factors that favor or disfavor collective governance. Of course, the answer in part depends on which Asian countries are to be included in the Asian Union. Homogeneous groupings are apt to fare better, but it is difficult to see any appealing supranational governance combinations when account is properly taken for cultural, historical, ideological, political and distributive factors. Let us then arbitrarily investigate the possibilities of an East Asian Union (ASEAN PLUS FIVE) encompassing Japan, South Korea, Taiwan, Singapore (Asian tigers), China, North Korea, Vietnam, Laos, Cambodia,

---

problem, even though advocates of the Common Market, the EU and the euro contend that trans-union administrative rationalization creates a level playing field and enhances competitiveness. It is conceivable that institutional aspects of the EU could save social democracy from itself, but close scrutiny of developments during the past twenty years debunk claims about the Union's miraculous powers.

These accomplishments (tempered by overregulation and related anticompetitive games) are not intrinsically socialist, except to the extent that regulations promote labor protection, limit private property rights and economic liberty, and increase the scale and scope of government by layering trans-union administration on top of each member's existing arrangements. Pluses may exceed minuses, but as shown in Fig. 12.1, not enough to compensate for the larger deficiencies of social democracy.

Socialism is not just a matter of condemning the side effects of Adam Smith's invisible hand, and the libertarian preference for small government (without Marx's harmonist presumption); it is a philosophy that makes basic principles like exploitation free societies, and egalitarianism absolutes. Where democrats tolerate conflicting claims about the *summum bonum* (highest good), socialists including those who call themselves social democrats contend that sovereigns have a superior duty to protect that transcends personal freedom and choice. Both share common humanist and Enlightenment views about the primacy of the individual and the virtue of autonomy in building worthy existences, but for socialists individual fulfillment takes a back seat to the higher good of egalitarianism and societal wellbeing.

Myanmar (communist/socialist), Thailand, Malaysia, Indonesia and the Philippines using an EU benchmark. The Europeans, with few exceptions, share a common 2000-year-old heritage founded on Athenian democracy, Roman law, humanism, the Enlightenment and socialism. They are committed to social democracy (welfare state), individual empowerment, egalitarianism, social justice, the rule of law, competitive markets and entrepreneurship. The dispersion of per capita income among core members is narrow despite significant population and territorial differences. Portugal, Greece and many new East European members are much poorer than the founders, but the disparity is nothing compared with the 15 to 1 per capita income differential between South and North Korea.

East Asia, by contrast, is homogeneous in very different ways. The rule of men, communities and religion take precedence over the rule of contract law. Rent-granting trumps competition. Protectionism, overtrading and excess dollar reserve holding are rife. This means that no matter how much Asians say that they are committed to a level economic playing field, the instinct of most is to strive for privilege and tactical advantage in ways that undermine supranational governance.[7] This defect is compounded by population and development asymmetries. The EU's richest countries are among its most populus. When smaller and poorer nations joined the club, risk perceptions declined sharply facilitating investment flows from advanced outsourcers to the EU's less developed periphery, spurring catch up and accelerating growth across the community. The polarities in Asia are just the opposite. Relatively poor, high population countries like China, Indonesia, the Philippines and Vietnam are net recipients of intraregional foreign direct investment, not donors. Any perceived risk reduction wrought by an East Asian Union would prompt some increased intraregional investment flows to late starters, but these could not amount to much on a proportionate basis. Japan, South Korea, Taiwan and Singapore could not invest enough fresh money to significantly affect prevailing regional growth trends. An AU economic miracle should not be anticipated on this score.

Macroeconomic asymmetries follow the same pattern. The small size of the PIIGS enables EU founders to face their sovereign debt crisis with

---

[7]Daisuke Hirataka.

comparative equanimity. It appears that Germany and France are prepared for "haircuts" (partial PIIGS' sovereign debt forgiveness). But how much of a helping hand could Japan, South Korea, Taiwan and Singapore give should bubbles burst in China, Vietnam and Indonesia? If they are AU members, there will be intense institutional pressure to do more than their systems can bear. Likewise, East Asia might consider emulating the EU's Schengen Agreement (1985) allowing visa free member mobility throughout the region. Unencumbered travel does not entail a right to work anywhere in the Union, but pressures of this kind have caused considerable discord, even though the illegal migrant problem faced by Germany, France and the UK is trivial compared to potential flows of more than a billion migrants from China, Indonesia, Vietnam and Myanmar into Japan, South Korea, Taiwan and Singapore. From a microtheoretic standpoint, these flows should be beneficial, however, from a social and cultural perspective they could be catastrophic.[8]

---

[8]The Taiwanese government decided to open its domestic labor market to foreigners at the beginning of the 1990s to alleviate shortages and dampen rising wages. Low-skilled labor, primarily from ASEAN countries (Tsay and Lin, 2001) immediately poured into Taiwan. Official data report that there were more than 300,000 foreign laborers in the Republic of China by the end of 2005, recently rising to 360,000. About 100,000 illegal workers need to be added to the total. Foreign brides (most of who are seeking work permits) account for another 420,000 to 450,000 outsiders. More than 10% of the immigrants qualify as skilled laborers. Foreign immigrants surprisingly have been concentrated not only in labor intensive but also in capital intensive industries, pressuring unskilled domestic employees to upgrade their skills. The phenomenon is most conspicuous in manufacturing, construction and services. Unemployment also has been correlated with immigration. Tsay and Lin (2001) indicate that unemployment increases 0.1% for every 15,000 foreign entrants into the domestic labor market. Lin (2002a; 2002b) finds that uneducated and low-skilled domestic workers not only have been "pushed" into new types of jobs, but often relocate. Domestic workers in the Taipei Prefecture, and less well educated laborers in the Taoyuan Prefecture have been the principal regional outmigrators. See Lin, J.P. (2002a), *"Impacts of Foreign Labor on the Internal Migration of Domestic Labor: The Case of Taiwan,"* in Taiwan Economic Association, ed., Taiwan Economic Association Conference Proceedings, 2001, Taiwan: Taipei, pp. 329–363. Lin, J.P. (2002b), *"Immigration 'Pushes' and Domestic Labor 'Flights': Impact of Foreign Labor on the Manpower Redistribution of Taiwan,"* Paper presented at the XVth ISA World Congress of Sociology, Bribane Australia, July 2002. Tsay, C.L., and J.P Lin (2001), *Labor Importation and Unemployment of Local Workers in Taiwan,"* Asia and Pacific Migration Journal, Vol. 10, pp. 505–534.

Finally, East Asians inevitably will have to consider the costs and benefits of monetary union following the EU example, even though ASEAN currently eschews the possibility. The Europeans created a European Central Bank (ECB) and the euro (1999) to lubricate intraregional transactions and earn seigniorage, with participating members agreeing to surrender independent monetary and foreign exchange rate policy. The benefits were palpable when times were good. The ECB vigilantly resisted the temptation to over-leverage, mindful of inflationary risks, and the euro has become an international reserve currency. Nonetheless, the 2008 global financial crisis and its aftermath soon revealed the monetary union's vulnerabilities. Sovereign debt laden PIIGS to their consternation found themselves mired in a severe depression, without remedial recourse to fiscal, monetary and foreign exchange policy. They wore out their welcome in financial markets, and surrendered their control over the money supply and foreign exchange rates to the ECB, leaving PIIGS to cope solely with deflationary instruments. An Asia version of this melodrama could take many forms, depending on who controlled the ACB (Asian Central Bank), China (notably tolerant of inflation) or Japan (inflation averse), but the potential for catastrophic outcomes given intraregional asymmetries is obvious. East Asians of course must decide for themselves whether risk adjusted benefits are likely to exceed the expected costs of an AU, but given the EU's disappointing results, it is difficult to see why the region should hasten to emulate Europe's mistake.

Economic Union isn't East Asia's only option. The formation of a United States of Asia beyond China's reacquisition of Taiwan is unthinkable, as is a Soviet-style common market (Comecon). However, Asia has vast experience promoting free trade through forums (APEC),[9] as well as with customs unions and regional security alliances. ASEAN has been particularly active, and a case can be made for the proposition that it should content itself with operating within the framework of an

---

[9]Asia-Pacific Economic Cooperation (APEC) is a forum of 21 Pacific Rim countries established in 1989, including Taiwan which is permitted to participate at a sub-prime misterial level. It is not a supranational organization with governance rights over members.

Asian Community (AC),[10] instead of pressing forward into the twilight zone of an AU. The best as the French are won't to say, too often is the enemy of the good.

12.4. Prevention

The 2008 global financial crisis neither spared the EU nor the ASEAN economic community. If the crisis were preventable, or ameliorable beyond the benefits of dirty currency floats, both the EU and ASEAN failed to adequately protect. Neither created an agency dedicated to this task, trusting politics as usual to carry the day.

ASEAN however did address the issue obliquely with its Chiang Mai Initiative(CMI), a free standing multilateral currency swap agreement among ten members of ASEAN, China(including Hong Kong), Japan and South Korea capable of dovetailing with and supplementing IMF arrangements as members prefer. It draws from a foreign exchange reserves pool launched March 24, 2010, worth $120 billion. The initiative began as a series of bilateral swap arrangements after ASEAN PLUS THREE met on May 6, 2000, in Chiang Mai, Thailand at an annual meeting of the Asian Development Bank. The proposal was intended to prevent a recurrence of the 1997 Asian Financial Crisis, but was criticized as being a band aid. CMI worked poorly during the global financial crisis of 2008–2010. China, Japan and South Korea account for three quarters of the swap fund.

It therefore can be safely concluded that supranational organizations, whether economic communities or unions don't in and of themselves prevent or mitigate bubbles and crises. They are not "bigger is better" panaceas for the shortcomings of nation states, but they can compound the misery as the PIIGS unhappily learned the hard way. ASEAN PLUS FIVE should not ignore the lesson.

---

[10]A "community" is a transnational governance institution covering various policies including a common tariff regime. A "union" extends cooperation to more fundamental aspects of governance including the adoption of a common currency.

CHAPTER 13

BUDDHIST CRISIS PREVENTION
AND MANAGEMENT

TEERANA BHONGMAKAPAT

13.1. Introduction

Financial crises have been experienced in a number of economies, both developed and underdeveloped, and the frequency of their occurrence has increased over the past 15 years. Crises in many countries in Latin America, Asia, Western Europe, and North America originated in the private sector and then spread to other countries in the region and the world. The Thai crisis of 1997–1998 took place swiftly after the Mexican crisis of 1995, and spread throughout Asia and some connected economies. The U.S. subprime crisis, which started in 2007, has been contagious globally causing great recessions and debt crises in many European countries. The contagious nature of crises seems endemic, suggesting the need for concerted international crisis prevention and management.

Global financial corrections are unavoidable whenever contagion and spillover effects are significant. They are artifacts of globalization. Nonetheless, it is important for economies to be strongly disciplined in both the private and public sectors to mitigate social distress. Ordinary citizens find themselves vulnerable to the machinations of speculators able to make big bets offering the prospect of huge rewards, at little personal risk. The government has a duty to protect these innocent victims by maintaining a level playing field and providing compensation where feasible, but often is remiss. Officials responsible for crises frequently have already resigned, and those in power do not consider themselves accountable for their predecessors' failings. Tirole (2002) showed in the Mexican case that domestic taxpayers were stuck with the full cost of the crisis. He found this outcome was typical for emerging market economies, with investors in troubled financial institutions also bearing a hefty share of the burden.

Better results are possible. First, governments must acknowledge their duties to prevent and protect instead of dithering and inventing excuses. Second, they must resist the temptation raise tax revenue unfairly by subtle ploys such as artificially low interest rate policies, investment subsidies, real estate incentives and excessive government borrowing because they pave the road for greater crises later. Third, prompt counter-crisis intervention is imperative because it is not practical to wait for global authorities to build a consensus. This study therefore focuses on the nation aspect of crises more than international connections.

Thailand's crisis experience during the late 1990s provides two useful lessons. First, the recovery process was weak because intervention efforts were distorted by privileged political influences. Second, better results would have been achieved if the government had abided by His Majesty the King's concept of Sufficiency Economy, concentrated on strengthening the rural sector and local communities. Had private interests been better coached about their Buddhist obligations for self-discipline, and their duty for compassion, Thailand would have avoided needless suffering. His Majesty the King's framework is consistent with Buddhist teachings on consumer awareness, business ethics, the environment, and sustainable development. It provides an excellent foundation for better prevention and crisis management.

This chapter reviews the macroeconomic recovery initiatives adopted during the Thai crisis of 1997–1998, focuses on Thailand's mounting indebtedness problem, elaborates the Buddhist Sufficiency alternative, and details the virtues that make it meritorious.

13.2. The Macroeconomic Approach to Crisis Management in Thailand

The early economic development literature blamed crises on policy errors in crisis stricken nations (see Krugman, 1978). Fixed exchange rates and inconsistent macroeconomic policies were said to be the main culprits in Latin America's financial crashes during the 1970s and 1980s, and in

Sweden during the 1990s. Floating peg exchange rates were implicated in the European community's 1992 crisis, and flexible exchange rates for America's bubble. It gradually became clear through trial and error that there were no crisis free exchange rate regimes, prompting theorists to shift their attention to other suspects.

Second-generation models attributed crises to speculative frenzies, where "pigs" imagined that there would always be "bigger pigs" willing to purchase inflated assets at ever higher prices. This self-fulfilling prophecy was sustainable for a while, creating huge bubbles that burst into full fledged crises.

Kaminsky and Reinhart (1999) demonstrated that "bigger pig" financial globalization was destructive. Developing countries that chose to financially liberalize turned out to be especially vulnerable. Thailand was no exception. During the boom of the early and mid-1990s, policymakers liberalized capital flows and intermittently adopted a tight money regime. This raised domestic interest rates, enticing a massive inflow of carry trade foreign capital, mostly from Japan, that ignited domestic speculation, setting the stage for a hot money crisis when bullish expectations were reversed in a fixed exchange rate regime. Mundell–Fleming found that the Thai crisis to be the inevitable consequence of a "trilemma," where policymakers could not preserve foreign exchange rate stability and simultaneously press expansionary fiscal and monetary policies.[1]

Bhongmakapat (2001) showed that the capital flight predictable from the Mundell–Fleming trilemma caused Thailand to abandon its fixed exchange regime during the 1997–1998 crisis. Thailand's external debt steadily rose in the 1990s as a direct result of its macroeconomic development policy, reaching 59.7% of GDP in 1996. The fixed exchange rate regime was a principal culprit. The baht was pegged to an appreciating U.S. dollar that made its exports increasing uncompetitive. Foreign reserves at the time were deemed sufficient to defend the baht, but when confidence was lost due to deteriorating current account deficits and high short-term external borrowing, the baht came under persistent attack until it collapsed in mid-1997. This caused external debt mostly denominated in U.S. dollars to rise to 72.4% and then to 93.9% of GDP in 1997 and 1998, respectively (see Table 13.1) Output loss

---

[1] Mundell (1963) and Fleming (1962).

Table 13.1.   Thailand's macroeconomic indicators.

	1995	1996	1997	1998	1999	2000	2001	2002
GDP (Bn baht)	4,186.2	4,611.0	4,732.6	4,626.4	4,637.0	4,922.7	5,133.5	5,450.6
GDP (Bn $)	168.0	182.0	150.9	111.8	122.5	122.6	115.4	126.8
Real GDP growth (%)	9.2	5.8	-1.4	-10.5	4.4	4.8	2.2	5.3
CPI inflation (%)	5.70	5.90	5.60	8.00	0.30	1.60	1.60	0.70
Policy interest rate*	10.33	10.50	11.50	12.50	5.83	4.00	3.98	3.46
Exchange rate (B/$)	24.92	25.34	31.37	41.37	37.84	40.16	44.48	43.00
Real exchange rate	111.24	116.14	107.15	92.30	95.63	92.21	87.55	89.47
Capacity utilization (%)	78.27	75.15	69.92	58.70	65.70	68.49	64.44	64.48
Government Budget (%GDP)	2.8	2.3	-1.9	-2.4	-2.8	-2.4	-2.1	-2.2
Current account (%GDP)	-7.8	-7.9	-2.0	12.7	10.2	7.6	4.4	3.6
External debt (%GDP)	60.01	59.74	72.38	93.89	77.52	65.02	58.49	46.94
Net Foreign Reserves (Bn $)	37.0	38.7	27.0	29.5	34.8	32.7	33.0	38.9
Money Supply, M2 (%change)	—	—	—	9.3	1.5	3.9	5.7	1.3

(*Continued*)

Table 13.1 (Continued)

	2003	2004	2005	2006	2007	2008	2009	2010
GDP (Bn baht)	5,917.3	6,489.4	7,092.8	7,844.9	8,525.2	9,080.4	9,041.5	10,104.8
GDP (Bn $)	142.5	161.1	176.1	206.8	246.7	272.2	263.3	318.5
Real GDP growth (%)	7.1	6.3	4.6	5.1	5.0	2.5	-2.3	7.8
CPI inflation (%)	1.80	2.70	4.50	4.70	2.30	5.50	-0.90	3.30
Policy interest rate	2.96	2.94	4.29	6.29	4.19	3.83	1.85	2.00
Exchange rate (B/$)	41.53	40.27	40.27	37.93	34.56	33.36	34.34	31.73
Real exchange rate	87.61	87.34	88.15	94.86	100.00	100.00	97.52	102.86
Capacity utilization(%)	69.81	71.55	72.07	73.91	72.51	67.64	61.0	63.2
Government Budget (%GDP)	0.6	0.3	0.2	0.1	-1.1	-0.2	-4.7	-2.0
Current account (%GDP)	3.3	1.7	-4.3	1.1	5.7	0.6	8.2	4.6
External debt (%GDP)	36.29	36.43	33.61	33.80	30.16	27.96	28.60	31.59
Net Foreign Reserves (Bn$)	42.1	49.8	52.1	67.0	87.4	111.0	138.4	172.1
Money Supply, M2 (%change)	6.2	5.8	6.1	8.2	6.3	9.2	6.8	10.9

Note: Using Bank rate until 2001 then after is End of day liquidity rate.
Source: Bank of Thailand.

was very substantial and the banking sector was beset by panicky, hot money driven withdrawals.

The IMF suggested that Thailand resolve the crisis after the horse left the corral with high interest rates designed to entice fresh capital inflows. The idea was to close the external current account gap and then concentrate on remedying the Keynesian output deficit, but the strategy backfired placing the adjustment burden on internal devaluation, that is, reduced wage rates, goods and asset prices. Thailand, eventually recovered, but the process was needlessly traumatic.

Later, in 1998, although the IMF preferred fiscal expansion to easy money, low interest rates were adopted to ease the financial panic and facilitate debt restructuring. The domestic balance was then given more emphasis. The policy interest rate was cut dramatically in the third quarter of 1998, reduced to 5.8% and 4.0% in 1999 and 2000, respectively (see Table 13.1). Real GDP growth recovered moderately from −10.5% in 1998 to 4.4% and 4.8% in 1999 and 2000.[2]

Domestic financial companies also contributed to the 1997 crisis. They accumulated huge toxic private debt that proved difficult to pare. The bulk of these bad debts accrued from the failure of 56 financial companies, plus one commercial bank at the crisis's onset. The Financial Institution Development Fund, FIDF (the nation's financial guarantee agency) was compelled to provide liquidity to the Bangkok Commercial (BBC), and its *de facto* affiliate, the Thai Fuji finance company shortly before the exchange rate crisis. It then quickly discovered that 15 other firms required liquidity assistance to the tune of 53,800 million baht. Ultimately, all became insolvent, and the FIDF was forced to provide 700,000 million baht in the process of closing them down in August 1997. The debt then was auctioned at fire sale prices that recouped a pittance of their cost.[3] Nonetheless, FIDF debts today remain large, amounting to approximately

---

[2] Stanley Fischer (1998) has noted that the IMF gave Thailand faulty advice because it underestimated the risk of regional contagion.

[3] During the period of the Thai crisis some economists suggested that the debt should be kept standstill rather being on fire-sale. See Miller and Zhang (1998), Krugman (1998), and Miller and Stiglitz (2010).

940 billion baht, despite the currency devaluation, a recovery in export demand and the restoration of a current account surplus.

On balance, Thailand managed to temporarily weather the storm, but laid the foundation for a more powerful tsunami later.

13.3. The Crisis' Aftermath and Persistent Indebtedness

Excessive debt remains a significant threat to Thailand's economic stability (McKinnon and Pill, 1996; Goldstein, 2003). The problem pervades the private investment community, households, and the public sector. Fiscal and monetary policies were very expansionary during the Thaksin administration (2001–2006). It introduced a multitude of populist measures through government programs and credits, while maintaining low interest and exchange rate polices.

These loose macroeconomic policies bolstered aggregate demand, but encouraged further debt accumulation in the consumer and public sectors. Table 13.2 provides statistics on household debt since 1996. It rose substantially during 2002–2006 and remained high thereafter due to continued populist pressures for easy state bank lending. According to the latest survey data, the household debt-income ratio increased slightly from 52.1% in 2007 to 53.7% in 2009, indicating that household debt was unaffected by the global crisis during 2007 and 2008.

Table 13.2.   Average Household debt.

(Baht)

	1996	1998	2000	2002	2004	2006	2007	2009
Debt Per Household	52,001	69,674	68,405	82,485	104,571	116,585	116,681	134,699
Annual Household Income	129,348	149,904	145,800	164,832	179,556	213,444	223,920	250,848
Debt/ Income Ratio (%)	40.20	46.48	46.92	50.04	58.24	54.62	52.11	53.70

Source: National Statistical Office.

Table 13.3.   Public debt.

Year	Government Debt	Government Enterprise Public Debt	(Million Baht) FIDF	Total	% of GDP
2003	843,207.03	853,214.50	1,205,960.20	2,902,381.73	49.05%
2004	824,317.33	932,446.53	1,364,039.00	3,120,802.86	48.09%
2005	831,058.54	1,036,962.48	1,428,018.31	3,296,039.33	46.47%
2006	825,480.69	914,531.67	1,360,584.03	3,100,596.39	39.52%
2007	888,036.91	939,271.09	1,324,674.32	3,151,982.32	36.97%
2008	986,217.48	1,047,262.93	1,148,516.79	3,181,997.20	35.04%
2009	1,455,519.89	1,097,956.12	1,215,244.71	3,768,720.72	41.68%
2010	1,860,322.04	1,078,805.56	1,172,683.87	4,111,811.47	40.69%
2011F	1,877,913.52*	1,072,101.07*	1,163,387.81*	4,113,402.40*	38.84%

*Public debt figures are of June 2011.
Source: Ministry of Finance.

The ultimate consequences of Thailand's easy lending policy will depend on the extent to which the government stimulus package raises productivity. Walter Heller and other Keynesian economists contend that fiscal stimulus spurs productivity growth,[4] but this claim must be taken with a grain of salt because it disregards country risks associated with high public debt.

The situation in this regard is disturbing. Thailand's public debt has risen from 15.9% of GDP in 1996 to 49.1% by 2003. As shown in Table 13.3, in 2003, almost 41.6% of total public debt was toxic FIDF inherited from the 1997 financial crisis. The proportion of government debt in total public debt rose from 29.1% in 2003 to 45.2% in 2010. Should these trends persist, they will blight Thailand's future.

Thailand's economy has been vulnerable to foreign business cycles. Its growth was coupled with the west's during the 2007–2009 crisis, and recovered slowly in tandem with most other countries the following year, unlike China and India which displayed robust growth throughout (see Table 13.4).

---

[4] For Heller's Keynesian policy initiatives, see Pechman (2008).

Table 13.4. Public debt, bank loans and economic growth.

Year	World growth	Growth in Developed countries	Growth in Emerging Asia	Thailand's economic growth	Public debt as % of GDP*	Bank loans as % of GDP	Public debt plus bank loans as % of GDP
					(Percent)		
2003	3.6	1.9	8.1	7.1	49.05	106.57	155.62
2004	4.9	3.1	8.6	6.3	48.09	105.01	153.10
2005	4.6	2.7	9.5	4.6	46.47	104.75	151.22
2006	5.2	3.0	10.4	5.1	39.52	99.66	139.18
2007	5.4	2.7	11.4	5.0	36.97	95.26	132.23
2008	2.9	0.2	7.7	2.5	35.04	104.59	139.64
2009	−0.5	-3.4	7.2	−2.3	41.68	113.24	154.92
2010	5.0	3.0	9.5	7.8	40.69	114.90	155.59
2011^F	4.4	2.4	8.4	1.8	38.84^	123.53^	162.37^

* Public debts here exclude BOT debt.
^ Public debt and bank loans are of June and August, respectively.
Source: Bank of Thailand.

The bloody political crisis in April 2009 also may have been a contributory factor, limiting the government's room for fiscal maneuver.

Investment expenditure accounted for less than 20% of total government spending, and its proportion was reduced to accommodate government spending on wage and salaries. The emphasis on consumption was exacerbated moreover by "quasi-fiscal" populist expenditures using off-budget tactics like subsidized state bank loans.

These contingent liabilities are not included in official public debt data. From 2003 to 2010, they grew from 19.0% to 25.9% of total loans (see Table 13.5).

13.4. Buddhist Sufficiency Strategy

During the late 1980s and early 1990s, Thailand was lauded as East Asia's fifth Tiger (*Fortune*, 1988). The economy grew rapidly and the nation was optimistic. Success however breeds corruption, prompting His Majesty the King Bhumibol Adulyadej to warn Thais not to succumb to greed, or

Table 13.5. Loan outstanding by commercial banks and specialized state banks.

			(Billion Baht)
Year	Commercial Bank Loans	State Banks Loans	Total Bank Loans
2003	5,110.82	1195.387	6,306.21
2004	5,432.84	1381.475	6,814.31
2005	5,795.97	1634.064	7,430.03
2006	6,013.58	1804.329	7,817.91
2007	6,245.83	1875.016	8,120.85
2008	7,393.25	2104.285	9,497.54
2009	7,691.51	2546.654	10,238.16
2010	8,607.21	3003.144	11,610.36
2011 (Aug.)	9,712.60	3368.732	13,081.33

Source: Bank of Thailand.

Lobha in *Pali* Buddhist language. Thais were advised to be self-sufficient and caring; concerns voiced earlier in other Royal speeches:

> ... We are not a rich country. We have some, enough to live on, but not a country which progresses extraordinarily. If we are a very progressive country, we are then to move backwards. Those who are advanced industrial countries will need to move backwards and frighteningly backwards. If we manage ourselves in the style of the poor, not too much attached to the textbook, we shall do it with harmony which is compassion, we will live on forever.

> (Dusit Palace, December 4, 1991, unofficial translation)

> ... Usually, people like to be optimistic, as we called it "Leng Phon Lert" (in Thai). They see Thailand as progressing. Finances, industries and trade are doing well and have good profits. For the other (pessimistic) way, I have to say that we are decaying. Mostly, the theory will address that there is such amount of money, or such amount of borrowing, the economy is meant to be advanced and the country is advanced and could be a superpower hopefully. I am sorry to warn them that the numbers were of course good, but if we are not careful about basic needs of the people, it is the wrong way...

> (Dusit Palace, December 4, 1993, unofficial translation)

In His Royal speech in December 1997, five months after the collapse of the exchange rate regime, HM the King remarked that:

> Recently, so many projects have been implemented, so many factories have been built, that it was thought Thailand would become a little tiger, and then a big tiger. People were crazy about becoming a tiger...
>
> Being a tiger is not important. The important thing for us is to have a sufficient economy. A sufficient economy means to have enough to support ourselves...
>
> It doesn't have to be complete, not even half, perhaps just a quarter, then we can survive...
>
> Those who like modern economics may not appreciate this. But we have to take a careful step backwards.
>
> (Dusit Palace, 4 December 1997, translated by UNDP, 2007)

This counsel differs sharply from the western notion that people can never have too much (nonsatiation), and the Keynesian corollary that during recessions consumption is virtuous and thrift vicious because excess saving is the root of deficient aggregate demand. Keynesians insist that people, including investors, should be encouraged to spend as much as they can instead of repaying debts, because this strategy provides a fast track to recovery and rapid economic growth. But His Majesty the King correctly recognizes that the Keynesian outlook is one-sided; that it makes a fetish out of "never enough," and disregards the danger of debt addiction. The right path requires comprehensively restoring equilibrium in all markets including debt, coupled with harmonious development.

Unfortunately, His Majesty the King's sage advice was ignored before the crisis. Thais overinvested and accumulated too much debt. The nation's current account surplus was inadequate to cover its potential obligations, and excess domestic spending was financed by borrowing from abroad. This imprudent behavior exposed Thailand to catastrophic risk, but policymakers failed to draw the right conclusions even after the economy plunged into depression. They continued relying on excess fiscal, monetary and financial stimulus at the expense of moderation hoping to finance excess debt with pie-in-the-sky productivity gains.

Self-discipline, moderation, and balance are not easily achieved, but if properly coached, Thais can do the right thing. They can live within their means, and channel their energies for harmonious progress by adhering to the precepts of His Majesty the King's Sufficiency Economy projects,[5] derived from the crown's experience helping the poor.[6]

The Sufficiency Economy Philosophy aims to construct a comprehensively harmonious society at the household, community, and national levels. As in His Royal Speech in 1974, HM the King remarked development should concentrate on assuring the necessities of life for everyone first, and then attending to special individual and local needs, avoiding imbalances and crises.

HM the King suggested a so-called "New Theory" aimed at teaching small farmers sound husbandry with simple "rule of thumb" techniques. His royal guidance is very scientific. Farmers, mostly small ones with about 15 Rai (6 acres) land holdings, are advised to divide their land holdings into four zones: (1) 30% for rice cultivation sufficient for a farmer household, (2) 30% for other crops and gardening, (3) 30% for water resources and fish farming and (4) 10% for home and living areas. This land use scheme stresses organic food production and crop diversification as a better alternative to rice monoculture dominant in Thailand since the 1960s. HM the King remarked that:

> Therefore, this New Theory will be able to expand, maybe all over the country, but it has to be slow because it requires significant amount of spending. We should work on it gradually, and should see it as a way to let the people live on accordingly: they may not be rich but have enough to live on, not being starved. The New Theory could therefore be useful, but it has to be done carefully.

> (Dusit Palace, 4 December 1994, unofficial translation)

---

[5] For its meanings and applications, see Puntasen *et al.* (2003), Piboolsravut (2004), UNDP (2007), and Wibulswasadi *et al.* (2010).

[6] HM the King involved with development projects since his early years of his reign. His first Royal Project was the Khao Tao project, which was to provide better irrigation and drinking water to small farmers and was completed as early as in 1953. His Royal Projects are presently over 3,000 projects (UNDP, 2007: p.27).

Table 13.6. Sufficiency economy and its degree of applications in practice.

	Not applicable (1)	Little (2)	Modest (3)	Substantial (4)	(3)+(4)
Agriculture	1.14	8.44	28.14	62.28	90.42
Education	2.04	17.30	42.34	38.32	80.66
Government	3.51	18.26	42.50	35.73	78.23
Commerce	2.04	22.55	45.88	29.52	75.40
Industry	3.18	20.72	49.97	26.13	76.10
Services	2.22	24.74	49.73	23.30	73.03

Source: Thai Rath Newspaper and Business and Economic Forecast Center, UTCC, 2007, cited in Wiriyapipat (2009).

HM the King, building on this foundation, further recommended the development of cooperative institutions at the community level to improve productivity. He counseled establishing local exchanges that tapped indigenous strengths, followed by the creation of external links to foster networking, knowledge, technology and cooperation with other Thais.[7]

The Philosophy of Sufficiency Economy is applicable to non-agricultural activities too. A survey revealed that 70% of participants sampled believed that the principles of the Sufficiency Economy were relevant in all productive endeavors (see Table 13.6).

The principles of Sufficiency Economy helped numerous crisis stricken businesses in 1997 by inculcating positive attitudes and teaching sound management techniques. The Chumphon Cabana Resort and Driving Center provides a good example. The hotel was nearly bankrupted by the crisis. The owner's son had to succeed his father and contemplated selling the hotel to pay off the debt. However, he decided instead to restructure the business, using some of his land to cultivate organic food. Productivity was enhanced, and the business was made profitable by training managers

---

[7] The three principles of the Sufficiency Economy include (1) Moderation (that is appropriate to personal and social conditions), (2) Reasonableness (that is consistent to scientific causations, legal regulations and morality) and (3) Self-immunity (that makes good preparation and smooth adjustment towards shocks). See Piboolsravut (2004) and UNDP (2007) for details.

and employees to give, not to take. The new approach was win-win, providing superior services to customers, and greater happiness for everyone involved in the business.

During the crisis, corporations adhering to the Sufficiency Economy Philosophy fared better than most (Puntasen *et al.*, 2003). They operated their factories efficiently, mindful of managerial ethical obligations to their consumers and employees. However, after the crisis, some succumbed to temptation.

The Sufficiency Economy Philosophy is completely compatible with Buddhism. It discourages greed and promotes loving-kindness, compassion, charity, and integrity. Other religions such as Hinduism, Christianity, and Islam share these values. HM the King is devoutly Buddhist and his advice reflects his faith.

Buddhism emerged over 25 centuries ago after the dominance of the ancient Brahmas, who laid the early foundations of Hinduism. The purity of Buddha's teachings is still preserved in many parts of the world. Buddhism and Hinduism both consider life to be a combination of mind (*Citta*) and matter, or body (*Kaya*), and emphasize the power of the mind to manage the body. Brahmas learned to control the mind as a tool for disciplining the body, whereas Buddhism focused on understanding, training and empowering the mind as a path to enlightenment, independent of the body.

Lord Buddha's Four Noble Truths and noble practices (*Ariya Magga*) provide guidelines for purifying contaminated minds from physical and spiritual impurities originating in the body. This is accomplished through analysis and enlightening insight. Buddhism considers the mind, not material things the key to worthy existences. Virtue is not a matter of blind luck, it depends on right actions.

Sufficiency Economy Philosophy is derived from these Buddhist principles. It requires people to follow Buddha's middle path. Buddhists are taught to avoid two extremes, lust and self-deprivation.[8] Unenlightened people crave material and sensual pleasures, even though their desires invariably bring them grief. Buddhism alerts believers to this danger and the alternative extreme of asceticism. It teaches them to shun materialism, consumerism, and

---

[8] This is the teaching establishment the Buddha gave to his first five disciples, called the *Dhamma-cakka Sutta* (the Wheel of the Law).

self-deprivation. This requires moderation. Virtuous Buddhists avoid excesses. They reject hedonism and asceticism, always treading the middle way.

People are taught in Buddhism not to allow their rational utility seeking to be corrupted by desire. They are advised to dispassionately utility maximize, labor honestly, conduct business fairly, and prudently save for the future. This is sometimes called "Knowing to be moderate, not having too much or too little for oneself" (*Mattannuta* in *Pali*, or "Ru-Jak-Por-Pramarn" in Thai). The Moderation principle in the Sufficiency Economy Philosophy is tantamount to following the Buddhist middle path within each individual's station and capacities. One shoe does not fit all feet. Buddhism and the Sufficiency Economy Philosophy take full account of each individual's special needs and local conditions. They don't reduce existence to a least common denominator as is sometimes done in the west.

Buddhism is scientific. It accepts the principle of cause and effect. Personal problems and economic disorders do not appear out of the blue. They have real causes with real effects that can be remedied with right actions in accordance with the precepts of the noble path (or *Ariya-Magga* in *Pali*). Issues of cause and effect are addressed in the *Paticcasamupada* (Law of Dependent Origination).[9]

The Reasonableness principle in the Sufficiency Economy Philosophy reflects Buddha's view of causation both in science and ethics.

> I want everyone to bear in mind the law of cause and effect. A result arises because of a cause, an action. Whether that result is good or bad depends on whether the action was good or bad. So to achieve any aim, you first have to study what is the appropriate means, and then proceed according to the law of causation with honesty and determination. Then everyone's work will have a good outcome, and taken together will result in the desired progress and security of our country.
>
> (Royal Speech, Chulalongkorn University, July 9,1970, translated by UNDP, 2007)

Buddhism stresses the importance of individual responsibility. The reality of cause and effect does not imply that people cannot influence

---

[9] See, for example, Buddhadasa Bhikkhu (1982).

outcomes by developing their mental, spiritual and material capacities to cope. Shocks happen, but their consequences depend greatly on awareness, preparedness, and sound response. People should be resilient and react prudently based on the fullest information at their disposal.

The vital importance of awareness and knowledge is stressed in the *Satipatthana Sutta* (Law of Mindfulness Foundations). Buddhist are exhorted to practice (1) *Sati* (Mindfulness or awareness) and (2) *Sampajanna* (Clear comprehension, or understanding the nature of changes) in order to calmly, competently, effectively and efficiently solve real problems.

From a Buddhist perspective, human conflict and environmental degradation are caused by greed, the lust for power, and other impure desires. These passions which originate in the body, fester in the mind as impure feelings (*Vedana*). Materialism is the wheel of improper desire. Buddhadasa Bhikkhu (1906–1993), a world famous Buddhist monk, repeatedly condemned materialism, and urged believers to embrace idealism (mind-focusing) instead:

> Looking without is materialism itself and it inevitably brings the fruits of materialism — namely, endless slavery to material things and endless problems. Because of materialism, our modern world is full of trouble. No matter who is fighting who, each side is fighting for materialism, Each side may hold to its own particular variety of materialism —a cruder variety or a more refined variety; a very extreme, unmitigated, thoroughgoing materialism, or a very subtle fine, barely discernible materialism — nevertheless they are all equally infatuated with materialism.
>
> There is absolutely no way that the present crises in the world can be resolved other than through both sides curing their mad obsession with materialism and becoming more concerned with idealism. We must understand that which has nothing to do with materialism, and which is the highest ideal. We require an inner or spiritual idealism. There will then be no need to outlaw war. People will stop fighting of their own accord and begin seeking the true happiness which comes without any loss of flesh and blood or expenditure of materials. People will live in supreme. Look at the cost of looking without and at the value of looking within. Do take an interest in

looking within, in the one and only way of penetrating to Dhamma, to Buddhism.

Buddhadasa Bhikkhu (1961)

Sufficiency Economy Philosophy is a practical set of Buddhist precepts that enable people to purify their minds enough to righteously solve practical problems. Lord Buddha discovered the ultimate power of mind development, and taught this ancient noble technique to monks and devotees so that they could attain "non-self" freedom, *Nibbana*.[10] Buddhism considers mind purification and development indispensible for achieving true individual and social happiness. Buddhist Sufficiency consequently must begin by purging minds and bodies of corrupt cravings, and then clear-sightedly and resolutely taking appropriate action. It is steadfastly anti-materialist.

13.5. Crisis and Mind Development

Crises are the result of extreme human misbehavior. The crisis looming today for much of the world is caused by people and governments borrowing excessively without considering the costs of default, or how they will manage to repay. His Majesty the King' Sufficiency prescription for remedying the problem calls for the government to save sufficiently when growth is robust, and spend when the economy turns into a great recession or depression. Keynes concurred with this prescription in *The General Theory of Employment, Interest and Money* (1936), but neo-Keynesians later chose to disregard his wise counsel under the influence of Walter Heller in the mid-1960s.

Buddhism concurs with the King's and Keynes's orthodox position. The Buddha encouraged Lay people to consume wisely and save part of their income for future needs, debt repayment and unexpected contingencies. Buddhists understand well that human beings find it pleasant to spend, but also realize that excess indebtedness causes misery.

---

[10] If interested, see Nyanatiloka Mahathera (1907) and Buddhadasa Bhikkhu (1958 and 1982).

However, western macroeconomists like Paul Samuelson, Paul Krugman,[11] and Larry Summers have talked themselves into the position that there can never be too much debt if economies are afflicted with high unemployment. Their attitude quickly became widely accepted with the result that western intellectuals and ordinary people alike consider it immoral to save when times are bad, and unnecessary to do so during booms because it is claimed that growth dividends, and price adjustments will settle capital accounts.

This compassion for the unemployed is laudable, but purblind because as Buddhism teaches people cannot change the laws of cause and effect merely by expressing good intentions. No one therefore should be surprised that national debt everywhere is on the rise. Before the Thai crisis started in 1997, the government budget was in surplus and international reserves were considered sufficient, but after the exchange rate collapsed, the government budget fell into deficit, while international reserves almost disappeared at the onset of the crisis.[12] The government wrongheadedly banked on boom time savings being adequate to tide the economy over hard times, but reality belied its wishful thinking.

Buddhist Sufficiency precepts if applied will prevent crises, or at the very least reduce their harmful effects. They foster prudent risk aversion, business and consumer awareness, ethical behavior, and social responsibility.

Buddhist Sufficiency precepts will help even when government policy is macro-economically conservative (rather than neo-Keynesian liberal).[13]

---

[11] Paul Krugman, "Nobody Understands Debt," Op Ed, *New York Times*, January 1, 2012. "So yes, debt matters. But right now, other things matter more. We need more, not less, government spending to get us out of our unemployment trap. And the wrongheaded, ill-informed obsession with debt is standing in the way."

[12] For international reserve, a conventional standard before the Asian crisis encouraged a country with fixed exchange rate to maintain international reserves at a minimum of 3 months of imports. According to other benchmarks earlier mentioned in Obstfeld and Rogoff (1995), such as international reserves per monetary base, Thailand also had much more enough international reserves. However, Thailand had suffered from heavy borrowings.

[13] Neo-Keynesians and Keynes share the view that markets are imperfect (especially the labor market) and therefore necessitates government regulation and crisis intervention, but the former expanded the microeconomic grounds for macro-failure, and favors bolder, more comprehensive and stimulatory government programs.

There are at least three reasons why conservatism by itself is inadequate to assure prosperity. First, risk assessment is pro-cyclical. Policymakers tend to underestimate risk during booms, and react hysterically during troughs. Business and government both are prone to fostering unsustainably high rates of growth for expedient short term gain. They seek to grab the speculative benefit afforded by asymmetric information, leaving the public to deal with the debt baby.

Second, cronyism, "animal spirits," and "herding" tend to intensify in times of crisis. Conservatism in and of itself is not enough to correct this vicious behavior.

Third, materialism warps people's perceptions. Households gorge themselves and businessmen throw caution to the wind during booms, and when economies sour, materialism continues to dull their judgment. Materialism is addictive and crippling.

Economic policy cannot solve any of these three problems, but Buddhist mental discipline and purification can be of great assistance. It trains individuals to be good, trustworthy, responsible, and effective.

Mind development is the crux of Buddhism. It trains people to be aware of corrupt desires and provides the discipline to resist. Enlightened success brings contentment (or "*Samtosh*" in *Pali*), a key Buddhist insight, shared perhaps in some degree by other religions.[14] "Wisdom" (or *Panna* in *Pali*) that comes from educating the mind, and mental discipline, enables people to detach themselves from the pain they experience during crises. Everyone can be spiritually happy in all circumstances, if he or she masters the art of wisdom. Mind training is the pathway to moral, peaceful and environmentally friendly happiness.

Happiness in Buddhist teachings is attainable in different degrees. Ordinary people mostly experience the lowest type, especially in the West. It is "Defilement Happiness" or sensual pleasure (or *Kama Sukha* in

---

[14] In Brahmas, or ancient Hinduism, contentment is called "*Apijjho*" (or "Mag-Noi" in Thai). "*Apijjho*" is the acceptance of small gains, and also encouraged in Buddhism. It is somewhat close to "*Samtosh*" in Buddhism. "*Samtosh*" is contentment in the sense that one prefers one own belongings or wealth, not being pleased with those owned or should be owned by others. *Samtosh*, contentment, sufficiency and "enoughness" are synonyms here.

Pali). They seek instant gratification from immoderately consuming goods and services, oblivious to their addictive consequences.

Superior *"Jhana* Happiness" rewards those who possess "immovable minds." The calm (inner harmony) achieved through deep meditation produces peaceful moments and bliss. The meditative techniques for attaining Jhana Happiness were devised by the ancient Brahmas (such as Raja Yoga), and similar practices are employed by some Buddhist monks and Lay disciples.

Supreme happiness, called *"Nibbana* Happiness," is only attainable through Buddhist meditation, the noble pathway to spiritual independence. Acquiring *Nibbana* Happiness is a slow process because it takes time for the mind to understand the ups and downs of beings, and learn how to detach itself from spiritual impurities (called *"Kilesa"*). Nonetheless, if practitioners are diligent they can shed cravings, anger, and delusion. They can learn what it is to have "enough" and attain "thoughtless" bliss; the calmness of mind accompanying wisdom.[15]

Materialism is an impediment, not an aid to achieving noble *Nibbana* happiness. Richard A. Easterlin recognized this when he cautioned that ordinary happiness derived from sensual pleasure, was not a positive function of income.[16] Bhongmakapat (2010) confirmed Easterlin's Paradox in a general equilibrium framework[17] and showed additionally that sustainable happiness is attainable through spiritual understanding independent of levels of national economic development. See also Indaratna (2007 and 2010).

"Enoughess," moreover is preemptive. It prevents crises and suffering from afflicting nations and people before they gain traction. If people are content, they will strive to preserve harmony, and refrain from chasing rainbows. Likewise, where economic misery is caused by externalities

---

[15] Insight meditation is called in Buddhism as *Vipassana* meditation.

[16] See Easterlin (1973) and Easterlin and Angelescu (2009). See also Layard (2005) and Frey (2008) for happiness functions, especially on income.

[17] This trade-off was hypothesized that individuals differently maximize preferences between (sustainable) happiness and income subject to differentiated types of individuals. Benjamin *et al.* (2010) also found that people might trade happiness for money. However, preference function addressed in Benjamin *et al.* (2010) was slightly different from that in Bhongmakapat (2010 and 2011) as it assumed that happiness was a function of income and non-income material factors, all of which were exogenous.

beyond the control of individual minds, the community of enlightened can easily agree to impose Pigovian taxes to deter pollution and suppress sinful businesses.

Thailand has not been successful yet in these regards, but should continue trying. As Benabou and Tirole (2010) show, it is essential for policymakers and social activists to persevere. The goal of a just and ecologically harmonious economy is attainable because spiritual education fosters altruism. Those who understand "enoughness" for themselves have no difficulty grasping the desirability of sacrificing for the greater good, or opposing the excesses of "pro-growth" advocates (Bhongmakapat, 2011).

Ethical behavior and social responsibility are difficult to teach effectively at the corporate level. Schneider *et al.* (2010) found that traditional approaches were ineffective. Buddhist strategies however have done better. Prayukvong (2010) found that they had a positive impact on product quality, long-term performance, working quality as well as social behavior and the environment.

Meditation as a personal development tool, likewise have proven to be very effective in building individual awareness, morality and trustworthiness. In Thailand, Buddhist corporate meditation programs have yielded excellent results. Khunthongjan (2010) found that regular meditation among managers and employees not only fostered good business practices, but promoted the Sufficiency Economy mission.

Mindfulness and wisdom, including integrity and compassion, are common among those who practice this noble type of meditation. Schneider *et al.* (2010) found that Brahmas or Hinduism meditation also produce good results. "Sahaja Yoga meditation," a modified variant of calm mind practice, had a strong impact on management decisions, and encouraged socially responsible behavior.

Buddhist meditation isn't easily mastered. It requires correct practice and experienced teachers.[18] The devotee must be diligent and many lack the resolve, making it unpopular. Nonetheless, the personal and social benefits of Buddhist meditation are potentially enormous and should be widely encouraged to prevent crises, cope, and create an harmonious society.

---

[18] There are various teaching lineages mostly available in Thailand and Myanmar, see Kornfield (1996) and Bhongmakapat (2010).

13.6. Conclusion

Stable growth obviously is preferable to crisis, yet governments paradoxically tend to promote destructive pro-growth policies that increase national debt to unsustainable levels and culminate in devastating crises. Thailand's national debt has been mounting dangerously for more than a decade, with little short term benefit to justify the catastrophic risks. There seems little unlikely that the nation can avoid hard times with conventional economic strategies.

Buddhist sufficiency strategy provides a superior alternative. It promotes the moral discipline, collective responsibility and practical guidance needed to construct a self-sufficient, stable and harmonious national economy.

Buddhist sufficiency strategy is not just looking at the form of governance structures, but the craving and corruption that warps economic behavior. It fosters a deep appreciation for an ethic of "enoughness" or contentment essential for combating materialism, consumerism, power-seeking and environmental degradation. In so doing, it deters economic crises and provides effective tools for coping when economies sour.

Buddhist sufficiency strategy is scientific. It accepts economic principles of cause and effect, but goes further by recognizing that economic dysfunction more often than not is rooted in impure desires and corruption that can be detoxified through Buddhist mind development and purification techniques.

There is no downside to the Buddhist sufficiency strategy, only the upside prospect of handsome rewards for people, the nation, and the global community.

References

Aguiar, Mark and Gita Gopinath (2005) "Fire-Sale Foreign Direct Investment and Liquidity Crises," *Review of Economics and Statistics*, Vol. 87, No. 3, pp. 439–452.

Benabou, Roland and Jean Tirole (2010) "Individual and Corporate Social Responsibility," *Economica*, Vol. 77, pp. 1–19.

Benjamin, Daniel J., Ori Heffetz, Miles S. Kimball and Alex Rees-Jones (2010) "Do People Seek to Maximize Happiness? Evidence from New Surveys," Working Paper 16489, October, Cornell University, mimeo.

Bhongmakapat, Teerana (2001) "Managing the Thai Crisis: Asset Bubbles, Globalization and Macroeconomic Policy," in Jere R. Behrman *et al.*, *Restructuring Asian Economics for the New Millennium*, Research in Asian Economic Studies, Vol. 9-B, Amsterdam: Elsevier Science, pp. 447–476.

Bhongmakapat, Teerana (2010). *Happiness Policy: Mind, Matters and Unlimited Wants*, January, Chiangmai: Public Policy Institute, in Thai, or its second enlarged edition, *Happiness Development for the Modern Society*, Bangkok: Sangsarn Books, 2011, in Thai.

Bhongmakapat, Teerana (2011) "Economics of Enoughness," Pillar of the Kingdom Public Lecture, Chulalongkorn University, February 4.

Buddhadasa, Bhikkhu (1958) *Handbook for Mankind*, Tenth English Edition printed by Mahachulalongkornrajavidyalaya Univerity, Bangkok, 2005.

Buddhadasa, Bhikkhu (1961) "Looking within," Lecture with the Buddhist Studies Group at Chulalongkorn University, Bangkok, Translated by Roderick S. Bucknell, December 15. Available at: http://www.what-buddha-taught.net/Books2/Bhikkhu_Buddhadasa_Keys_to_Natural_Truth.htm.

Buddhadasa, Bhikkhu (1982) "The ABCs of Buddhism," October 14. Available at: http://what-buddha-taught.net/Books6/Buddhadasa_Bhikkhu_ABC_of_Buddhism.pdf.

Easterlin, Richard A. (1973) "Does Money Buy Happiness?" *Public Interest*, Vol. 30, pp. 3–10.

Easterlin, Richard A. and Laura Angelescu (2009) "Happiness and Growth the World Over: Time-Series Evidence on the Happiness-Income Paradox," IZA Discussion paper No.4060, March.

Fischer, Stanley (1998) "The IMF and the Asian Crisis," Paper Prepared for Delivery as the Forum Funds Lecture at UCLA, March 20. Available at: http://www.imf.org/external/np/speeches/1998/032098.HTM.

Fleming, J. Marcus (1962) "Domestic Financial Policies Under Fixed and Floating Exchange Rates" *IMF Staff Papers*, Vol. 9, pp. 369–379. Reprinted in Cooper, Richard N. (1969) *International Finance*, New York: Penguin Books.

Fortune (1988) "The New Powers of Asia," March 28.

Frey, Bruno S. (2008) *Happiness: A Revolution in Economics*, Cambridge, MA: The MIT Press.

Goldstein, Morris (2003) "Debt Sustainability, Brazil, and the IMF," Working Paper No.03-1, Institute for International Economics, Washington, D.C., February.

Indaratna, Kaemthong (2007) "Sufficiency Economy: A Happiness Development Approach," Paper Prepared for the Third International Conference on Gross National Happiness, Nongkhai and Bangkok, November.

Indaratna, Kaemthong (2010) "Happiness: An Economic Bottom-line," Invited Paper Presented at Annual Conference of Contemplative Education Center, Mahidol University, held at Rama Gardens Hotel, Bangkok, December 2–3.

Kaminsky, Graciela L. and Carmen M. Reinhart (1999) "The Twin Crises: The Causes of Banking and Balance of Payments Problems," *American Economic Review*, June, Vol. 89, No. 3, pp. 473–500.

Khunthongjan, Supavadee (2010) *Study of SME's Business and Entrepreneur Characteristics that Facilitate the Movements of Sufficiency Economy*, Bangkok: Office of the Royal Development Projects Boards, in Thai, Forthcoming.

Kornfield, Jack (1996) *Living Dharma: Teachings of Twelve Buddhist Masters*, Boston: Shambhala.

Layard, Richard (2005) *Happiness: Lessons from a New Science*, London: Penguin Books.

McKinnon, Ronald I. and Huw Pill (1996) "Credible Liberalizations and International Capital Flows: The Over-Borrowing Syndrome," in Takatoshi Ito and Anne O. Krueger, *Financial Deregulation and Integration in East Asia*, Chicago: University of Chicago Press for National Bureau of Economic Research, pp. 7–48.

Miller, Marcus H. and Joseph E. Stiglitz (2010) "Leverage and Asset Bubbles: Averting Armageddon with Chapter 11?" *Economic Journal*, Vol. 120, No. 544, pp. 500–518.

Mundell, Robert A. (1963) "Capital Mmobility and Stabilization Policy Under Fixed and Flexible Exchange Rates," *Canadian Journal of Economic and Political Science*, Vol. 29, No. 4, pp. 475–485, doi:10.2307/139336. Reprinted in Mundell, Robert A. (1968) *International Economics*, New York: Macmillan.

Nyanatiloka, Mahathera (1907) *The Word of the Buddha: An Outline of the Teaching of the Buddha in the Words of the Pali Cannon*, First English edition, Ceylon: Buddhist Publication Society.

Obstfeld, Maurice and Kenneth Rogoff (1995) "The Mirage of Fixed Exchange Rates," *Journal of Economic Perspectives* Vol. 9, (Fall), pp. 73–96.

Pechman, Joseph A. (2008) "Heller, Walter Wolfgang (1915–1987)," *The New Palgrave Dictionary of Economics*, Second Edition, Steven N. Durlauf and Lawrence E. Blume, Palgrave Macmillan.

Piboolsravut, Priyanut (2004) "Sufficiency Economy," *ASEAN Economic Bulletin*, Vol. 21, No. 1, pp. 127–134.

Prayukvong, Wanna (2010) "A Buddhist Economics Approach to Business Management: Three Case Studies in Thailand," Ph.D. Thesis in Integral Development Studies, Ubon Ratchthani University.

Puntasen, Apichai, Sorravich Premchuen and Pichet Keitdejpunya (2003) Application of the Royal Thought about the Sufficiency Economy in SMEs, Bangkok: Thailand Research Fund, in Thai.

Schneider, Susan C., Maurizio Zollo and Ramesh Manocha (2010) "Developing Socially Responsible Behavior in Managers: Experimental Evidence of the Effectiveness of Different Approaches to Management Education," *Journal of Corporate Citizenship*, Vol. 39, (Autumn) pp. 21–40.

Tirole, Jean (2002) *Financial Crises, Liquidity, and the International Monetary System*, New Jersey: Princeton University Press.

UNDP (2007). *Thailand Human Development Report 2007: Sufficiency Economy and Human Development*, Bangkok: United Nations Development Program.

Wibulswasdi, Chaiwat, Priyanut Piboonsravut and Kobsak Pootrakool (2010) *Sufficiency Economy Philosophy and Development*, Bangkok: Sufficiency Economy Research Project, The Crown Property Bureau.

Wiriyapipat, Nipa (2009) "Business Leaders and the Sufficiency Economy Movement in Organization," Journal of the University of the Thai Chamber of Commerce, October–December, Vol. 29, No. 4, in Thai.

PROSPECTS

STEVEN ROSEFIELDE

Financial crises are frequent catastrophic events that repeatedly take government policymakers by surprise. The title of Reinhart's and Rogoff's treatise "This Time Will be Different: Eight Centuries of Financial Folly,"[1] tersely expresses the point, wryly implying that humanity is condemned to repeatedly suffer because financiers and governments refuse to put public welfare above private interests.

This volume, surveying the Asian bubbles of the 1990s, the global financial crisis of 2008–2010, and the unfolding EU and American sovereign debt drama finds little to contradict Reinhart and Rogoff, but provides further corroborative evidence. It demonstrates that contemporary governments do not want a duty to prevent to interfere with their short-term public and private agendas. They can, but do not devise early warning institutions, and fail to rein deficit spending, monetary expansion, and financial excesses. The handwriting is on the wall, but policymakers choose to act as if "this time will be different."

This callousness seems to be intensifying across the globe. Government leaders are digging in their heels, not with words, but with their deeds. They remain committed to expanding state programs, morally hazardous state–private partnerships, lax financial regulation, excessive monetary expansion, levering, tolerating burgeoning global imbalances, and promoting dysfunctional supranational organizations, shielded by theories

---

[1] Carmen Rheinhart and Kenneth Rogoff, *This Time Will be Different: Eight Centuries of Financial Folly*, Princeton, NJ: Princeton University Press, 2009.

like the "Great Moderation," "divine coincidence," "white swan business cycles," and inexhaustible endogenous growth. They also deceive themselves with "stress tests," protocols, regulatory tweaks, automatic stabilizers, and cooperative intervention mechanisms that are innocuous, but do not address the fundamental sources of speculative disequilibrium. The invisible hand, potent as it is, cannot save the globe from mega-folly.

Nothing precludes world leaders from having an epiphany. Some are interpreting the appointment of Yoshihiko Noda on August 31, 2011, as the Japan's rejection of the sort of populism that failed to extricate the nation from two "lost decades," while saddling it with an onerous domestic debt. Perhaps, the EU and ASEAN will back away from supranationalism, China will substantially reduce its hard currency reserves, and governments everywhere including the U.S. will trim their national debts to optimal size. Taxes can be raised, programs curtailed, financial institutions placed on a short leash, global imbalances amicably resolved, and the burden of government inefficiency and waste on private productivity lightened.

Should this come to pass bubble prevention will be superfluous, and the book closed on eight centuries of financial folly. The trend however is not encouraging. Leaders around the globe seem determined to tough things out, insisting that they are mostly right. Solutions, they claim, only require fine tuning and modest belt tightening. There are no serious discussions of radical governance reforms, or potent early warning systems.

Consequently, the likelihood that there will not be a next time is slight. The tsunami warning is blasting, people say they are alert, but are still blithely strolling along the Tohoku coast.

INDEX